LONELY

LONELY

A Memoir

EMILY WHITE

HARPER

An Imprint of HarperCollins*Publishers*
www.harpercollins.com

The names and identifying characteristics of all the individuals discussed in this book have been changed to protect their privacy.

HarperCollins books may be purchased for educational, business, or sales promotional use. For information, please write: Special Markets Department, HarperCollins Publishers, 10 East 53rd Street, New York, NY 10022.

FIRST EDITION

Designed by Leah Carlson-Stanisic

Loneliness induction exercise © Professor Robert Weiss. Used by permission.

UCLA Loneliness Scale © Dr. Daniel Russell. Used by permission.

Library of Congress Cataloging-in-Publication Data has been applied for.

ISBN: 978-0-06-176509-4

10 11 12 13 14   ov/wcf   10 9 8 7 6 5 4 3 2 1

To the memory of my father

Please close your eyes.

You live in an apartment. You are there alone. So far as your feelings go, you are entirely alone. You have no one to call, no one to talk to. There is no one sharing your life, no one at all. This is the way it is, this is the way it is going to be. If you were to go out, you would still be alone.

Please take note in your mind of how you feel.

Now open your eyes and write down what your feelings are.

Loneliness Induction Exercise
Professor Robert Weiss

CONTENTS

UCLA LONELINESS SCALE

INSTRUCTIONS: The following statements describe how people sometimes feel. For each statement, please indicate how often you feel the way described by writing a number in the space provided.

NEVER	RARELY	SOMETIMES	ALWAYS
1	2	3	4

1. How often do you feel unhappy doing so many things alone? _____

2. How often do you feel you have no one to talk to? _____

3. How often do you feel you cannot tolerate being so alone? _____

4. How often do you feel as if no one understands you? _____

5. How often do you find yourself waiting for people to call or write? _____

6. How often do you feel completely alone? _____

7. How often do you feel unable to reach out and communicate with those around you?   _____

8. How often do you feel starved for company?   _____

9. How often do you feel it is difficult for you to make friends?   _____

10. How often do you feel shut out and excluded by others?   _____

SCORING: A total score is computed by adding up the response to each question. The average loneliness score on the measure is 20. A score of 25 or higher reflects a high level of loneliness. A score of 30 or higher reflects a very high level of loneliness.

LONELY

THE VISIT

F ive years ago, I took an introductory painting class. The class was housed in a large white studio, one with huge windows that let in the early evening light. The instructor, a young man with curls and perfectly round eyeglasses, settled a huge stack of books on a table at the side of the room. He'd attached Post-it notes to various pages in each of the books, and he told us to choose a book, and then select one of the paintings to try to copy.

"The goal isn't to produce an exact replica," he said, "but to pay attention to things like light, and shadow. Ask yourself where the focal point of the painting is, and how the artist draws your attention to that point."

I selected a painting I'd never seen before. It was an 1899 print by an artist named Félix Vallotton, called *The Visit*. I chose it because the color scheme—a mix of purples and blues—was relatively manageable, and I liked the straightforward arrangement of it. It showed a couple simply embracing at the edge of a room.

I tackled the furniture first, congratulating myself on absolutely nailing a velvety-looking armchair and its accompanying side table. I painted the walls, and a doorway, and a carpet with a pattern of circles and waves. I didn't paint the couple until the end, both because I needed to block the scene out before I added them, and because they were more technically complex than the furniture and rugs.

I did what the instructor told us to do. I told myself not to paint "a couple," but to concentrate instead on following the artist's line. I carefully set out the man's shoulder, and the straight leg of his trousers, and the fall of the woman's skirt as it draped over her shoes. I noticed that their hands came together—they were holding them at chest height, as though they had just finished a slow, quiet waltz—and then I ran into problems. The line I was trying to follow disappeared. The area between the man and the woman—where their clothes should have met and mingled, and where their bodies should have brushed up against each other—that area was all darkness and shadow.

This aspect of the painting hadn't been immediately obvious. In fact, I'd been staring at the reproduction for almost two hours before I noticed it. When I'd first glanced at the painting, I'd seen two bodies. It was only in trying to reproduce the outline that I realized the artist had—through an extremely delicate use of shading—actually fused them into one figure.

And the intimacy communicated by that shadow—even through a cheap reproduction, and across a span of what was more than a hundred years—caught me like a blow to the chest. I'd signed up for the painting class because I'd been intensely lonely, so lonely that I was willing to pay for at least one evening a week that wouldn't see me returning to my empty flat on my own. Even though the class didn't offer much in the way of conversation—most of the students were focused on their easels—it did offer company, and it gave me the chance to see my behavior reflected in the actions of those around me: I liked the synchronicity of us all opening our tubes of paint, carefully glancing from palette to canvas, and squinting at the fruit and bottles set up at the front of the room.

As the course wore on, and as I grew more familiar with my fellow students, I told myself that I was doing OK, and that I was managing—with nothing in the way of real guidance—to put some distance between myself and the loneliness that seemed to have followed me for the past several years.

That was before I saw the painting. The sight of the man and woman standing so closely together made me remember what real warmth and proximity was like. It made me recognize what I'd been missing.

You've been without that for so long, I thought, staring at the picture. The memory of close connection made my throat tighten; it wasn't soothing so much as painful and disorienting. I felt as though I were being shown a photo of someone well loved, and long dead. I didn't want to be reminded of what I no longer seemed to have.

It was with a sense of defeat that I stopped painting. I was sitting on a hard wooden chair in front of my easel, and I simply dropped my arms to my sides, paintbrush in hand. Suddenly tired, I gathered up my things, and grew quietly angry with my fellow students as they continued to paint. My loneliness, by that point, had become twinned with frustration, with a borderline rage that surfaced whenever I was confronted with the lack of belonging that had come to define my life. I felt the need to escape the studio and lose myself in the summer crowds outside. It wasn't sociability or a sense of connection I was seeking, but just heat and noise and furious movement—anything that would block out my sudden and searing sense of aloneness.

———

I still have my painting of the couple in the living room. For some reason, even though the painting isn't finished, I've carried it through three moves and across two provinces. I think I keep it as an emblem, as a token of how bad things had gotten, and of how much I still had to endure before my life would change and improve. I keep it also as a reminder, not just of my past, but of what might be my future: no one's discovered a vaccine against loneliness; there's no prayer or charm or safeguard I've discovered that can be relied on to keep the state at bay for good. The painting is a warning, a message from my own life: *Do everything you can to keep the state from returning*, it seems to urge. *You don't want to go back to those years that you lived.*

Many people, over the course of the past several years, have asked me why I would want to write a book about chronic loneliness. The subject, they hint, is embarrassing; it's best kept unmentioned. And loneliness, they say, isn't "real"—at least not in the way that depression or bipolar disorder are real. Every word I've written has been penned against a chorus of "Don't" and "Why bother?"

"It's too trivial," I've been told, "too shameful," "too irrelevant." And it was, after all, just me. Even if my own loneliness was somehow significant, even if it did change my life, derail my health, cloud my intelligence and turn me into someone I didn't used to be—all of that was just *my* problem.

One of the things I made sure to do when writing this book was talk to other lonely people. Before every conversation, I thought about my own experiences, and drew up questions meant to probe how closely their battle with loneliness mirrored my own. I used to be a lawyer, and what I was looking for was evidence. I wanted to prove that what I went through as a lonely person was neither immaterial nor unique. I phoned loneliness researchers in places ranging from Arizona to Scotland; I talked to lonely people across the continent. I asked about symptoms, manifestation, mortality, disease, responses, rates. I plowed through hundreds of articles, followed up footnotes, searched the Internet, and paid for out-of-print books that were shipped to me long-distance.

Throughout this entire process, I've been fueled by the conviction that I had to give voice to an experience that mattered, one that affected people far and wide. What I wanted throughout my years of loneliness was recognition. I needed others to see and understand my state as a real problem. I needed others to ask me about it, help me through it, and view it as something valid and potentially life-altering. I also needed to hear *other people* talking about it. Right now, loneliness is something few people are willing to admit to. There's no need for this silence, no need for the shame and self-blame it creates. There's nothing wrong with loneliness, and we need to start acknowledging this through a wider and more open discussion of the state.

The fact that I'm the author of this book is little more than coincidence. The story set out in the pages that follow is my own, but I think any lonely person could have written a similar account. The state, I've discovered, is something of a universal, afflicting people from a variety of age groups and backgrounds, and affecting men and women in equal measure. The only thing that perhaps sets me apart from other lonely people is that the worst years of my loneliness coincided with years in which I was repeatedly instructed—as a lawyer—to examine everything. No question was to leave my desk until it had been answered; no argument was to be put forward until every angle had been explored. And so it became natural for me—once my rage had subsided after painting class, and I was back out on the streets of Toronto, walking and walking in the darkening evening—to start asking questions, and begin wondering whether my state had substance, whether it was in fact as significant as it felt.

Given the choice, it's not a journey I would have gone on. I would have preferred to have lived a life of connection, one in which loneliness did not assault me on a daily and yearly basis. But we don't get to choose the main facts of our lives. Loneliness was something I was born into, something that claimed me as its own. The only thing I could do in response was to try to follow and understand it, to chart it as fully and cleanly as I could. If it was clutching me, the least I could do was twist in its grip and really look at it. If I couldn't ward it away, I could at least see it as clearly as it saw me.

Part I

ARRIVAL

Chapter One

PREMONITION

Waiting for the state to strike

I've had periods of loneliness my whole life. Since research shows a genetic basis for loneliness, with some people being born with an ingrained tendency toward the state, I now see these periods as natural, almost inevitable. Or, rather, I see them as inevitable from the perspective of the adult I've become. I'm the sort of person who likes to play "What if?" What if I hadn't dropped physics? What if I'd married my first boyfriend? What if Henry Ford had mass-produced bicycles instead of cars? And I can engage in this sort of shuffling and reshuffling of reality when it comes to my loneliness. I can daydream about a childhood in which my sisters and I were closer in age, and my parents stayed together, and my whole family remained in the South. In this way, I can whip up an alternate version of my life, one in which my genetic predisposition toward loneliness doesn't slam up against the experience of early isolation.

But the fact is that I was a solitary child born into circumstances that saw me too much alone. I don't mean that I was friendless. One of the overriding ironies of my life has been that, although I've struggled with loneliness for years, sociability has rarely been a problem for me. I grew up with much older sisters—Christine and Theresa were ten and eight years older than me—and while the age gap set us apart, it also meant I had the benefit of role models. By the time I was nine, I had the manners of a much older child. I knew how to be polite with parents, deferent with teachers, and funny with friends. I had a best friend—a beautiful Trinidadian girl with the pretty name of Stacey Lea—and other girls used to crowd around me in the schoolyard, asking if they could be my second best friend, or my third. This sort of flattery never made me disdainful or vain, and that's because the isolation that characterized the other aspects of my life worked to keep my little ego in check. I'm not sure exactly when I became conscious of my motivations, but I realized fairly early on that the reason I was better than other girls at making friends was because I needed those friends more acutely.

This was something the kids around me didn't seem to notice. Stacey, for instance, had a big, sprawling house. It was a bungalow that had sprouted additions as the family grew and grew, and the erratic architecture made it an ideal place for playing, with an unfinished attic, blind spots in the yard, and dead-end hallways that could be cordoned off with sofa cushions. Stacey used to like a game where we dared each other to climb into a crawl space under the kitchen—it was a damp and gravelly spot that smelled of soil—and she never seemed to realize how uncomfortable the game made me.

"I'm here," she'd call out, as I cringed with nerves at the entrance, afraid she might just disappear. "I'm putting my clip down as a marker. You have to pass it," she'd say victoriously, emerging from the crawl space with dirt in her hair and cobwebs stuck to her sweater. And I could never do it. A foot or two into the crawl space, with daylight just an arm's length away, I'd panic, and scurry back out. "You have no guts," Stacey would say dismissively, already forgetting the game and heading up to the kitchen, and I'd follow along, patting the big German shepherd that slept on the stairs and not letting on how frightened I'd been.

Because what Stacey didn't know—and what she, with five brothers and sisters, would probably never understand—was that I had a fear of empty places, a fear that I recognized as embarrassing and irrational even at ten. There seemed to be two versions of my life. There was the public version, which saw me eating cabbage rolls at Stacey's huge dining room table, playing dodgeball at school, and reading the notes that the girl behind me would slip over my shoulder in class. And then there was another version, the one which I think my friends' mothers detected but which no one ever mentioned. This other me, this private me, saw me on my own a great deal of the time—unlocking the back door after school and calling out to the cat for company, or going to the corner store on my own, or sitting on the back porch in the early evenings and fiddling with marbles when the empty house became too dark and scary.

In many ways, I had it easy as a kid. Not only was I popular, but my family was reasonably affluent, and I saw none of the abuse or put-downs that some of my other friends had to deal with. The difficulties I faced had nothing to do with people behaving badly toward me and had everything to do with people not being there at all.

The 1970s—which saw families start to seriously fall apart—also witnessed the beginning of the vogue for family trees. My third-grade teacher had a particular fondness for these creations—they must have eaten up a lot of class time—and she made us cut leaves out of bristol board and glue them onto painted trunks and branches. There wasn't a lot of sensitivity, within the Catholic school system in the mid-1970s, to the fact that some family trees had blown apart, and I had to muster all of my precocious social skills to deal with the challenge.

"Mrs. Twaite," I said, holding a "Mother" leaf and a "Father" leaf. "What if they're not on the same tree anymore?"

"What do you mean?" Mrs. Twaite answered. I blushed, and Mrs. Twaite seemed to come to her senses. My sisters and I were famous—we were the "divorced kids"—and Mrs. Twaite was clearly unsettled by our lack of conformity.

"Maybe you can create a second tree," she said uncomfortably.

I looked around the classroom. There was no way I was going to have two trees when everyone else just had one, so I defiantly glued "Mother" next to "Father." I liked the way the tree looked—with the mommy and daddy leaves hovering protectively over the little kid leaves—but when I hung it up on the wall, I knew it was a lie. I had no memory of ever seeing my mother and father together, and when I thought about our family tree, I pictured something being dismantled, like the artificial pine my mother and I took apart every Christmas.

It hadn't always been that way. There seemed to be two families in my family. First, there was the intact unit that my sisters had spent their childhoods in. This was in Kentucky, before the move to Canada and the divorce. This grouping had seen my sisters and parents living in a big white house in Lexington, on a street with the magical-sounding name of Sycamore Road. My mother kept a photo of this house tucked in a drawer in Toronto, and I used to study it when I was little. I'd look at my sisters standing in matching white dresses on the sunny front steps, at the big oak tree in the corner of the frame, and the edge of my father's shadow in the foreground. There was a peacefulness to this portrait that mesmerized me. I always tried to insert some image of myself into the frame—perhaps looking out from an upstairs window—but I could never fully convince myself that I belonged in the picture. And that's because, even though I held the photo in my hand, the move to Canada seemed to have ripped its contents in two. Perhaps the absence of aunts and cousins had revealed fault lines within their marriage, but—for reasons that were never explained to me—my parents split up shortly after the move, when I was four. The divorce meant that I saw my father only on Sunday afternoons, and that I saw my mother barely at all. Confronted with the sudden demands of single parenting, she had to hustle for work, and she ended up teaching English as a second language to other newcomers at a college downtown. Her hours, as well as the long commute, meant that she was often not at home, and her absence meant that I had to be self-sufficient.

"You never gave me any trouble," my mother said fondly, years later, and what she really meant was that I could get by on my own. I relied a lot on Theresa for company in my early childhood—Christine left for university when I was eight—but, as we grew older, Theresa became understandably preoccupied with boyfriends and band rehearsals. By the time I was nine, I'd become adept at entertaining myself. In many ways, it was something I was good at. The relationship between loneliness and solitude can be hard to delineate: the former is often seen as canceling out the legitimacy of the latter, as though a lonely adult or child is simply not entitled to want or need time alone. But the feelings of isolation that accompany loneliness are entirely different from the more sated and creative feelings that accompany solitude, and it's entirely reasonable to feel lonely and yet still feel as though you need some time to yourself.

"If you don't want to stay, say yes," my mother would quietly instruct me, when I called from a friend's house to ask permission for a sleepover. My mother liked time alone as much as I did, and she never criticized my desire for solitude.

"*Yes*," I'd reply, trying to sound as enthusiastic as possible.

"Sorry, hon," she'd say more loudly, "I need you at home tonight."

And when I got home to find my mother there, I'd be entirely happy to lose myself in daydreams about being the Hardy Boys' little sister, or I'd just lie on my bed and listen to my mother writing letters and diary entries on the big electric typewriter downstairs.

The problem was that the solitude I enjoyed when my mother was at home disappeared completely when I was on my own. And this meant that what my family saw was a contented aloneness, while what I experienced, when there was no one else in the house with me, was a frightened isolation. On weekday afternoons and evenings—when my mother was still hours from the end of her workday, and Theresa was at the mall with her friends—I'd fall prey to all the habits and superstitions of a child left too much on her own. I'd refuse to go to upstairs. I'd race to the downstairs bathroom and then scurry back up to the main floor as quickly as possible. I'd try to stay rooted in the kitchen, where I could keep an eye on both the front and back doors, on guard against possible intruders, and I had long, nervous talks with my imaginary twin brother, Randy, someone I suspected I should have gotten rid of years earlier but whose presence comforted me.

The person who was best positioned to respond to the isolation I was experiencing was my father. As a university professor, he had flexible hours, and the fact that he had remarried quickly and well meant that he wasn't struggling with the feelings of isolation and distress that seemed to trouble my mother.

The problem was that the court had limited his access to Sunday afternoons, and my father didn't seem to know what to do with me during such a short time period.

"Isn't that terrific?" he'd ask, as we stood in the atrium of the Toronto art gallery, staring at an enormous canvas. I can still see this painting precisely. It's a late 1960s Ellsworth Kelly print of a huge blue circle against a pure white backdrop. I'd be hard-pressed to say something intelligent about this painting now, and when I was eight, I was absolutely dumbfounded. Standing with my father's hands on my shoulders, I'd fall silent, and my father would misinterpret my confusion as dissatisfaction. He'd grow anxious that I wasn't enjoying myself, and I'd feel guilty at having let him down. Our Sunday afternoons together were often marked by a sort of cool emptiness: we were often in drafty museums, or barnlike auction houses, or half-deserted restaurants. There was an enervation to our outings—I think both of us would rather have been tucked up inside somewhere, reading—and I often only relaxed on the drive home, when I could close my eyes and gobble up my dad's sheer presence. I'd breathe in the smell of him—spicy shaving lotion mixed with the scent of his clean cotton shirt—and imagine a more ordinary life in which he woke me in the mornings, and read me stories, and stroked my hair when I was tired.

But the drives with my father always ended. We'd pull into the driveway of my mother's house, and I'd open the car door to let in the cold air. "I'll see you next week," my father would say, not quite looking at me, and I'd head in our big front door to find my mother in the kitchen, half listening to the radio and making sandwiches for the week ahead. The sight of her alone at the counter always filled me with a sense of dread, with a feeling I'd later learn to call a premonition. It was as though, in witnessing her isolation, I was seeing the shape and content of my own future, as though exposure to her loneliness would further guarantee the advent of mine.

Because despite her gifts—her intelligence, her generosity, and her surprising wit—my mother's life was marked then by a sort of isolation. What little family she had was in the States, her husband had left her, and she spent her days working with people who didn't speak English. Her flat, midwestern accent was wrong in Toronto, she was an atheist in a Catholic neighborhood, and she was divorced at a time when you weren't supposed to be. Sometimes I used to find her in the kitchen—like me, she found it a comforting spot—and she'd be asleep with the lights on, her head resting gently on her arms, a day of work and night school having left her exhausted. Although it shames me to admit it, I don't think I went to her at these times. I was not so sturdy a child as to lead my own mother to bed. Instead, I'd leave her sleeping and tiptoe back to my own room, where I'd be acutely aware of the emptiness in the house, of the way it seemed to echo around my mother and me in our separate spaces.

I don't want to suggest that I was lonely all the time as a child. I wasn't. There were perfectly normal moments of sitting with my eyes closed as Theresa practiced her makeup skills on me, or letting my mother brush and braid my hair, or racing with Stacey on our banana-seat bikes. The problem wasn't that I was always lonely, but rather that loneliness had presented itself right at the beginning of my life, just as I was starting to define myself. There was no time for me to assemble a self-portrait in which loneliness was not a prominent feature. And this meant that my relationship with loneliness became charged. I couldn't dismiss the state. I came to feel, from a very young age, as though it had a special significance for me, as though it were a fuse that was set to ignite.

"I can't see this changing," I wrote when I was nineteen, a year after I'd left my mother's house and headed to university. I was caught, at the time, in the difficult interval that many young people face. I'd given up most of my high school friendships and was trying to create new and more complex relationships in a city hours from home. This transition is challenging enough to trigger loneliness in just about anyone. What was unique about my reaction was the way in which short-term and perfectly understandable feelings of loneliness seemed to portend something much worse. "All I can see is more loneliness," I noted in the diary I'd begun keeping. "Just more solitude, a life lived at a distance from everyone else." My descriptions of the state, even when it had barely settled, were full of alarm and intensity. The feeling, I wrote, was "knife-like"; it was something "poised to spill my own blood."

There are two ways of approaching statements of this sort. On one hand, they display all the melodrama I was prone to in those years. I didn't, in my late teens and early twenties, seem able to turn my emotional volume down: even without drugs, snow crystals were endlessly mesmerizing and conversations wildly intense; a documentary about the porn industry could send me into a tailspin about women's rights that lasted for weeks. On the other hand, I was, in the course of all my private scribbling, actually making predictions that came true. In a way that makes me slightly uneasy now, I can turn to pages that are twenty years old—soft, worn sheets pulled from coil-ring notebooks and covered with my eager script—and see myself setting out a great deal of what would eventually happen to me. "I'll never have children. I'll never marry. The idea of law school seems deadly to me." It was as though, during that brief interval when everything was rushed and new, a sort of chronological porthole opened up, and I was able to catch glimpses of what my future would hold.

And loneliness was part of that picture. In the same way that other women might worry—even at nineteen—about never finding a husband, I worried about becoming lonely. Saying that I suspected, in my teens and early twenties, that severe loneliness was going to emerge a problem in later years sounds slightly fatalistic. It's as though I simply internalized the image of my lonely mother and wasn't imaginative enough to conjure up a different sort of life. There's certainly some truth to saying my mother's modeling of loneliness was powerful, and that I've been subconsciously battling it for years. But my awareness of and sensitivity to loneliness went further than that. People with mood disorders often write about having emotionally intense childhoods, of being unnaturally prone to highs and lows, crying uncontrollably, or being queerly elevated by a shift in the weather. And if we accept that loneliness is a psychological problem in its own right—which is what researchers are trying to impress on us—then I don't think it's unusual or impossible for someone to have a sense of that problem gaining a foothold in their life. When I became lonely in my late teens and early twenties, I was aware of what I can only describe as the edges of something. It was as though I were seeing someone at a distance and through a crowd, and this stranger was waving patiently at me, confident that in time we'd draw much closer together.

By my midtwenties, I'd turned into someone who wasn't chronically lonely so much as chronically alert to the risk of loneliness. In much the same way that depressives try to orga nize their lives so as to avoid the blues—exercising obsessively and getting precisely eight hours of sleep a night—I grew into someone who put the need to avoid loneliness at the center of my life. My first attempt to stave off loneliness involved moving in with a sweet, insanely rich, and paternal redhead named Martin, who was the son of a stockbroker but who had the distinctly rural ambition of becoming a folksinger. He was rumpled, with the J. Crew shirts his mother bought for him falling out of his jeans, and he was talented, but full of insecurities that he tried to offset by finding stories of unlikely success.

"Did you know, sweetie," he'd say, lying on the futon we used as a couch, tipping his cigarette into the ashtray settled on his belly, and reading the insert from a cassette, "that John Prine used to be a postman?"

"See," I'd reply, as positively as possible, "anyone can do it. It's not your background that matters so much as how good you are. And you *are* good."

He was: he had a low, smoky voice, one of the most gorgeous I've ever heard, and my encouragement of him was sincere. I helped him with his application for a music management program, scanned the lyrics he jotted on the backs of cigarette packs, and cooked while he sang and strummed guitar in our back bedroom. Helping Martin certainly went some ways toward easing my feelings of aloneness. Experts agree that "nurturing" others, in the form of teaching, child-raising, or fostering stray animals, is an excellent antidote to a sense of isolation. The problem was that, in supporting Martin's dreams of becoming a musician, I wound up pushing him into a world that I couldn't enter. I didn't like the smoky bars late at night, or the rehearsals that saw Martin's friends using my pots and dried bean jars as instruments. I couldn't handle the endless drinking, and I never knew how to respond to the strange mix of calculation and dissolution that characterized the booking agents and talent scouts Martin was always trying to impress.

We lived a few blocks away from the law school at the University of Toronto. I used to pass it twice a day on the bus on my way to work at a film library. I liked the calm air of it, the way it was surrounded by manicured lawns and wrought iron gates. I'd seen legal dramas, such as *Law & Order*, and I thought of law as offering a sort of enforced collegiality. When I thought about becoming a lawyer, I pictured long, intense evenings around boardroom tables, hurried conversations in courthouse hallways, and whispered talks behind closed office doors.

"At least you'll have a paycheck," Martin remarked one night, as I sat beside a timer and scribbled out answers to LSAT questions. It seemed clear to us both that, in applying to law school, I was choosing a different sort of life over the one he was offering. Oddly, we never really argued about this. Martin seemed resigned to my impending departure; what seemed to bother him was the fact that I was leaving him for something so curtailed and dull.

"Some of us don't have trust funds," I replied, rather sharply, and Martin shrugged, as though his wealth had nothing to do with him.

"You could make money some other way."

"It's not *about* money, Martin."

"What's it about, then?" His question was entirely genuine. Martin was—to this day—the most gregarious person I've ever met. He didn't have a circle of friends so much as a pack of people who followed him to and fro wherever he went. Being at home with me was as close to *alone* as he ever came.

"You wouldn't understand," I replied, and as soon as I said this, I realized I didn't quite understand it myself. I didn't have any real interest in law, and the analytical exercises I was doing struck me as empty and hollow. What I was going for was to-getherness, a sort of bounded camaraderie which—much like the army—would see me dressing and behaving like everybody else. Although I could never have said so to Martin, who was socially gutsy, what I was looking for was a buffer, a shortcut into a life so intensely peopled that loneliness couldn't find me.

At least initially, my little feint against loneliness worked. In my first two years of law school, I was abundantly social, and happy to be surrounded by smart people with big ambitions. Loneliness, of course, continued to present itself, but I actively engaged in what I'd later recognize as cognitive behavioral therapy. When a negative thought about loneliness presented itself, I tried to counter it with a more objective assessment of the situation. If I saw others leaving a classroom without me, I'd tell myself that I'd been slow getting my books, and that I shouldn't interpret their departure as a sign of anything mean-ingful. Sitting alone in the library hour after hour, I'd force myself to actually write down my list of friends, in order to counter the familiar voice saying I was friendless.

The problem I ran into in those years wasn't a lack of so-ciability so much as a failure to connect. I made a very close friend during first year—a sweet human rights campaigner named Laura, a girl so attuned to injustice that she cried during a mock trial—but for the most part there was a gap between me and the other students.

"How is it that we're able to do this?" asked Brian, a law student I dated in second year. He was sinewy and handsome, and we were hiking along the edge of a sunlit field an hour north of Toronto. The field was part of a network of trails, all of which crossed private land, and Brian seemed preoccupied with trying to identify the mechanism that gave us free access to other people's property.

It's an easement, I thought, dutifully calling up the right term. But the thought of saying the word, of polluting the bright day with talk of laws and rules, seemed exhausting to me. There was a dog rushing toward us on the trail up ahead— the sun glinting off its neat black coat as its paws pounded the dust—and I tried to turn the conversation away from property rights.

"It's a Lab," I said enthusiastically. "Did you have dogs when you were little?"

"No. But think. If one of us got hurt right now, who would we sue, the province or the farmer?"

Conversations such as these would leave me feeling half drowned, as though I'd just woken from a dream in which everyone else was speaking a different language. And I couldn't even blame Brian for being a stiff. He was doing exactly what a law student was supposed to be doing—filtering everything through the sieve of a new vocabulary. I was the one who was, in a sense, refusing to engage with reality. I had daydreams of being a writer, and I'd often leave the law library, cross the street to a different college, and hide in its American literature section, perched on one of the little metal stools that most people use for standing on. I found a novel called *Anywhere But Here*, and the title seemed to capture the ambivalence I was beginning to feel about my situation. I'd walk into a three-hour securities lecture, look at the students swapping business magazines and doing penny trades on their laptops, and make a wish: *Anywhere but here*. The phrase became a mantra that popped up whenever I found myself trapped in a conversation about shareholder rights, or interviewing with a tax lawyer, or attending a wine and cheese reception and listening to a senior partner talk about his boat.

There are two lines of thought about the relationship between loneliness and depression. Some people see long-term loneliness as leading to the noonday demon, with aloneness taking such an emotional toll on the lonely person that he eventually runs out of resources and succumbs to chronic feelings of the blues. But it's also been shown that an episode of depression can leave someone more vulnerable to loneliness. Since it curtails the ability to socialize, creates a certain degree of secrecy, and can hasten the arrival of a double or triple self—in which some people are privy to certain facts, while others aren't— depression can be seen as a "predictor" of loneliness, with a bout of the blues increasing the likelihood that loneliness will follow in the years to come.

And it was depression that I hadn't counted on when I'd been drawing up plans for how to sidestep aloneness. In retrospect, I think my failure to connect with people at law school disappointed me, and the constant sense of not saying the right things and not appreciating the right ideas reminded me of all of those afternoons with my father, when I hadn't been able to enjoy the paintings and sculptures he was trying to entertain me with. Law school comes with a future mapped out—you do your clerkship at one firm, find a job at a different firm, then become a partner—and my inability to imagine myself partaking of this future quickly collapsed into an inability to foresee any future at all. I began sleeping ten to twelve hours a day; my hands shook; I developed a genuine anorexia, in which food tasted like chalk; and it soon became routine for me to start crying the minute my apartment door was closed and my book bag hit the floor.

"Do you feel you might do something?" asked Laura gently, standing in her winter coat and not complaining about the cold. I'd called her from my apartment in the middle of my clerkship at a large litigation firm. It was late at night, midweek, and I'd been overcome by a sense of panic, by a powerful feeling that something bloody and dreadful was about to materialize. Laura had taken a cab to my apartment, and then hustled me into a second cab, which had deposited us on the big wide sidewalk in front of one of Toronto's hospitals.

"Do you want me to go get someone?" she asked, reaching for my elbow. She had on a bright red hat and scarf, and I remember thinking how cheerful she looked, and how wrong it was of me to infringe on her happiness.

"It's *OK*," she stressed, reading my mind. I felt suddenly exhausted, and began to cry. Even though I'd been the one who'd suggested the hospital, the prospect of stepping into the emergency ward, with its bright lights and injured people, struck me as suddenly undoable.

"Maybe we'll go home," I said weakly.

"I'll go with you," Laura said, without hesitation. "And make you some hot milk." She stepped toward the road to call for the third cab of the evening, but then turned back to me with an ultimatum. "We're only going if you agree to get help. Do you agree?" she asked, in a very lawyer-like tone.

I did. I saw my GP for a psych referral, and in late 1999 was sent to one of the most shockingly attractive men I'd ever seen. In his midforties, with loose brown curls and a perfectly urbane fashion sense—cashmere sweaters, pressed trousers, Prada shoes—he diagnosed me as clinically depressed. After my symptoms stabilized, and I'd mastered the trick of looking at him without blushing, he suggested not just continued medication but the full removal of myself from the environment that was distressing me. My clerkship had to last twelve months, and there was no way I could lobby for a shorter period. There was no real requirement, however, that the whole year had to be spent at the same office.

"Can't you go somewhere else?" Dr. R. asked, writing out another prescription for Zoloft.

"I'm not sure."

"Well," he replied, handing over the script, "you can keep seeing me until your term there ends—and I'm fine with that— or you can come up with an exit strategy. You seem like a creative person. Be creative."

Feeling the need to prove my creativity, I used the firm's phone lines for a series of complicated long-distance calls, and wound up arranging a transfer to a government office in Iqaluit, Nunavut, in the eastern Arctic. The idea was to put as many miles as possible between myself and the sadness that had found me in Toronto, and the plan worked perfectly. The North—be it Alaska or the Northwest Territories—has a reputation as a haven for misfits, and I found this reputation to be well earned. Many of the people I met in my small Arctic town were there because they found "the south" too constricting: they were too smart for an ordinary city, or too hooked on booze, too easily bored, too restless. I liked the fact that no one questioned my description of the rough, dirt-blown place as "relaxing," I liked it that the sun never set, and I loved the three-hour hikes I took across the tundra most evenings. I was still talking to Dr. R. every week by phone, but by the end of my fourth month in Nunavut, in the summer of 2000, I was able to sit on the deck in the clear midnight light and write one word: "Cured."

And I meant it. Six years later, long after my clerkship was over, and after I'd emerged on the other side of a loneliness that had nearly undone me, I began to talk to publishers about the possibility of writing about my experiences. In having these discussions—which, since they saw me naming loneliness as a fundamental problem in my life, were incredibly unnerving—I expected to be met with a lot of negative reactions. I expected to be stigmatized. I expected to be judged. What I did not expect was for people to tell me I was *wrong*.

"Maybe you were just *depressed*," I heard, time and time again, from editors and marketing reps interested in the project. Lexicographers—people who write dictionaries—often talk about the death of words, about having to delete terms and phrases that have been in use for centuries, simply because they've fallen out of common usage. It was with the sense of having to battle a death of meaning that I countered the assertions that I had, despite my awareness of the problem and my ability to analyze it, been suffering from the blues.

"I wasn't depressed," I'd reply, in an etymological spirit. "I was *lonely*."

"Same thing."

No, it's not. In 2007, after I'd secured a contract for this book (at least one editor recognized that loneliness and depression were separate states), I created a blog called LongTerm Loneliness.com. My goal was to connect with other lonely people, something that's very hard to do in the course of ordinary life. Loneliness—especially chronic loneliness—is a state most people work incredibly hard to hide. It's not something alluded to in even intimate conversations. I quickly discovered, however, that the Internet provided a fast and novel way of bypassing the general taboo against admitting to loneliness. My blog allowed me to post photos of myself, so that potential respondents could see me, and I used the site to write about all the things that were bothering me, such as the silence surrounding loneliness, and the idea of lonely people as unattractive. I complained—in that breezy, carefree way that's really only possible on the Internet—about stereotypes of the lonely as socially awkward; I posted summaries of research findings; and I wrote rather urgently about the need to pull long-term loneliness into public view. I posted ads about my blog on Craigslist, and asked other lonely people to contact me if they were willing to talk. With almost no difficulty, I assembled a research pool of about twenty lonely people from across North America. All of them agreed to share their stories, provided I kept their real identities secret. (It's for this reason that all names and identifying details of the lonely people presented in this book have been changed.)

One of the first things I mentioned in the interviews—which I conducted in 2007 and 2008—was the frustration I felt at being told that my loneliness was really depression. Rachel, a forty-two-year-old homemaker from Florida, knew immediately what I meant. "I used to think it was depression," she says, referring to feelings of aloneness that have troubled her for years. "But I don't think it is. I think it's loneliness. It's just *loneliness.*"

"Being lonely is somewhat sad," says Sonia, a copywriter in her late thirties from the West Coast. She falls silent for a moment as she tries to tease loneliness and depression apart. "I might have short bouts of feeling depressed when I'm lonely," she says, "but there's no long-term depression where I might need medication."

While some of the lonely people I spoke to did struggle with depression, everyone who contacted me stressed that their loneliness was a difficulty in itself. If they were depressed and lonely, they described themselves as having two problems, not one. "It's definitely a bit of both," says James, a Quebec-based engineer in his late fifties who suffers from both depression and loneliness. James describes the situation he faces as "chicken and egg," with one state feeding into the other, but he stresses that loneliness is likely the core of the problem. "I ask myself if I'm depressed because I'm lonely, or if I'm lonely because

I'm depressed. And I think a lot of the depression comes from being lonely."

Loneliness is certainly not an upbeat emotion, but then, neither is grief, and we manage to see it as something other than depression. In my case, the loneliness that unfolded in my thirties was certainly marked by lows, but these lows never came to dominate the core of my emotional life. Depression, for me, has always been marked by a sort of presence, a presence that's often evoked, by others, through the imagery of "black dogs." Depression really does feel like something hounding and snapping at you. It's as though you've been set upon by something vicious you can't see.

With loneliness, that sense of a presence begins to vanish over time. What lonely people find themselves drowning in is absence. They have to struggle with the unnerving sense of being too much on their own, and having to rely on themselves in an effort to meet their own needs. And once the self has been searched and patted down for a sense of companionship—which is something it can't provide—what the lonely person is left with is a worn-out, edgy sense of insufficiency. "It's just this emptiness," says Adam, a forty-five-year-old illustrator from Rhode Island. "I think there can be a really good emptiness, when things are really harmonious, and you're content. But this," he says, referring to days and nights spent entirely alone, "this is shameful. It makes me want to not do anything."

I'm not suggesting that loneliness is full of joy, or that it doesn't bear a passing resemblance to depression. What I am saying is that we need to start seeing loneliness as something separate from the noonday demon. The social psychologists and neuroscientists who work with the lonely are careful to stress that they know what they're doing. They're not, with all of their advanced degrees and methodological training, accidentally mixing up depression with loneliness, and foolishly confusing one state with the other.

"I'm quite careful about what it is that we're studying," says Dr. John Cacioppo, a University of Chicago neuroscientist who is one of the world's leading loneliness researchers. I'd called him, very nervously, in the fall of 2007, after reading close to a dozen of his papers. Getting him on the phone was, from a loneliness perspective, sort of like calling God, and I'd made myself memorize my list of questions before dialing his number. One of the first things I asked about was the notion of loneliness as a problem in its own right, and it was a balm to hear him confirm what I'd long suspected.

"Loneliness is related to depression, but it's *not* the same thing," he stresses. "If you see loneliness as just an aspect of depression—and that's really how it's been conceived—then it doesn't require any special attention."

What Cacioppo and his fellow researchers are stressing is that loneliness *does* require special attention. Using statistical analyses, specialized scales, physiological assessments, and careful interviews, Cacioppo and others working in the field have demonstrated that loneliness—in itself—can lead to dementia, early death, physical illness, and behavioral changes. "We are fundamentally a social species," says Cacioppo. "If you take other people away, we *don't* do well."

Conversations with lonely people tend to reveal difficulties that can't be reduced to depression—such as a persistent sense of isolation, a troubling lack of intimacy, and an unwelcome jealousy that erupts when confronted with other people's rich social ties. Many lonely people refer to depression as not just a different state but a state capable of pushing loneliness to the margins. "I was crying, I was sad, I was having these crazy thoughts," says Rachel, referring to a depression that overcame her after the birth of her second child. That depression, she says, was terrible, "but it blocked out the loneliness, because it was quite a different feeling. It was when the depression lifted that I began to feel lonely again."

One reason we're comfortable saying that loneliness is "just depression" is that we don't have enough information about the state. Loneliness isn't widely written about, and findings about loneliness don't make the evening news. In this sense, the lack of awareness about loneliness is understandable; if it consti-tuted the extent of the problem, it could be excused. But there's something else in play as well—a sluggishness, a failure of the imagination. Studies suggest that close to 10 percent of North Americans struggle with persistent loneliness, but we don't want to think of what life is like for these millions of people. We don't want to imagine what it's like to feel lonely day after day and month after month. We don't want to dwell on the cir-cumstances of a life marked by strong feelings of isolation, and by long stretches of aloneness. Telling ourselves that loneliness is just depression is a way of closing the door on the state. It means we don't have to hear from the lonely, we don't have to understand what their lives are like. We can say, "You were just depressed," and in this way completely shut out what the lonely might be trying to say.

It took me some time, after my return to Toronto in August 2000, to notice things going awry. After my clerkship, I had to prepare for my bar admission exams, which involved a class every morning and an exam every two weeks for a period of four months. In fairy tales, major life changes are often pre-ceded with long, deep sleeps—think "Sleeping Beauty"—and the strangest thing about my bar admission course was how often it saw me napping. After class, I'd study from about one o'clock to three o'clock, then collapse onto the bed with the windows wide open and fall into a thick, gluttonous sleep. I'd wake at six or seven, cold and confused about the day and about whether I'd missed class.

Even at the time, I felt as though the sleeps had some significance, but I couldn't discern just what it was they were trying to warn me about. In any event, the naps were interrupted by my return to work. I'd decided, during my bright nighttime hikes across the tundra, that I had to dedicate myself to something meaningful, and after my bar exams were over, I chose to become an environmental protection lawyer. I went to a small boutique firm that offered me the sort of light, flexible schedule my psychiatrist had encouraged me toward, and bought a tight tweed jacket, which I thought of as my "environmental law coat." I spent my early weeks at the firm arranging plants, gathering binders, and ordering books on deforestation. I noticed that the office was often fairly empty. My bosses spread themselves thin and kept strange hours, and an environmental practice meant attending to landscapes hours away, with official contacts being little more than voices on the phone, and the real clients being trees. There were law clerks in the back office—cheerful young women who did excellent work while keeping up an unbroken dialogue about mortgages, therapists, and vacations—but the front office, where I sat, was often still. We were in a converted loft space with massive skylights, and I began to feel as though there wasn't enough physically present for the light to hit on. Mine would be the only office occupied, and I could wander from doorway to doorway in my stocking feet, encountering no one.

The fact that I'd chosen a highly specialized field meant I began to lose touch with classmates who'd stayed at the big

litigation firms, and—just as my professional life was contract-
ing—my personal life began to winnow itself down as well.
One day in October 2001, my father went to the emergency
ward with an inexplicable 104-degree fever. By December he
was dead, consumed from within by a sharklike cancer that
had encircled him without warning. My reaction, as my father's body began to shrink and he lost the ability to grip the
books he'd always loved, was, *Here we go again*. His death, in
many ways, felt like a repetition of the loss I'd experienced in
childhood, when I must have watched him move out, never to
return. And the uncanny thing about this second departure
was that it signaled a recurrence of the isolation I'd struggled
with in childhood. After his death, I quickly learned the details of his will—my sisters and I had inherited nothing, while
my stepmother inherited everything—and this left me furious
with Mary-Ann, whom I'd previously felt quite fondly toward.
I felt cut off from my sisters, who were engrossed in the issue of
how to handle their children's grief, and I was struck, just as I
had been in childhood, by my mother's interminable aloneness.
Given the acrimonious nature of the divorce, she hadn't been
given any role at the funeral, and I sat and watched numbly
from the back of a limousine as she stood outside the funeral
home and tried to find a ride to the cemetery.

I was thirty-one when my father died. This meant, of course,
that I had resources at my disposal that I hadn't had as a child.

"You have amazing friends," said Juliette, a confidante from
college, shortly after my father's death. Not only had Juliette,
Laura, and other friends supported me during my father's hospi-
talization, they had—while I was dealing with funeral arrange-
ments and trying to absorb the worst of the shock—painted
my entire apartment. I'd signed a lease two months before my

father died, and they hadn't wanted to see me coming back to a place that was dingy and chipped.

"I know," I replied, looking at my cream and sage walls. In the weeks following my father's death, I often thought of my friends standing together in the snowy graveyard as my father was being buried, and this memory was surprisingly comforting—it was a way of reminding myself that I wasn't as alone as I had been in childhood.

And that sense of reassurance might have been enough. I might, with friends in place and a career beginning to unfold, have sidestepped loneliness. I was single at the time, but I don't think that a life filled with only work and friends is necessarily a lonely one. The problem was that, almost without my realizing it, a gap had opened up. The Canadian poet Michael Redhill talks about loneliness "metastasizing," and the one person who had kept my sense of isolation from dividing and subdividing had been my father. Even though he'd been absent for much of my childhood, when I looked at him, I'd seen myself. There was something about his quietness and reserve that mirrored my own; there was a steady, unwavering gentleness to him that made me feel safe. I'd started seeing a new therapist, a deftly intelligent Jungian analyst named Genevieve, when my dad entered hospital, and I told her about the dreams I'd been having about his impending death. I'd be snapping pictures of him, and he'd be disappearing from frame to frame, or aliens would be leading him up a path of light to a spaceship.

At the time, even though my father was very sick, the doctors kept telling us that he'd pull through, and both of my sisters seemed to believe this. After my dad died, I asked Genevieve why I'd been the only one who seemed to think that his death had been a certainty.

"It's possible that you were attuned to your father in a way that others weren't," she replied.

I asked her what *attunement* meant, and she told me that it meant silent connection, a wordless sense of identification. I made a mental note of the term—it seemed slightly academic at the time—but I think that was what I found myself increasingly missing as the months wore on. The sense I'd had of matching with at least one other person had disappeared, and—as this feeling evaporated, and perhaps because it had evaporated—my relationships with others began to winnow out and thin. In 2002, in the months following my father's death, my close friend Simon and his wife realized they were expecting another child, and this discovery pulled them closer into a home-based world that had less room for me. Laura began an internship with a women's law organization in Nairobi; Juliette became heavily involved with her job at a film company; and Georgina, a soft-spoken friend from law school, left for another town. I began an affair with a tall, dark-haired professor, but the substitution function Ron was serving—he was so clever and bookish, so coincidentally like my dad—became so obvious and disturbing that I ended the relationship before it had the chance to bloom.

My office was near King Street West, the core of Toronto's financial hub. A few blocks away from my office were the huge sixty- and seventy-story towers that housed tens of thousands of employees. I used to love the morning rush. I liked the sight of everyone hurrying from the subways, briefcases in hand, coffee mugs at the ready, newspapers folded under elbows. One of the things I liked to do in the evenings was watch the reverse of this process. If mornings were marked by a slightly regimented aspect, with everyone arriving at the same time and looking slightly pressured, evenings were a more casual affair, with people chatting as they waited for the streetcar, or talking on their cell phones as they wandered toward the subway entrance, or idly counting out bills as they drew money from the bank machines.

One warm night in early fall, about nine months after my father had died, I was engaged in what I called my Friday-evening dawdling. I went to a bookstore and bought *Life of Pi*, then wandered back out to King Street to have a mint tea at Starbucks. With my tea finished, I went into a cheap clothing store and browsed through the flashy, flimsy acrylic sweaters on sale. They weren't my style—I liked wool and heavy knits—and I realized, upon leaving the store, that I had nothing else to do.

The subway entrances in downtown Toronto are bordered by thick silver rails: the steps descend from one direction, and opposite the steps is a concrete barrier with the rail on top. The rail is positioned at chest height, so that you can lean on it and watch people as they enter the station. What I found myself doing, after I left the sweater shop, was standing at the railing to King Station and looking down. Although I didn't know any of the people I was seeing, I felt I had some sense of how their evenings were going to unfold. The leisurely pace, and the look of relaxation on many faces, spoke of home lives, of boarding a northbound or southbound train to meet a wife, or boyfriend, or best friend.

And I suddenly realized that my life was no longer like that—that I had no one to visit, no one to return home to. I juggled the weight of my paperback in its plastic bag, and began to feel slightly anxious. My after-work loitering suddenly assumed a different hue. I hadn't been *dawdling*, I realized. I'd been avoiding something. And what I'd been trying to put off was my inevitable return to an empty apartment, and to a weekend that offered little or nothing in the way of company.

It was one of those perfect, windless, cloudless evenings,

with the sky a rich indigo that made the streetlights seem incandescent. There was something about the beauty of the evening, the Indian summer feel to it, that made my loneliness seem suddenly stark. It was as though the world was full of riches that had escaped me. The strategies I'd been deploying against feelings of aloneness—reading, window-shopping, wandering—suddenly struck me as childish, as forms of evasion that were bound to fail. Although I'd later come to associate loneliness with weight, I felt, as I stood at the rail, suddenly too light and unfixed, as though there literally weren't enough to me to keep me grounded.

There was a tide of people heading down the steps, and I began to feel as though it were pulling me toward it. I tried to think about diversions, but came up empty-handed. The financial district would shut down in another hour or two, leaving me with nothing but smoke shops and courier depots. I could head to one of the movie theaters or malls farther north, but doing so would only buy me some time. What I couldn't avoid, and what I could feel myself stiffen against as I lifted my arms off the rail, was an evening of aloneness. I soon found myself joining others in the march down the station staircase, and heard a train rumbling along the northbound track. The train pushed warm, humid air from the tunnel into the station as it came to a stop and opened its doors. Without being quite aware of what I was doing, I boarded the train, and as the doors closed, I began to feel as though the stranger I'd been aware of all my life—the one who'd been waiting to make my acquaintance—had found me and was pressed up against me, ready to follow me home.

Chapter Two

TRUTH

*Struggling with popular notions of
what loneliness should be*

I n retrospect, it strikes me that the onset of my loneliness—
in late September or early October of 2002—was actually
well timed, in that the state was taking hold just as winter was
setting in. This may sound counterintuitive, as though the last
thing a lonely person needs to deal with is windchill, but it's
been my experience that loneliness is actually more manageable in the winter. One of the main problems with loneliness is
what I think of as "visibility," the sense of having your loneliness witnessed by others, and of being *seen* as being too much
on your own. Winter—at least in Canada and the northern
United States—offers something of a reprieve from this feeling
of fluorescence. The fact that darkness fell early meant that I
could take after-work walks through my neighborhood in privacy. Most people weren't out, and those who were out were so
busy navigating snowbanks that they barely glanced at me.

Although I know that I was doing things during those winter

months of early 2003—still seeing my family for Sunday brunches on occasion, still going to my friend Simon's house to talk about his dreams of becoming a filmmaker and his excitement over the new baby, still taking walks with Juliette—what comes to mind when I think about that season is my kitchen. I lived on the third floor of an old triplex, and the fact that the apartment was wedged into the roof meant its ceiling sloped sharply downward. There was a skylight cut into the slope, and as the snow piled on top of the window, the whole room came to take on a ghostly white light. I spent a lot of weekends sitting below the skylight at my kitchen table, with the radio on for companionship and my diary open in front of me—since no one came over, I never bothered to put it away. Despite its proximity to the roof, the kitchen was always extremely warm, and I tended to remain fixed there, as though the room's peacefulness and gauzy light could substitute for the comfort I needed to take from others.

It was when I was at the table one day, writing in my journal, that I first noticed something going wrong with words. I'd been writing about my visit to a church near my office. St. Andrew's was a century-old cathedral in the downtown core, and I'd started going there during my lunch hour to see if I could summon up the sort of connection I used to feel in church in grade school. A day earlier, during the workweek, I'd decided to add a slightly mercantile aspect to my experiment with belief. I thought that if I *paid* for a prayer, I might feel a stronger sense of belonging. I was writing about the church—the muted light, the cracked stained glass, the plaques to generations of war dead—when I realized I'd forgotten how to describe the candle I'd paid to light. It was a votive candle, of course, but I sat at the table, chewed my pen, and thought, Motive candle? Devotive candle? Devout candle?

The University of California social scientist Robert Bell, writing in the journal *Communication Monographs*, has shown that lonely people have more trouble recalling things—after a conversation, they'll remember less of what their partner has just told them—and I realized that a certain porousness was beginning to affect my vocabulary. Reading an article in a women's magazine, I had to struggle to picture what a saucer was; on the phone with Simon, I said I'd become a "celebrity."

"A what?" Simon asked with a laugh.

"You know," I said, awkwardly scanning my stack of nouns and hoping he'd provide me with the right one. "One of those people who don't have sex."

"And that would be a celibate."

"Right. I just forgot."

But it was more than just forgetting. The more time I spent without companionship, the more it began to seem as though words were spinning out of my control. This was something I wasn't used to. I've always been precise. One of the things I'd done during lonely times in childhood was write out dictionary definitions and make myself memorize them. This isn't as entirely nerdy as it sounds. Words were something I cottoned to from an early age, and I loved flipping through the big dictionary my father had left behind. The problem was that, as a lonely adult, all the words I'd made myself learn seemed to take on lives of their own. Either they darted away just when I reached for them, or they lunged back up at me with exhausting force.

Because my inner life, as I spent more and more time on my own, was becoming an increasingly noisy one. My kitchen table had only four chairs, and I, of course, occupied only one of them. But I often felt as though I were at a table of six, with everyone talking simultaneously. A trait I came to describe as "conversationitis" began to dominate my life. Even as I longed for quiet, a constant, vivacious line of chatter wound its way through my mind. If I'd had a talk with someone at work that afternoon, the discussion would replay itself as though it were on a loop. Bits of songs raced through my head, as did imagined responses to radio phone-ins, recollected disputes with Martin, and lively, completely honest exchanges with Georgina, who'd fallen out of touch.

Am I going crazy? I thought, after an afternoon in which an imagined talk with Martin had reduced me to tears. I knew—everyone knew—that hearing voices was an early sign of schizophrenia, and I worried I was beginning to manifest the signs of something disturbing.

"Because they're like *real voices*," I said to my therapist, Genevieve. I'd gotten to the point where I'd started shaking my head in an effort to clear the voices out, and this behavior struck me as so patently unbalanced, I knew I needed help.

Genevieve adopted a curious, compassionate look, as though she saw something quite clearly, but wasn't sure how much of her insight she was prepared to reveal.

"It's because you're lonely," she said, very gently. The words hit me like a slap. Although I should have seen her response coming—and probably should have been able to spot the source of the problem myself—I was entirely shocked, and profoundly embarrassed. Everything about her statement was new and unwelcome. I wasn't used to having anyone comment on my loneliness. I wasn't used to hearing anyone name it as a problem in my life. I'd seen Dr. R. for at least two years, and although problems with loneliness had surfaced during those years, he'd never alluded to it. With Dr. R., I'd been the over-achieving lawyer who had a problem with depression. I *liked* the depression scenario. I liked the way it left my personality out of the picture, the way it seemed to keep attributes such as *smart* and *successful* intact.

Genevieve was saying something much more damaging, and more threatening. Her comment made it clear that she saw the gaps in my personal life, and these were gaps I didn't want anyone seeing. Nobody knows, I told myself when I came home on a Friday evening to an empty apartment, or when I went to bed on a Sunday night after having spent the weekend alone. It was comforting to me that, even if loneliness was emerging as a significant problem, it was at least a problem I was able to hide. And hiding it felt crucial. Loneliness, at the start of the wired-up twenty-first century, was so totally nowhere, so crushingly uncool. The word itself made me cringe. The state jarred with the image I tried to project, which was that of a clever, together young woman who had few emotional needs—or at least few needs that weren't being met. Having someone spot my loneliness made me feel outsmarted, as though I were a child caught out at a game. And, childishly, I wasn't able to tell Genevieve that she was right. Instead, I squirmed in my chair and equivocated.

"So long as it's not schizophrenia," I said, trying to sound lighthearted and casual, as though this loneliness she'd mentioned wasn't a problem of mine. "Anything else I can deal with."

But the fact was, I really didn't know how to deal with it. I did what I'd always done—I wrote—but my diaries began to seem like printed versions of the conversations I was struggling with. There were simply too many of them. What I would have said to a partner or best friend got funneled into my journals, until the pages began to grow fat and sweaty-looking. And what I didn't like about the diaries I'd started keeping—what set them apart from the journals of my more sociable law school years and my years with Martin—was that they were filled with little scribbles and graphs.

Social network theorists often ask lonely people (and their nonlonely counterparts) to imagine themselves at the center of a circle, and to plot out where others fall in relation to their central spot. A spouse or best friend might be directly beside them, their boss might be two spots away, their neighbor might be three or four places removed.

I found myself drawing up these little maps of my social life, always with dissatisfying results. It was as though the pleas I'd listened to so glibly when I was young—*Can I be your second best friend? Or your third?*—had come back to haunt me. There was no one that I could cast in the empty spot directly beside the word *me*. Laura, who was probably my closest friend, had come back from the law clinic in Kenya and begun dating an economist, a change that made me feel as though some distance had opened up between her name and mine. My friend Simon had a whole ring of people—wife, children, co-workers—around him. Juliette, my friend from college, had moved in with a young man she'd met at her film company. Ron, the professor I'd had the short affair with, was lost in his work. My sisters were fairly far away, on the other side of town, and my mother—whose relationship with loneliness seemed to have changed—was surprisingly busy with lunch dates and socials. No matter how I tried to tilt and rig the graphs, I couldn't seem to spill anyone else's name closer to my own.

As the days grew brighter, in the spring of 2003, I began to feel my aloneness more acutely. The sight of families in playgrounds and young couples on park benches was hard to witness. The abundance of light was bringing more people outdoors, and I began to lose the sense of privacy and invisibility I associated with my evening walks. The clerks at work were growing slightly giddy, making plans with their boyfriends for patio dinners and barbecues, and my firm announced it would be keeping summer hours: beginning in July, the workday would end at four. The bright warm light and longer days, the leaves coming out on the trees, the sparrows lifting up off the lawns, the grass turning a rich, luscious green—all of this felt like an accusation, as though I weren't participating in life in the way that it was meant to be lived.

Laura was aware of my solitary state, and was bothered by it. In part, I think she felt guilty about having a boyfriend when I was single, but I think she also saw, perhaps more acutely than I did, how seriously my isolation was affecting me. Laura had met her economist boyfriend, Ben, on Lavalife, and she encouraged me to try it.

"What are your requirements?" she asked as we sat one day in her bright, leafy apartment, in front of her laptop. Her question sounded like a job offer from a law firm, asking me about salary expectations. I told her I wasn't sure what she meant.

"Things like education and religion, body type, whether they smoke or drink—all that sort of stuff."

"You can search for all that?"

"Sure," said Laura, cheerfully clicking boxes off for me. She decided I needed someone tall, with a postgraduate degree, who didn't drink or smoke and who enjoyed volunteering, photography, and social activism. She hit "find" on the search engine, and I was astonished to see photos of agreeable-looking men pop up. Sitting at Laura's desk, I became overwhelmed, not with sexual desire, but with the desire to connect. Looking at the pictures of potential partners, I felt as though the end of my loneliness might be in sight, and this outcome was so enticing I felt winded. It was as though my body were made up of iron filings, and the computer was a magnet. I was riveted. I might connect with *that one*, I thought excitedly, hurrying down the list and looking at the photo of a smiling, dark-haired man, or *that one*—a blond—or *him*, a redhead who bore an uneasy resemblance to Martin.

The sense of possibility persisted as I set up dates. I was a pro at writing my personal description. I quickly realized, in scanning the better ones, that the trick was to downplay feelings of aloneness and emphasize instead how full and social your life really was. The desired tone seemed to be one of harassed busyness, as though someone were dragging you from the keyboard even as you tried to type. I mastered this satisfied voice in a snap. "My apartment is filled with books and plants and sunshine," I wrote. "All I need is a significant other to add to this colorful, cheerful mix."

It's become a cinematic cliché to show Internet dates unfolding one after another, with one disastrous scene leading directly into the next. This portrayal might seem contrived on the screen, but my experience with Internet dating actually felt like this. I went to the same café time after time. It had large, street-level windows, and I figured the people-watching could always provide a subject if conversation stalled. (When I told a law school acquaintance about my preference for a single location, he said, "Oh, you've got a graveyard," meaning I'd never see any of those people again.) Among my dates was the man who told me, apropos of nothing, that he had a powerful phobia of dogs (*"Even puppies,"* he stressed, in case I thought there might be hope for him), and the young techie who described himself as being heavily into gaming, but who never gave me the chance to ask what gaming actually was. I liked talking to Jordan, an accountant with a quiet demeanor. He told me he loved reading, and I thought we might have something in common. Then he told me about a cross-country trip he'd taken, and about how he'd wound up snowbound in Manitoba for nearly a week.

"But it was OK," he said, happily, "because I had my Erasmus with me."

I was completely stunned. Most people, heading out on the road, pack Jack Kerouac, or condoms, or a half-carton of cheap cigarettes. Jordan had packed a theological text by a sixteenth-century Dutch academic. Not only had he packed it, he'd *read* it.

I fumbled for a response. "Erasmus," I repeated, trying to sound informed. And then I heard myself saying, in something of a panic, "I really enjoyed Gregory of Tours." Gregory of Tours was a sixth-century French bishop I'd been forced to read in history class, and who I remembered solely for his description of a man sharing his bedroom with a pig. I had a sense that the pig story wouldn't appeal to Jordan, and—since I had nothing else to talk about—I fell silent as he grew enthusiastic about our apparently shared appreciation of medieval theology.

"I'll call you," I said, as we stepped out of the café onto the street. It was a gorgeous April evening, and a couple was laughing as they locked their bikes to a parking meter a few feet away. Even as I was saying good-bye to Jordan, I knew I'd never call. I knew this silence would disappoint him, and I realized that, despite my innocent intentions, I might wind up adding to someone else's sense of isolation. It was with the sense of not wanting to spread my loneliness around that I gave up on Internet dating and decided that rule number one in my battle with aloneness would have to be a refusal to harm anyone else.

There's an idea in loneliness literature that refers to "situational loneliness," and it means that the loneliness has presented itself for a specific reason, such as a move, a divorce, an illness, or a bereavement. Situational loneliness is usually seen as being just as severe as chronic loneliness. Both situational and chronic loneliness evoke feelings of threat and insecurity, as well as an overpowering sense of isolation. What sets situational loneliness apart from chronic loneliness is that, with an explanation attached to the state, it's possible to imagine a life without it. That is, the situationally lonely person can tell herself that, once she's fully settled in the new town, or adapted to the new school, or remarried, her loneliness will wane. The problem with situational loneliness becomes not endurance but management. How, the situationally lonely person tends to ask herself, can the circumstances of a life be changed so that loneliness recedes to the background?

Although I'd been having problems with loneliness since childhood, I was still—at this relatively early point—trying to cast my problem as situational. I didn't want to see my state as indicative of a chronic psychological problem. I wanted to see it as something accidental. My original plan had been to attach my loneliness to my dating status, the idea being that if I met the right person, my problems with loneliness would just disappear, as though they'd never been a strong part of my past. Even after my foray into Internet dating imploded, I didn't want to give up on the idea of situation. As a result, I simply shifted my focus from dating to place. If only I were *living* somewhere else, I reasoned, I wouldn't be so endlessly lonely.

Without my bosses being aware of it, I began to look for job opportunities in Alaska, the Yukon, and the tiny northern

Ontario town of Moose Factory. I never considered more cosmopolitan locations, such as Paris or New York City, because I wanted a place so small and remote that it would provide me with an instant sense of community. Trying to convert my loneliness into something it wasn't, I told myself that feelings of aloneness provided me with a license to "live larger." With no dependents to support, and no spouse to keep me rooted, I could go wherever I wanted. I'd experienced less loneliness in Iqaluit, Nunavut, during my clerkship—I think that being in a place where most people came up alone, and where it was common to lack close ties, made my aloneness much easier to bear—and I became fixated on the idea that if I just moved, I'd have my loneliness solved.

Or at least that's what I told myself. Looking back, I'm not sure that I wanted to move so much as I wanted to be met with fierce and passionate opposition to the prospect of my moving. Because the strange thing about my goal of removal was that, even though I received job offers from the University of Alaska and from the legal clinic in northern Ontario, I couldn't seem to find the traction necessary to get up and go. I liked telling people about the possibilities in the North, but that's because I wanted to hear others say I should stay.

"Why would you want to go to Moose Factory?" asked my eldest sister, Christine, when I told her about my possible job change. "That's crazy. There's nothing up there. Nothing. I mean, you have to take a *boat* to get there."

This sort of response was pretty typical. My friends and family thought my desire to transport myself out of Toronto was odd, but no one seemed poised to stand in my way. With no one trying to bar the door, my desire to depart for some distant, barely settled town began to seem a bit ill-thought-out and desperate.

"It's just a thought," I told Christine. "A way of, you know, getting closer to nature."

"There's a lake right down the street," she replied, not un-kindly. We were in her big house near Lake Ontario, and she was heading to the kitchen to make lunch for her kids. "You could grab a bike and go commune."

And so I did, in a sense. Throughout the summer of 2003, I embarked on a strategy of what I called stoicism but which was really repression. When I went to Simon's house and found myself feeling lost amid the noise of his two young kids, I'd leave and tell myself to shelve my sense of having lost a close connection. When I called Juliette only to find out that she'd forgotten our weekend lunch date and had made plans with her mother, I'd grab the edge of the bed, stifle my sense of distress, and tell myself I could get by alone. When I began to feel invis-ible at a family brunch where conversation revolved around the kids' grade school teachers—Christine's and Theresa's kids were the same age—I'd grip my fork and think, That's OK, you have a rich life of your own.

Except I didn't. When I'd been struggling with depression during my clerkship, a friend had given me the *Feeling Good Handbook*, and I remembered the author's advice to people feel-ing anxious about empty chunks of time: break the hours up, write down small, self-contained activities, and attend to each activity in turn. I never went so far as to actually write down a schedule, but I definitely engaged in this sort of planning ex-ercise in my head as the summer wore on. At work, toward the end of the day, I'd mentally spell out my evening: subway, dinner, walk, book, bed. The problem was that parceling out my evening this way didn't make me feel calm. It made me jumpy. Seeing my evening stripped to its component parts drew my attention to the fact that I'd be undertaking each activity alone, and the prospect of impending aloneness made my stomach drop, as though I'd just peered over the edge of a cliff.

"I think we need to turn to the emptiness," said Genevieve. My weekly appointments with her were becoming indispensable. For at least an hour, I'd be the focus of someone else's unbroken attention and concern. I wouldn't be alone. I often felt some ambivalence toward Genevieve during these sessions. I craved the sense of connection she provided, but felt a certain degree of anger about the fact that such connection wasn't available in the course of my ordinary life. "You're right," she said immediately, when I raised the issue. "You shouldn't have to rely on me." But the fact was that I *did* have to rely on her. Outside of her consulting room, intimacy was starting to seem like a distant thing, a prize handed out to everyone else but me. Awash with the sense that everyone but Genevieve was retreating, and that my need for her was becoming too pronounced, I started trying to hide the existence of the need itself. I'd show up late for appointments, or I'd breeze through her office door talking airily of people at work.

What I was much less ambivalent about was the fact that I was able, with Genevieve, to slowly start naming loneliness as a problem. After Genevieve's first, loaded introduction of the subject, she'd refrained from mentioning it directly. What she did instead was create openings in our conversation that allowed me to practice saying the words *me*, *alone*, and *lonely*. She'd ask how I felt about my bosses being so often out of the office, or whether I felt distant from friends who were becoming parents. I was still, in the summer of 2003, uncomfortable saying too much about loneliness. I'd name the state only to back away from it, or I'd describe myself as lonely and then try to make myself sound less lonely by launching into a long story about Laura, or one of my sisters. But I was at least taking the first steps toward admitting to loneliness. Within the confines of Genevieve's consulting room, the state was a problem I was beginning to describe as mine.

I'd hesitantly told Genevieve about trying to plan out my evenings and distract myself from loneliness. She clearly disagreed with this haphazard strategy.

"I think your loneliness is trying to tell you something."

Profound, I thought. I knew what my loneliness was trying to tell me: I needed more people in my life. I could hear coins go *ca-ching* as I briefly considered the money I was spending. Genevieve was quick, and she caught my irritation.

"I think if you really turn to it, you'll be surprised at what it has to say."

And so, trusting Genevieve, I went home one evening and sat at the kitchen table with paper and pen. I closed my eyes and did as I was told. I "turned" to the loneliness. Feeling a bit like someone receiving messages from the afterlife, I wrote down every thought and phrase that came to me. At first, the words were nothing more than the stock terms I'd been scribbling for months. "Me, myself & I," I doodled. "Always, always me. Why, why, why?" And then boilerplate words and phrases— the ones I barely thought about—seemed to snap and give way to something else. "It's like a wind," I found myself writing. "Its color is white. It feels rough, like sandpaper, and big, like a blanket spread out. Its edges are jagged. Sometimes it feels like something pressing up against my mouth and nose, as though it were trying to suffocate me."

I paused in my description, and opened my eyes. There was a pounding feeling behind my temples, as though my blood were rushing too quickly through my veins. I felt I had seen something—not a feeling, not a transient mood, but a real object. The sensation was like suddenly noticing a house in a far-off field, or a bird quickly taking flight. The whole time I'd been dealing with loneliness—and it was nearly a year by this point—I'd been trading in ephemeralities, telling myself the sensation didn't have substance, that it was closer to a mirage than a diagnosis. But as I wrote, my loneliness was presenting itself in a substantive way—as something with texture, color, sound, and intent. "It wants to be seen," I found myself adding. And then I stopped writing. I felt as though my hands were full, as though I'd just been presented with something cool and metallic, like a medallion or charm I could handle and clutch.

My sudden recognition of what felt like a real state made me uneasy. I wasn't sure I was ready to start thinking of loneliness as something present and tangible in my life. There was a sense of safety in not seeing, in dismissing my loneliness as a passing phase, or as something as immaterial as my preference for the color blue. But as a lawyer, I was struck by the sheer logic of what my list was trying to tell me. I'd known for some time that I was dealing with something other than depression. "I'm not depressed," I'd write over and over again in my journals, subconsciously using the process of elimination as a means of trying to arrive at the real problem. But even as I was ushering the diagnosis of depression out, I wasn't sure I could usher the diagnosis of loneliness in. I wasn't sure that loneliness could *be* a diagnosis. Loneliness was supposed to be a light, minor, and occasional problem, not a difficulty in itself.

But my description—one whose emphasis on air and whiteness and a steady, monotonous roughness still feels right to me—had been the description of something meaty, something with substance, like my desk lamp or my knee. In the years to come, I'd talk to neuroscientists and psychologists about loneliness as an affliction in its own right, one that manifests itself through significant changes to mind and body. In 2003 I hadn't yet had these conversations, but I'd hit on the same conclusion nonetheless. I'd written about my loneliness as something real and purposeful, as something that was, in itself, sweeping, risky, and wide.

One of the reasons I knew I wasn't struggling with depression was that my loneliness was affecting me in ways depression never had. Around the time that I was conducting my experiment in "listening" to loneliness, for instance, I'd begun to experience what I called "mild highs." These weren't frenzied, energized episodes of hypomania, but rather stretches of time—maybe three or four hours at most—that would see me *not needing* anyone. That is, the problem I was dealing with seemed to come bundled up with its own escape valve. At least within that first year, my sense of isolation was broken, perhaps once or twice a month, by the sense of being "lifted," a reprieve that would see me feeling contented and connected and whole. This wasn't because my need for affection and sociability was being met, but rather because my mind was temporarily— through some means that I'm not able to pinpoint—producing a break from that need. Since loneliness has profound psychological, behavioral, and physiological effects, the possibility that we might have developed an ability to at least briefly turn the state off makes sense. It's as though the mind is giving itself the chance to recuperate from the considerable stress it's facing.

My inner resources also seemed to be working overtime at night, in a way that was entirely new. When I'd been depressed, I hadn't dreamed of happiness. But the first year of my loneliness saw me indulging in dreams of close connection. I'd be married, and would be happily suiting up three young children for a day at the beach; or a woman would be wrapping her arms tight around me, and letting me tilt my head against her neck; or someone would be trying to tell me I was single, and I'd be laughing, and hauling out all the mail addressed to my partner, saying, "Look, look, I told you he was real." There would be a period, between sleep and wakefulness, when I'd re-experience the comfort and calm I'd known during the most connected times of my life—when I'd first started dating Martin, or when I'd first met Laura at law school. Even as my dreams receded, leaving me with nothing but fragments, I'd try to hang on to the feeling of belonging, knowing I needed it for the day ahead.

The isolation I was experiencing was also leaving me profoundly anxious. When I wrote that my loneliness was trying to "suffocate" me, what I was picking up on was the change that seemed to have overcome my breathing. It had become shallower. If I hurried or tried to run, I had a harder time catching my breath. My neck and shoulders were often tense, and—in a development that should have raised alarm bells with me, but which I didn't understand the significance of at the time—this tension began to increase when I was with other people. Coming home from a dinner with my friend Juliette, I'd shut my apartment door and realize that my jaw was clenched, and that it had been all evening.

What I should have done at this point was return to my psychiatrist for help, but I couldn't see myself approaching him with a complaint about loneliness. The state—even after I'd sketched it out as something real—seemed to lack the legitimacy of other afflictions, such as depression or bipolar disorder. My loneliness didn't seem like an ailment so much as a flaw, a problem I'd somehow brought upon myself and had to overcome through will alone. "It seems like a weakness," says Sonia, the copywriter from the West Coast. I ask why she hasn't sought treatment for a condition that has lasted so long—she describes feelings of aloneness as being in place for most of her life—and she stresses that it's because she can't point to anything significant about it. "It seems like it's not really something to complain about, because you're supposed to have the power to just fix it."

The only aspect of my experience that didn't seem to translate into notions of self-blame or inadequate will was anxiety, and—with my breath catching like an engine turning over—I eventually presented myself at my GP's office, where I heard myself saying I'd become jumpy, that I'd started suffering from a high-grade edginess I couldn't understand.

"Any major changes?" he asked, the trees of a ravine looking cool and green in the window behind him. "A breakup? A move?"

"No," I replied, feeling blatantly dishonest. There had been a change—I'd been overcome with loneliness—but I felt too ashamed to mention this. I'd just begun acknowledging the state, in private, with Genevieve. I certainly wasn't ready to burst forth and start announcing myself as lonely to the wider world. And my doctor wasn't exactly opening the door to a discussion about isolation. His desk was covered with photos of his wife and children, and I couldn't imagine admitting to an aloneness he obviously didn't feel. "It's sort of generalized," I said, using a word I'd picked up in *Help and Hope for Your Nerves*. "I don't know what's causing it."

With generalized anxiety disorder so prevalent—global rates for the disorder hover around 5 percent—and with its symptoms so open and vague, my doctor readily wrote out a prescription for clonazepam. He also gave me a brochure for a mindfulness-based meditation clinic being offered at a hospital in the west end, and suggested I attend.

"A lot of patients find it helpful," he added noncommittally, making it clear he wasn't in much need of it himself.

I'd heard about mindfulness, of course. The modern fiction of us all leading such busy lives comes with a corollary, which is that we all need time for ourselves. Increasingly, this time alone has been commodified into something that can be bought—in the form of yoga classes and meditation retreats—and I soon signed up and paid for the eight-week program my doctor had recommended. The program's promotional materials talked about meditation as a form of self-nourishment, and I found this concept intriguing. The idea seemed contradictory—nourishment, as far as I knew, was something that came from outside, either in the form of food or love—but the prospect of being able to provide myself with my own nourishment was attractive. If I had to be so much on my own, perhaps I could contort myself into being my own source of comfort.

The classes were moderately useful. I liked the cat stretch, and it was pleasant to sit cross-legged on the floor with a dozen other adults, as though we were all briefly back in kindergarten. But I balked every time the instructor told us to open to the sources of strength within us. After a year of being very much on my own, my inner sources of strength were pretty much tapped out. Every session ended with us lying in the corpse position, with the instructor telling us to create loving energy around ourselves. This instruction always made me want to lunge forward and spin my head around. I had no clue how to create my own loving energy, and I felt like announcing this in a dramatic fashion. Obedient by nature, however, and not wanting to alarm the others, I remained silent, and wondered about the metaphysics of loving myself. Was there a part of me that could detach and love the other part? Or was I supposed to generate some sort of emotional wave that would roll down my body from head to toe? Whatever the precise mechanism, I was never able to find it, and the sessions usually ended with me feeling slightly failed, and frustrated about my inability to cater to my own needs.

It's unfashionable to say so, but I have to admit that, in the contest between meditation and meds, I preferred the pills. I liked it that my prescription for clonazepam didn't come with any overt ideology attached, and I was reassured by the way in which swallowing a tranquilizer seemed to calm the voices in my head. What I found unnerving about taking clonazepam was the fact that, since the pills had been prescribed for a different problem, they didn't provide me with a context for what I was experiencing. Normally, when you pay for a prescription at the pharmacy, you get the meds along with a "patient information sheet" describing the difficulty the meds are designed to address. I received one of these sheets, telling me that anxiety could cause people to be worried or tense much of the time, but since anxiety wasn't the core of my problem, I didn't really feel informed.

What I needed was a sort of scaffold for my loneliness, something I could stand on as I tried to understand the condition afflicting me. In September 2003, about two months after I'd sketched out loneliness as a significant problem in my life, I began to toy with the notion of researching the state. I'm still not entirely sure why this idea came to me. Pop culture, then, was all I had access to when it came to thinking about loneliness, and nothing within pop culture was telling me that the state was anything worth researching. I know that part of my interest in gathering information flowed from how I was spending my workdays. At that point, much of my practice involved complex legal research assignments. It was routine for me to spend eight hours a day pondering a legal problem and sifting through case law until I'd come up with a solution. My automatic response, when presented with a difficulty of any sort, was to reach for authorities, analyses, and arguments. The fact that I started to nudge my loneliness toward a legal research framework is slightly odd, but as soon as I began to think about my loneliness as a kind of legal problem, like pesticides regulation or hazardous materials transportation, I found I could neutralize it and in this way soften its emotional blow.

But something else was drawing me to research as well. There's a massive library at the University of Toronto, and in the evenings after work, I'd often find myself walking there. I wasn't really sure why I was going, or what I expected to find. The building just seemed soothing. As soon as I hit the entrance to the library—which was home to the third largest collection of books in North America—my cluttered breathing would begin to slow, and I'd start to feel an odd sense of connection. It's only now, in 2009, that I realize where that sense of connection was coming from. The library—a huge, spidery, strangely industrial place of fluorescent lights, metal shelves, and painfully uncomfortable wooden chairs—used to be one of the few places open during the Sunday afternoons I spent with my father as a child. I had dim memories of following him through the literature stacks, helpfully clutching the biographies of John Dos Passos and William Carlos Williams that he'd hand to me. I can't picture my father too well in these memories—he's just a thin, almost booklike presence up ahead—but some trace of our visits must have remained there, not just in my memory but in the stacks themselves. The place always made me feel less alone.

So it was due to an unusual mix of training and history that I wound up in the library's computer commons, punching the word *loneliness* into the online catalog. I was surprised, on my first visit, to see few titles emerge. Thinking I'd simply typed the wrong keyword, I wrote down the call number—which I've since seriously considered having tattooed across my ankle, the way a different type of woman might settle on a dove or a peace sign—and made my way to the psychology section.

As soon as I arrived at the section, I was struck by two things. First, the English language had played a little joke on lonely people, since any book on loneliness would be forever tucked between happier volumes on laughter and love. Second, the collection itself was old and worn. Most of the books dated from the 1970s or early 1980s, as though loneliness were something akin to feathered hair or the Thompson Twins, a phenomenon that had flourished decades ago but had fizzled out as the years wore on.

I signed out the books that were there—rapidly shoving texts with the word *Loneliness* across their fronts into my bag as soon as I could, so that no one else could see the titles—and started reading them at home. In doing so, I felt as though I were entering something of a different world. Not only was loneliness being openly discussed in the books I signed out, it was being set out in substantial and serious ways. All through the fall of 2003, I flipped through analyses of loneliness among American and Middle Eastern youth, I read about the important role of attachment, and I tried to wrap my head around the notion of loneliness flowing from the perceptions of the lonely person. What puzzled me about the books I was reading was the fact that they seemed to grind to a halt in the late 1980s.

Even though the library had a huge purchasing budget, its collection didn't include many recent texts on loneliness (the love and laughter sections, of course, were an embarrassment of riches). Writing about the subject, based on what I could find in the stacks, seemed to have stopped in 1989, when I was just nineteen.

Being a modern citizen, I understood that the information I was looking for might have simply migrated from the library shelves to the Internet. I started running searches at work—typing "loneliness" and "isolation" into Google—but stopped when I realized, with a great deal of alarm, that our part-time IT consultant (a person I rarely saw) would likely be able to track my entries. Worrying that knowledge of my loneliness might affect my employability, I switched to running my searches at home. This arrangement—working alone in my study—had the advantage of offering privacy, but it also removed the more social aspects of the office. At least at work, I'd been able to hear others talking and laughing in the background as I'd conducted my searches on aloneness.

I quickly realized that searches for "singledom," "singleton," and "alone" would turn up a lot of information about "quirkyalones," who were said to inhabit singledom as a "natural resting state" and who were, by force of personality and inner strength, "rebels." I tried to see myself in this light—quirkyalones seemed cool in a way that the lonely absolutely did not—but I couldn't summon up the necessary rebelliousness. My solitary nights were not bittersweet, and they did not seem to be bringing me wisdom. I was spending my solitary nights lying on the kitchen floor, listening to radio programs featuring 1950s big bands. Much as I wanted to become one of the smiling people on the Quirkyalone page, I was too lonely to make the cut.

With loneliness having edged out quirkiness, I was left with a down-market digital world of italicized fonts and black backdrops. Lonely people didn't post pictures of themselves on the Internet, and many people, if they wrote about their affliction at all, did so under pen names such as Lonely Wife and Still Alone. There was advice for the college-aged—"You can feel lonely at a football game with hundreds of screaming spectators"—as well as new age perorations that I "take control" of the state (control being taken by buying one of the self-help books on offer and somehow rewiring my entire personality so that loneliness no longer emerged as a problem). There was an uncomfortable amount of bad poetry—*My loneliness is so arresting / My solitude becomes detesting*—and some alarming stream-of-consciousness pieces linking loneliness to death and a lacerating lack of self-esteem. Unlike depression and problem gambling, which came with helpful online quizzes and lengthy lists of support groups, loneliness seemed like an affliction without moorings. The state seemed to occupy a data-free world filled with suggestions that I might want to lose weight, or take an assertiveness training class, or perhaps sign up for a course offered by a life coach in the areas of self-awareness and articulating one's thoughts and feelings.

I didn't want a life coach. I didn't need much help in the area of articulation. What I was looking for was a sort of emotional mirror, something I could hold up and see myself in. This may sound like a vague goal, but I'd had this experience with fiction. Novelists seemed willing and able to define the contours of severe loneliness with a clarity that was simply lacking elsewhere. Loneliness seemed to *exist* in the world of fiction in the way that it didn't seem to exist in real life. Feeling hungry for information, I soaked up the portrait of the solitary, loveless butler in Kazuo Ishiguro's *Remains of the Day*, and the picture of Caryl Phillips's outcast and exhausted refugee in *A Distant Shore*. Reading about loneliness didn't make my condition worse. Fictional characters have always felt real to me, and the lonely people I found in books felt like fellow sufferers, people whose companionship left me temporarily less alone in my loneliness.

It was this sense of fellow feeling that collapsed as soon as I stepped from the fictional world to the world I actually happened to live in. As someone in her thirties, who had grown up with the usual barrage of ads, television shows, and magazines, I considered myself media-smart. I would have been amazed if someone suggested to me that the sort of companionship portrayed on *Friends* or *The L Word* characterized the norm for normal people. I was the sort of young woman who'd taken courses focused on "deconstructing" cosmetics ads, and I tried to draw on this questionable background when faced with representations of togetherness. I told myself that the close-knit relationships on *Grey's Anatomy* were the product of a screenwriter's pen, that the endless marriages and love affairs presented in *People* masked an otherwise total lack of editorial content, and that the extended family on the breakfast commercial was actually an assemblage of poorly paid actors.

I tried to be ironic about images of sociability. I tried to be shrewd. But it was tough. It was very hard to feel isolated and to live in a culture in which sociability was presented as easy to achieve. Although I tried to tell myself that loneliness was an entirely natural and humane feeling, the lack of reference to the state made me feel unnatural. One of the John Prine songs that Martin used to sing was called "Unlonely," and it was this nonsense word that the media seemed to beam out at me. The characters in action films were *unlonely*. The smiling models in ads were *unlonely*. The newly married celebrities, the expectant

mothers with baby bumps, the entire cast of *The Sopranos*—
these people were all *unlonely*.

By November of 2003, I was simply confused. On one hand,
I had the books that I'd signed out of the library, and I was
starting to understand things about loneliness that weren't popularly discussed: how it affected large numbers of people, how
it could be measured, and how it could last for a lifetime. On
the other hand, I had the world of pop culture, a world in which
long-term loneliness either didn't exist or existed only for those
who were unattractive, maladapted, and unlovable.

Not knowing who to side with, I found myself waltzing
from one idea to the next. Walking to the subway on my way to
work, I'd ponder the word *true*, and move it from category to
category. The things the academic texts were telling me might
be true, or the social displays I was seeing on TV might be
true. Maybe it was true that a lot of people felt lonely, or maybe
it was true that I was the only one. Maybe truth rested with the
idea of the media portraying an impossibly high social standard; maybe my social circle had shrunk to such a point that
any portrayal at all would seem like an impossibility.

By the time I reached my subway stop, I'd be worn out,
unsure of how common my condition was, how serious it might
be, and how earnestly I should take it. I'd leave the station with
my head swimming with ideas and data, not knowing who to
trust, or what to believe.

It was because I couldn't fully part company with pop culture—because I couldn't, then, really accept the idea that loneliness mattered and that a lot of people suffered from it—that
I began to struggle with a profound sense of not fitting in. Despite the reading I was doing, I couldn't shake the idea that my

loneliness was unique. And this misperception led to one of the worst aspects of my loneliness: deceit. I've never been a good liar, and had never previously had much use for an extended campaign of dissemblance. But toward the end of November I found myself creating an alternate version of my life, a more peopled edition that didn't really exist.

Many people think that lawyers work constantly, and that there are never enough hours in the day to get things done. While this might be true for some lawyers, especially those who work in areas such as mergers and acquisitions, it's certainly not true for everyone. My own work schedule was fairly light, and much of my work involved dealing with government officials who weren't at their desks after five o'clock. By five thirty, I would often have nothing to occupy myself with. I'd check my e-mail, and surf the Internet, and head to the back office for a chat with the law clerks about their evening plans. Then I'd go back to my desk and look at the little clock in the corner of my computer screen. Six o'clock. Six thirty.

"Aren't you leaving?" asked Adele, a pretty blond secretary who was always kind to me. She had a huge tote bag slung over her shoulder, and her hair tied back in a knot. "It's late," she said, looking at her watch. "Don't you want to get home?"

"Just finishing some things up for tomorrow," I said, shuffling papers.

Adele looked at me strangely. She had an almost canine sense of what stage all the firm's files were at, and she knew better than anyone that I didn't have anything pressing.

"Plus, I'm heading out for dinner," I lied. "I don't want to go all the way home and then have to turn around and come back downtown."

"OK," Adele said slowly. She seemed on the brink of saying something more, of asking me if I was all right, but then her boyfriend honked from where he was parked on the street below, and she hurried toward the door to join him. "If you need anything done," she added uncertainly, "you can just leave it on my desk."

"Will do," I called out, mentally adding this exchange to the memory of the person I was beginning to think of as "the other me." This other me had brunch dates to tell my bosses about, and completely fictional romantic interests that I dropped subtle hints about in the back office. If someone mentioned that I seemed a bit off and scattered, I'd reply that I was "really tired," or "a bit mixed up about things," as though the demands of my social life were so exhausting they were leaving me worn out. No one at work was familiar with my pre-firm life, so I hauled my relationship with Martin forward a few years, to make it seem as though I'd been single for less time than I had. And the other me was beginning to play a leading role in my personal life as well. I told Laura that work was consuming a huge amount of my time, I hinted to Juliette that my work-place was as happily social as hers, and when I finally left the office on a Friday night to wander alone along busy downtown streets, I'd return home to a friend's phone message and report that I'd been out with someone for drinks.

What I couldn't do, within the context of my everyday life, was admit to my loneliness. There was actually an inverse relationship at work, one that I now know is common enough to have attracted research attention. The longer my loneliness lasted, the more reluctant I was to mention it. We tend to think that the more a problem intensifies, the more likely the sufferer is to talk about it. In the case of depression, which can progress from a diffuse sense of sadness to powerful and harrowing thoughts of self-destruction, this progression from silence to speech is more of a norm. Other afflictions, such as anorexia or

problem gambling, seem to follow the same trajectory from secrecy to admission, even if someone else might have to broach
the subject at the start.

Loneliness is different. Although we tend to think of loneliness as easy to spot, studies show that there are few telltale
signs that might lead others to identify the state. Similarly,
since the lonely person is in control of the stories and anecdotes
he decides to tell, it's easy for him to camouflage the problem.
"Others don't know," says Daniel Perlman, a social psychologist at the University of North Carolina who's looked at the
ability of loneliness to fly under the radar. When I ask him *why*
other people don't know, he replies, "Partly it's a matter of a
failure to reveal, and partly it's a failure to recognize loneliness.
Some of the cues are clear, but not all of the cues." Since many
of the traits associated with loneliness—such as disrupted
sleep, ill health, and anxiety—aren't generally associated with
aloneness, the state can advance and entrench without anyone
but the lonely person being aware of it. Secrecy can lead to the
creation of an alternate self—the sort of cheerful, connected
self I created for my coworkers—and the distance between this
fictional self and the real one can make the lonely person feel
even more alone.

The way out of this trap seems obvious. The lonely person,
according to conventional wisdom, is to hack through their
aloneness by reaching out to someone else and admitting to the
problem. The difficulty with this piece of advice is that it
doesn't correspond to the reality of loneliness. So much shame
and stigma attaches to the state that it's extraordinarily hard to
talk about, even in a culture that prides itself on being self-
revelatory. In addition, the lonely person may know that many
of the people around them don't want to hear about loneliness,
since the admission may point, or seem to point, to problems

within the relationship in question. It's also the case that many lonely people (though not all) lack the close confidants they're supposed to be opening up to. If there's no best friend in the picture, no spouse or close sibling or best buddy at work, then who, exactly, is the lonely person supposed to tell?

The unmentionability of my loneliness left me in something of a conversational bind. Even when friends asked if I was all right, I couldn't summon up the courage to tell them I was feeling horribly alone. The words that had begun to flow in Genevieve's office—*me, lonely, always*—bottled themselves up in more ordinary conversations. This was partly because no one was asking me about the state, and partly because I was steering the discussion away from loneliness. I always felt as though I'd be asking too much of people if I referred to a problem murkier and more incomprehensible than the blues. And pop culture was always so definitive in its portrayal of loneliness. The state was reserved for widows, the unemployed, the newly arrived. Someone like me—with full citizenship, a job, and youth on my side—wasn't supposed to be lonely. Loneliness had somehow, through some tidy cultural twist, emerged as a feeling I wasn't permitted to feel.

So I continued to hide my state. I kept silent about it. Just as, in childhood, I hadn't wanted to accept that my divorced family was any different from other kids' intact ones, I didn't, in adulthood, want to acknowledge my state of loneliness as any different from the temporary feelings of aloneness my friends sometimes mentioned. Even though I was beginning to see the outline of my life veering from the script other people's seemed to follow, I couldn't—because of my sense of failure, and my embarrassment, and my sheer confusion about what I was dealing with—step forward and name my loneliness as a serious concern.

With my loneliness unmentionable, I found myself trying to simply distance myself from it. I gravitated toward settings where my loneliness felt like less of a burden, where I could pass an hour or two without noticing it. I liked the pool at the nearby gym, where the sun shone through the tall ground-level windows and rubbed the surface of the water until it shimmered like glass. There was something hugely comforting about being in the presence of the other swimmers. Without my glasses, everyone looked blobby, wet, and unthreatening, and the shared activity—*Are you using this flutter board? Oh, no, after you*—gave me a soothing and welcome sense of togetherness. In order to achieve at least a bit more in the way of contact, I began volunteering at a weekly soup kitchen, a gig that provided me with enough emotional outrage—children eating side by side with homeless men!—that my loneliness would temporarily wane. And with evenings falling early once again, I returned to long walks through my neighborhood.

My apartment was on the edge of a hill leading into a schoolyard, and after strolling past the big houses in the nearby streets, I often came to a stop on the hill opposite my flat. If I looked across the empty square of schoolyard, I could see directly into the windows of my apartment, and I used to sit there in the cool evenings and try to understand the problem of my aloneness.

Pulling at the grass, I'd try to identify just what mistake I'd made to turn my life so ragged and thin. I scrolled past unlikely solutions—running into an old flame on the subway—and I sometimes let myself fantasize about the lives of others, about kids and a partner and shared mornings in the kitchen. I tried to adopt different attitudes toward my loneliness. I tried to accept it. I tried to ignore it. I tried to argue it into retreat. But my loneliness never budged, and what I was usually left with, as I sat alone on the hill, was a sense of worried resignation.

Dog walkers came by sometimes, their squat dachshunds and snappy little terriers nudging round to sniff at my hands and ankles.

"Nice night," the owner might say, pulling back on the leash.

And I, trying to force myself to participate in the social world around me, would reply as brightly as I could.

"Lovely. A wonderful evening."

And then whoever I was talking to would nod and walk away.

Part II

IMPACT

Chapter Three

THE LONG HAUL

*Recognizing chronic loneliness
as a problem in itself*

At some point during the winter that followed, in 2004, my loneliness began to change. I remember that season as being particularly cold, the sort of cold that makes you catch your breath when you leave the house and forces you to pull a scarf up to your eyes, so that—between the brim of your hat and the top of the scarf—the world shrinks to what you can see through a two-inch gap in fabric. I remember snow piling up on my kitchen skylight, and the windows of buses frosting over, and steam escaping up through the sewer grates.

I continued to try to visit with people. My apartment was downtown, but it was in the north end. Most of my friends lived in the west end, and my sisters and their kids lived to the east. Toronto is a big city, so the distances involved were considerable. To get from my apartment to my friend Laura's could take forty-five minutes; traveling to my sister's place involved a one-hour trip. It strikes me as odd now that I should have chosen a place so far removed, but when I'd signed my lease, I'd been attracted by the gardenlike feel of the neighborhood, with its big trees and well-tended yards. Anticipating my father's death, I think I wanted a place that was soothing and quiet, fenced in by nothing more challenging than the schoolyard and the ravine.

The problem was that, in the unwritten rules that governed my city, people flowed from north to south. Laura sometimes made trips up to see me, but most of my friends and family expected me to make the journey to what they called "the real downtown." I saw things this way myself. I knew that I'd chosen an out-of-the-way location and that it was up to me to cover the miles and ride the rails in an effort to get to the more densely populated parts of the city.

This meant that my socializing that winter was marked by long journeys in low temperatures. I'd go to my friend Simon's to have a low-key dinner in his messy kitchen after the kids were in bed, I'd go to my sister Christine's for a big, expertly prepared Sunday brunch, and I'd meet my friend Juliette for croissants in a café downtown. The difficulty was that the sense of connection I took from these outings was never enough to offset the isolation I was otherwise facing. The trips would see me, both literally and metaphorically, traveling from the cold to a place of warmth and then back out into the cold. Each visit ended with me back on my own, tucked into a corner seat on the subway, closing my eyes and curling up against the wall as the train traveled north.

The question of why these visits weren't enough is an interesting one. In one sense, the problem was one of quantity. A busy month for me, then, might entail four or five social visits, while what I needed was eight or ten or twelve. In other words, while I was seeing people, I wasn't seeing enough people—or seeing them for long enough—to put a dent in my loneliness. It was also the case that, during those freezing months, I really did not want to be out. I didn't mind gearing up for outdoor walks through the snowy ravine, but I had a deep dislike of, and basic confusion about, combining more fashionable clothes with my parka, big winter boots, and thick mittens.

When it came right down to it, I didn't want to be traveling miles to go see people. I didn't want a sense of connection that lasted an hour or two and then left me to return to face the rest of my weekend alone. I'm the first to admit that there were more activities I could have participated in during that winter. I'd signed up for an outdoor sports league, for instance, but failed to go to any of the skating parties or snowshoe lessons I received e-mails about. My reluctance to throw myself into things could be explained partly by loneliness itself—it was beginning to change my behavior and motivations—but also by the fact that I didn't want to be socializing. What I needed was someone at home with me, someone whose breath I'd hear as I sat reading, whose footfalls would sound in the hallway, whose voice would reach me from an adjoining room.

What I wanted was the quiet presence of another person. My visits, in a sense, felt like noise. To the extent that they involved the grinding of subway gears, and the scraping of snowplows, and the knocking of my own knuckles against heavy front doors, they really were noisy. In a follow-up exercise to the stream-of-consciousness writing about loneliness I'd done at Genevieve's command, I sat and asked myself what my loneliness needed. The first word I found myself writing down was *food*—an allusion I'd come to understand through my research—but the second word on the list was *peace*. I needed the steady, calm companionship that a friend, lover, or family member could offer, and without it, my loneliness persisted.

There's a general division in the loneliness literature between short-term and chronic loneliness. Short-term loneliness is the sort that's usually being referred to when someone happens to raise the issue. It's the type of aloneness that finds us right after a breakup, or when we're trapped at home on a rainy Tuesday afternoon. Loneliness of the short-term variety is, by definition, a passing emotional event; it's a *mood* that often eases through the passage of time.

Chronic loneliness, on the other hand, is a vastly different experience. Chronic loneliness usually arises through a combination of genetics and circumstance. Some people are simply born with a greater tendency to feel alone, and the facts of their life might propel them toward an isolation that lasts. It's chronic loneliness that researchers are starting to zero in on as a significant psychological problem. That is, the state is beginning to lose its status as a "mood," and is being recognized as an affliction—as something capable of changing the thoughts, behavior, and body of the lonely person in question.

When we think of chronic loneliness at all, we see it as a rarity, as something that simply doesn't happen to people, but research shows that the state is surprisingly common. The first studies of loneliness were undertaken in the United States in the mid-1960s, and they showed that occasional loneliness was a problem for approximately 25 percent of the people surveyed. Sociologists commenting on these studies noted that a 25 percent rate was high but not particularly troubling, since the loneliness under examination was being framed as temporary. It was only in the late 1970s that psychologists began to understand that for about 10 percent of U.S. and Canadian populations, loneliness would simply *last*, month after month and year after year.

The reason that researchers were able to uncover the truth about the duration of loneliness was that a reliable scale had been developed. Before 1978, loneliness was often cast as a state too subtle to measure, too mysterious and otherworldly to pin down. This portrayal of loneliness was damning, since it meant the state couldn't be set out and studied in a lab. Without close scrutiny, the role of loneliness in people's lives couldn't be properly understood. What researchers at UCLA did in the late 1970s was challenge the view of loneliness as ghostly and clingy. Working with students who self-identified as lonely, as well as with hundreds of psychology undergrads, a team led by the psychologist Dan Russell began to test questions that probed feelings of attunement, isolation, and persistent aloneness. (A modified version of the scale they finally arrived at—the UCLA Loneliness Scale—is set out in the opening pages of this book.)

One thing the scale allowed researchers to do was test and retest given populations, to see if loneliness was persisting from one test period to the next. They found that, for many individuals, high loneliness scores held steady. "People's situations change," says Andrew Steptoe, the British Heart Foundation Professor of Psychology at University College London, "but there's quite a lot of stability as well. So if one measures people after three years, or five years, those people who are scoring high on the loneliness scale at one point are typically scoring high at the later point. There's variation within that, but— within large populations—that's what you find."

The dividing line between short-term and chronic loneliness isn't clear-cut. Some researchers peg the jumping-off point at one year, others at two. What everyone in the research community agrees upon, however, is that loneliness that presents itself over a period of months or years has to be seen and understood as something different from a transient mood. "There are some people for whom loneliness is one of the defining qualities of their lives," says the University of North Carolina's Daniel Perlman. "And for those people I think they stay lonely a great deal of the time." Some lucky individuals will experience only short-term and transient feelings of loneliness; they'll neither know nor understand a loneliness that lasts. Others, however, will find themselves struggling with a loneliness that's all too familiar, one that persists for years.

I'm not sure when my own loneliness jumped the boundary line from short-term to chronic. I do know that, after the year mark, as I was forcing myself to socialize in the depths of winter, the "mild highs" I'd been experiencing began to disappear. I no longer had periods of not needing others. Rather, my sense of need was present and piercing much of the time. It was also the case that, during that winter, my dreams began to change. I stopped dreaming of warmth and close connection, and began to dream of loneliness. I'd be at a pay phone, trying to call around to find the location of a party, but wouldn't be able to reach anyone who could tell me how to get there. Or I'd be lying in bed and waiting for someone to join me, but hour after hour would go by, and I'd wind up alone on the mattress in the weak dawn light. It was as though, after more than a year of battling loneliness, my mind had temporarily run out of gimmicks and resources. It could no longer sustain what must have been an enormous effort to offset my sense of isolation through dreams and needlessness. Although I'd ultimately come to settle on a different compensatory scheme, my mind, at the time, seemed to temporarily drop its defenses and succumb to the aloneness around me.

The idea that loneliness might *last*, and simply persist year after year, is in many ways an odd one. There's an ingrained notion in our culture that loneliness is a temporary condition, a self-indulgence that can be fought off through a surge of self-determination. In some important ways, it's as though we accept short-term loneliness but not chronic loneliness. Not only is short-term loneliness culturally sanctioned, with little attaching to it in the way of stigma, chronic loneliness is generally denied even as an emotional possibility. With no strong and solid representations of chronic loneliness available, the state begins to seem like an improbability, an oddity, a minor deal.

When I started looking for people suffering from long-term loneliness—which I did through my blog—I initially worried that no one would describe a loneliness like my own. I'd accepted the idea of chronic loneliness as an unlikelihood, as something that I was unique in feeling. Even though I'd read several papers, such as those prepared by the U.S. National Institute of Mental Health, describing chronic loneliness as a surprisingly common state, I couldn't shake the notion that I was the only one who struggled with it.

My concerns about being the only one were groundless. As soon as my conversations with lonely people began, I started to hear about periods of loneliness that had lasted for five, ten, or twenty years. "Sometimes I can sort of trick myself into thinking it's circumstantial," says Claire, a forty-year-old financial services employee from Saskatchewan, who told me that she's been lonely for most of her life. "You know—maybe my life has gone in this direction, and for whatever reason that's why I'm lonely now. And then I'll think the same thing five years later."

Many of the lonely people I spoke to stressed that the state had been with them more or less for life. I thought I'd been unusual in feeling lonely in childhood, but Rachel, the home-maker from Florida, emphasized that childhood loneliness had been a reality for her as well. "I remember being in kindergar-ten," she says, "and we were all sitting in a circle, the way you do in kindergarten, and the teacher was very nice, and she was handing everything around, and everything was lovely, and I remember feeling like I really didn't belong. There wasn't that feeling of inclusion. And even though I wasn't being excluded, I never felt that sense of inclusion. I was like an outsider looking in at what was going on. And that feeling lasted throughout my childhood, and my adolescence, and right through until now."

"I honestly would say it's probably been a lifelong issue," agrees Anne, a thirty-five-year-old social worker from Illinois who compares the state to chronic pain. "I would say there's probably a baseline that's always there. Sometimes it's not something that bothers me, it isn't really something that's no-ticeable or that affects me, but it hasn't gone away—it's just not a big issue then. But there are other times when it gets worse, and I'd say it affects how I'm leading my life."

As soon as I got lonely people on the phone, one of the first things I did was probe more deeply into the relationship be-tween loneliness and depression. I did this because I knew from my own experience that many lonely people who tried to allude to their state would be told that they were struggling with the blues.

"When someone's lonely," says Chris Segrin, a behavioral scientist at the University of Arizona, "and they come in to see a psychiatrist or a psychologist, they tend to be diagnosed as depressed or socially anxious more often than not. In other words, there are comorbid conditions that seem to have diagnostic priority. So loneliness has, I think, always been kicked around as the bastard child of psychology, and I think that's a bad thing. I think sometimes depression is secondary to loneliness, but when someone comes in, the psychiatrist says, 'Oh, your problem is you're depressed.' "

The diagnosis of depression reflects the confusion that exists between the two states. For some practitioners, loneliness is simply not a problem in good currency. It's not something they ask about when a patient comes in for a consultation. "A lot of the time when I'm talking with people clinically," says Ray, a fundraiser from Philadelphia who's suffered from both depression and loneliness, "they're mostly focusing on the depression, not the loneliness, even though they can go hand in hand." Doctors, of course, can't shoulder all the blame for the muddy diagnostic waters. A lot of the confusion between loneliness and depression arises from the fact that lonely people choose to tell clinicians that they're depressed instead of lonely. "I was chronically lonely all the time," says Claire, thinking back to one isolated period, "but I would just tell my doctor that I was feeling depressed, feeling down, feeling low. And I instinctively knew it was because I was interacting less and having less quality interactions. But I didn't come right out and say that I was lonely, because you can't really take a pill to treat loneliness."

I quickly realized that the demarcation point between loneliness and depression would vary from person to person. As I noted in chapter 1, some of the lonely people I spoke to had no problems with depression, while others had a history of struggling with the mood. Even in conversation with those who were receiving treatment for depression, however, it became clear that in discussing loneliness, they were talking about something that differed from depression. "Depression results from virtually anything," says Daniel Perlman. "And loneliness results from very specific antecedents. There has to be an interpersonal aspect to loneliness." It was this sense of an interpersonal shortfall—a degree of aloneness and disconnectedness—that came to the fore as soon as I asked lonely people to describe the state.

Anne, the Illinois social worker, stresses that when she's depressed, she knows that social ties are available and that she has connections in place, even if she doesn't choose to draw upon them. When she's lonely, however, this sense of connectedness just disappears. "I may *not* be depressed," Anne says, describing her loneliness. "I may be very functional, and yet I'll be very much feeling like there's no one really who understands what I'm doing or where I'm at." For many of the lonely people I spoke to, the problem wasn't the shapeless dissatisfaction of depression, but rather a very clear and focused distress about the lack of intimacy in their lives. "I can be around people and still feel alone," says Sonia, the West Coast copywriter. "I don't feel like I make connections with people. For me, anyways, I don't necessarily feel like I'm understood or maybe cared about too much. I just feel a lack of connection with people, even when I'm around people."

"I had a really interesting conversation last night," says Adam, the illustrator from Rhode Island, who was trying to explain his sense of social relations as too glancing and thin. "A friend asked why I wasn't coming to the gay running group anymore, and why I wasn't doing this and that, and I said, 'You know, I go to these things, and when I'm there, people pat me on the back and say, "Adam, it's so great to see you." But I don't know what it is. It doesn't feel like anybody, when I'm not there, is saying, "Where's Adam?"' And I was kind of struggling for words to describe it, and my friend said, 'Nothing sticks.' And I said, 'Yes, that's it exactly.' Nothing sticks."

The notion that a life might feel chronically underpopulated, or that existing relationships might feel too loose and inconsequential, is something that many lonely people insist others fail to understand. "You don't know it unless you've been there," says James, the Quebec-based engineer, who's suffered from loneliness for over ten years. "I mean, most people define loneliness as, 'Oh, gosh. I haven't seen my boyfriend or girlfriend in a week, and I'm lonely, and I'm sitting here waiting for the phone to ring.' That's not what a long-term situation is. You can be functioning quite normally in society and still be *unbearably* lonely." The lack of awareness about loneliness means that trying to raise the issue with a health-care provider can lead exactly nowhere. "I've mentioned it to my doctor," says James, "and he's kind of brushed it off, saying, 'You should get out more. It will do you good.' Trying to explain it to him—it doesn't register."

What doesn't register is the fact that loneliness can start to feel rooted into your life, as central and definitive as your work or your marriage. Like James, Claire stresses that when most people think of loneliness, they tend to think of short-term varieties of the mood, and they have a hard time imagining the emotional reality of someone for whom the state is roughly constant. "Loneliness might be something they experience as a fleeting sensation," she says, "but it doesn't really carry with them throughout the years, where they can think back to *long* periods of time when they've felt that way every single day. And I don't know if you can know what that's like unless you've experienced it."

The fact that the lonely live with a problem that's not widely understood means they have to grapple with issues of confusion and self-evaluation that don't generally present themselves in the course of depression. "You can really fly that one around," says Rachel, referring to the noonday demon, and sounding slightly chagrined at what she sees as a degree of unfairness. "You can talk about depression, and everyone feels that it's a problem that can be managed. Whereas if you say you're lonely, it's like, 'What do you *mean*? *Why* are you lonely?' And people consider it a flaw, a personality flaw that can't be cured."

When lonely people refer to chronic loneliness, they're not talking about a mood. They're pointing to a state that's been with them for years, a state others don't understand, and one that—in addition to causing them emotional difficulties—is linked to shame and confusion.

"The fact that it's been going on for so long," says Adam, "both in and out of relationships, makes me feel maladjusted somehow. It's just not something I'd want others to know about."

Conversations with chronically lonely people reveal the paradox attached to the state. The longer it lasts, the less you're supposed to mention it. The more closely it attaches to your life, the more you're supposed to pretend it's not anything you feel.

I wasn't prepared for some of the odder ways in which chronic loneliness would begin to affect me. I'd rented my apartment in the north end, for instance, because I had no problems with the subway. I liked the pockets of companionship the trains provided, the warm bodies, the glimpses of people sleeping and reading. Toward the middle of my second year of loneliness, however, this sense of camaraderie began to unravel. The more time I spent alone, the more difficult I found it to be around others, especially strangers. The most harmless people—teens coming back from a basketball game, businessmen staring at their PalmPilots, women checking their watches to make sure they'd get home before their kids—began to seem vaguely threatening. I'd worry about people getting too close to me, and I'd feel insufficiently guarded, as though there wasn't enough to me to keep risk at bay. As I traveled home, the sense of threat would become overwhelming, and I'd often disembark and wait for the next train, hoping it would provide me with more in the way of space. If the next subway was too crowded as well, I'd disembark once more. This little routine could repeat itself, over and over, until a twenty-minute journey had fanned out into nearly an hour. On really bad nights, I'd leave the transit system entirely, and hike the last few miles between the subway and my flat.

My behavior—which struck me as bizarre—was one of the things that made me curious about John Cacioppo's research. In arguing that chronic loneliness needs to be seen as something different than depression, Cacioppo has pointed specifically to a sense of stress and threat as one of the factors that sets the two states apart.

"Loneliness is not just a *sad* circumstance," he explains. "It's a *dangerous* circumstance. When you're lonely, something's gone wrong with connections, and you're motivated to reconnect, because it's really dangerous to not be part of a group. Especially in evolutionary time—it's dangerous to be out there by yourself in a hostile world." Loneliness, according to Cacioppo's analysis, might make us feel demoralized and unhappy, but what it does most of all—and what depression doesn't do—is make us feel insufficient and unsafe. Since loneliness draws our attention to potential dangers, it's hard to feel lonely without also feeling uneasy. The world, when you're lonely, simply starts to seem like a more threatening place.

This has actually been demonstrated. In 2003, Cacioppo decided to equip 135 University of Chicago undergrads with diaries and with beepers that sounded nine times a day. Every day for a week, the students were asked—at the sound of the beep—to record what they were doing and to reflect on how stressful and threatening they found the activity in question.

By the end of the seven days, Cacioppo had collected thousands of individual moments, and he was able to reconstruct rough outlines of the weeks of the lonely and nonlonely students. Somewhat to his surprise, he found that there was no real difference in how the lonely and nonlonely were spending their time. The lonely were just as likely as the nonlonely to be studying, doing errands, relaxing with friends, and attending lectures.

What differed between the two groups was the sense of threat and stress cued by each activity. Across the board, lonely students rated their main activity as more stressful and threatening than the nonlonely, and they rated themselves as less able to meet the demands of the activity in question. Since the lonely students weren't actually engaged in different activities, activity levels couldn't account for the different stress responses. Similarly, since both the lonely and nonlonely groups had been screened for life changes and possible traumas, background events couldn't explain the difference. Finally, since all of the students had tested as low in depression, depression couldn't be cuing the heightened threat response.

With other possible causes ruled out, Cacioppo had to conclude that loneliness itself was triggering feelings of threat, that the mere perception of isolation was making the students feel tense and inadequate. That is, the ordinary demands of under-graduate life—waiting in line at the caf, searching for books in the library, and taking notes on Pip's psychological devel-opment in *Great Expectations*—all seemed more stressful and threatening simply because the students were lonely.

Cacioppo's findings make sense within an evolutionary framework. Loneliness was making the students feel threat-ened and insecure, and these feelings of stress and threat were spilling outward to discolor the week as a whole. *Stressed* and *threatened* would actually be good ways of describing how I felt when lonely. Even when my life was objectively fine, it began to feel unmanageable. I made a lot of money—I was very lucky that my loneliness did not coincide with financial straits—but I began to worry compulsively about my savings. Even after receiving a substantial raise, I was preoccupied with not having what I thought of as "enough." This wasn't because I needed more money. With little in the way of a social life, I had almost no use for a wardrobe, and I had no debts or dependents. Rather, I felt the need to buttress myself somehow, and I came to fixate on money as the answer.

"Tabitha," I said one day at work, heading to the book-keeper's desk and feeling as though I were about to cry, "my Visa bill wasn't paid." I said this as though I were announcing the sudden torching of her home. It seemed like an *enormous* problem.

Tabitha looked slightly surprised. The bill contained a $700 charge for my annual licensing fee, and it was routine for the firm to refund me the cost.

"No problem," she replied. Tabitha studied alternative heal-ing in her spare time, and—like other people in the office—she'd begun to suspect that something was wrong with me. "I can do up a check for it right now. But if it were me, I think I'd see this as an opportunity for an inward journey. The bill's only a week overdue. You might want to take time to explore your issues with money."

"I don't have issues with money."

"You're a little excited about this bill."

"That's because it was *supposed* to be paid, and it *wasn't* paid, and now it's *late*."

I was clearly arguing, and Tabitha—as an administrator—wasn't really in a position to argue with me. Sounding as though she'd say something quite different if our roles were reversed, she repeated her promise to pay the bill, but couldn't resist adding, in a whisper, "Every worry is a chance to wonder," and it took everything I had not to pounce on her.

Dealing with Tabitha was relatively easy, because I could pull rank. The office's pecking order meant that, no matter how curious they were, Tabitha and the clerks couldn't go too far in delving into my personal life. The situation was completely different with my bosses, who had no problems prying into what they were beginning to see as increasingly odd behavior.

"Do you know that you are *radiating* anxiety?" Grant, one of the firm's partners, asked me one afternoon in March. He was standing in the doorway to my office, dressed in his usual enviro law garb of jeans, battered hiking boots, and a button-down shirt, and looking at me as though he were about to launch into a cross-examination.

"I'm not," I said, as my heart raced and I struggled to work my feet into my shoes.

"You are," Grant replied, matter-of-factly.

Personal boundaries! I felt like shouting. *Personal boundaries!* But there was no stopping Grant.

"For the past couple of weeks you've been coming in here looking like you've seen a ghost. *What* is going on?"

I stared at my computer screen, trying to think of an excuse. This was three years before I had the chance to speak with Dr. Cacioppo, and I couldn't explain my behavior to myself. All I knew was that—in feeling isolated—I'd become jumpy and apprehensive. My anxiety had become something I couldn't control. I couldn't say this, of course. Since I didn't feel able to mention my loneliness, any trait associated with it became instantly verboten. With the most significant aspects of my life emerging as conversationally off-limits, I found myself trying to arrange my facial features into a non-anxious display and come up with something convincing.

"It's my files," I said finally, reaching for the all-purpose law firm stressor. "I think I've got too much on my plate."

"You should have said something," Grant replied, reaching for the chair that sat in the corner of my office. "Let's look at what you have."

The entire time that I was reviewing my files with Grant—going over environmental assessments of pipelines and attempts to stop roads from running through wetlands—I was trying to come up with ways to appear less anxious. Discussing a proposed sewage plant, I decided I needed some help. I was still seeing Genevieve, but she worked slowly, sifting through memories and dreams and sometimes returning to the same theme, such as the mysterious workings of trauma, week after week. This approach was fascinating—I always felt as though I'd just stepped into 1930s Vienna—but with Grant staring at me, it became clear that I needed an approach that was more hands-on and bracing.

Because of their stated aim of treating not the disease but the patient, and because they offered hour-long appointments that promised to be long on talk and short on actual investigation, I decided to go to a naturopath. Gabriella was a big-boned young woman, heavily pregnant, who listened with care as I described some of my symptoms: a chronic sense of being unguarded, overwhelming stress, disturbing dreams (which, in fairness to her, I made out to be more like ordinary night-mares than scenarios of isolation). I mentioned, truthfully, that headaches were becoming a problem and that my sleep—which was usually fine—had become jumpy and broken, meaning my anxiety was starting to feel laced with exhaustion.

I'd told her I was a lawyer, but I hadn't mentioned much about the nature of my practice.

"How many hours do they keep you each day?" she asked.

My bosses didn't keep me at all—they were like permissive parents who let me come and go as I pleased—but I had the sense that this admission would throw off Gabriella's conclusion.

"Long hours?" she suggested, gently.

All I could do was nod.

"And maybe not enough time to see the people you really need to see?"

Right.

She had a diagnosis: chronic stress. My adrenal glands, she said, describing the ins and outs of the endocrine system in a way that I found hard to follow, were overworked. In response, I was supposed to take a cow-derived hormone supplement and focus on restoring my work/life balance.

"When our lives become unbalanced," she said, jotting something about my chronic stress in a chart, "our bodies will respond. You need to start focusing on the nonwork aspects of your life."

I didn't tell her that it was work—with its seven to eight hours a day of limited social interaction—that was actually keeping me sane. She asked if I wanted to schedule another session. She seemed interested in my childhood, and she suggested that we take time to explore the ways in which feelings of stress as a child might be contributing to my sense of stress as an adult. There seemed to be something to this line of inquiry, and—although I ultimately saw her only once more—I told her I'd book another appointment. As I was leaving, she told me she'd forgotten something.

"What I find useful with all my patients," she said, pushing herself away from her desk with both arms, to give her ample belly more room, "is to encourage them to keep a symptom log. It's still the case that we're not entirely sure what we're dealing with. It can be a lot easier to identify a problem when you have a clearer picture of it."

In order to gain this clearer picture, I was to write down everything that struck me as out of the ordinary—physical symptoms, cravings, sleep disturbances, fevers, dreams.

"It can take a couple of months," she added, "but sometimes we're able to see some really strong patterns emerge."

The notion of the symptom log intrigued me. It coincided completely with my natural tendency to take notes, and I liked the way it seemed to combine diarizing with medical observation. Borrowing a hardback notebook from work, I started to describe what was happening to me, and was eventually surprised—just as Gabriella said I would be—by the picture that emerged.

Ever since loneliness research began in the 1970s, psychologists have been emphasizing that there's a *content* to the state, that it manifests itself in specific, observable ways. "Loneliness is *there*," argued the University of Massachusetts sociologist Robert Weiss, who was and remains incredibly influential in the field of loneliness research. "It has symptoms, expressions, and a set of characteristics," just like any other ailment.

One of the first symptoms Weiss pointed to was a sort of pressured restlessness, an inability, when lonely, to feel at ease with what you're doing. "I'm not able to concentrate or just *be* where I am," says Sonia, the copywriter, reflecting on the restlessness that overcomes her when she's lonely. "I just feel like I should be somewhere else, or doing something else. I just feel a lot like I should be *doing* something else. I find that I get fed up. I have these moments where I'm just fed up with not having something."

The sense of *not having* something can be a powerful force. Weiss, in considering what role loneliness might be playing, chose to focus on it as a "proximity promoting device." By this he meant that it functioned as a mental nudge, alerting us to the fact of our aloneness, and urging us to connect more closely with other people. From an evolutionary standpoint, the need for such an emotional mechanism makes sense. As a species, human beings are distinctly lacking in size, speed, and physical strength. We are, as one researcher happily told me, "delicious bits of walking meat." What's kept us safe over the millennia has been our tendency to form groups: we're simply safer in one than outside of one. With the presence of others enhancing our safety, it's no wonder we've developed an alarm bell that begins to ring when we find ourselves too alone, and it's also no surprise that the alarm in question is hard to ignore.

"Physically," says Claire, the financial analyst from the prairies, "I just have to get up and move around, or I feel the urge to work out, or to go for a walk or something, because to be sitting still, it's just very—I don't know how to describe it—it almost feels too intense, to be sitting still and being alone."

The problem with loneliness is that, compared to other motivators, it's not one that's readily satisfied. If you're hungry, it's hopefully easy to find food. If you're afraid of the bear, you can hustle toward the car. But when you're lonely, other people—almost by definition—are not available. This means you can be left with a keyed-up energy that you can't turn off. If you try to direct the motivational energy into something like work or reading, you'll be left feeling oddly off balance, and—even if you do recognize that what you're looking for is another person—you'll feel unfocused and dissatisfied until that other person is found.

The fact that loneliness drives us to look for something—or someone—means that it can be accompanied by a pronounced distractibility. I saw the distractibility that came over me in my second year of loneliness as both unusual and unique. During more embedded times of my life, such as my early years at law school, I'd enjoyed a robust attention span: I could brave three-hour real estate lectures; I could work my way through the Expropriations Act without passing out. As my loneliness began to span out, however, my attention simply fractured. I went from reading novels, to reading magazines, to finally giving up on paragraph form entirely and flipping through books of comic strips like *Dilbert* and *Calvin and Hobbes*. At work, I became an Internet junkie, following minute-by-minute match reports of sports I didn't know how to play. After work, I was easily and maddeningly distracted by anything my attention might light on: posters taped to telephone poles, the sounds of other people's conversations, neon store signs, ads on buses. My distractibility was irritating—I saw it as something I should simply *get over*—and I was intrigued to see it emerge in the findings about lonely people in general.

The idea of the lonely as more distractible than the nonlonely was first noted in the 1980s by Daniel Perlman. He found that if you gave lonely and nonlonely students an assignment to complete in noisy conditions, the lonely would have more trouble completing the task than the nonlonely. The distractibility of the lonely was scrutinized more closely by John Cacioppo, who put lonely and nonlonely students in listening booths and asked them to pay attention to sounds presented to their right and left ears. Generally speaking, if you're a right-handed person, you'll be able to focus more easily on information presented to your right ear—shifting to your left ear requires concentration. What Cacioppo found was that, when lonely students were asked to shift from a right-ear to a left-ear focus, they were less able to do so. That is, the lonely were more likely to remain focused on sounds being presented to their dominant right ear, even after they had been told to make the switch, and even when this was all they were being asked to do. Cacioppo now argues that this relative inability to control attention might partly account for lonely people's tendency to withdraw in new or complex social situations. If you can't properly focus your attention, and if your environment feels overwhelming as a result, withdrawal becomes not just a welcome but a possibly unavoidable response.

One of the reasons that distraction is such a problem for the lonely is that the state is often accompanied by the sort of pronounced anxiety my boss noticed at work. If you give lonely people the UCLA Loneliness Scale, as well as a measure of anxiety, the two scores will correlate. The more lonely someone is, the more likely they are to have symptoms of anxiety. "I'm usually able to handle stress," says Frank, a freelance journalist from Seattle who suffers from a loneliness that has lasted at least three years. "But over time, at least in more recent times, it's not even stress that sets off the anxiety, it's just nothing. It's not even big things that will make me anxious, but just small everyday things that seem to affect me a lot more."

Loneliness, in many ways, functions *as* anxiety. As soon as we recognize an aloneness that can't be remedied, alarm bells go off, and the alarm continues to sound until the security of another person or group is found. The notable aspect of anxiety within this schema—and what sets loneliness apart from conditions such as generalized anxiety disorder—is that the sense of strain is often responsive to companionship. There were times, after anxiety had emerged as a problem, when I'd find myself feeling calm after a long talk with Simon, or soothed after an afternoon of doing crafts with Laura. The chattering in my head, the feelings of threat and vulnerability—these things would fade for the stretch of time that I was connecting with someone in a meaningful way.

Frequent, meaningful companionship was not something I had a lot of, however, and this meant that the anchored feelings cued by togetherness tended to wane as I spent more time on my own. My anxiety would return, and when it did, it tended to undermine my sleep. In part, I was contributing to my own sleep problems by shifting from room to room. During my second year of loneliness, I began falling asleep on the couch in the study, directly above my neighbors' living room, so that I could drift off to sleep comforted by the sound of their voices. The conversation downstairs would inevitably end, however, and the silence that found me at two or three in the morning would shift me into a queer wakefulness. I'd move into my bedroom and sit leaning against the pillows, or I'd drift into the kitchen with conversations racing through my mind, unable to settle down.

Broken sleep is actually one of the most common—and most

critical—symptoms that researchers have fastened on as an indicator of loneliness. When researchers in the United Kingdom, who were studying 250 middle-aged civil servants in London, asked lonely participants how they had been sleeping, the answer that came back was a resounding "Not very well." Regardless of the person's age, sex, or marital status, lonely individuals in the British study complained of taking a long time to fall asleep, waking more frequently during the night, and experiencing greater dysfunction due to sleepiness the next day. Interestingly, the same description of sleep—or lack of it—was offered by lonely elderly individuals in Chicago, and by lonely young students at Ohio State University. The results could be viewed as an instance of the lonely simply exaggerating, or viewing every aspect of their lives through a negative lens, but this doesn't seem to be the case. When lonely individuals at Ohio State stayed at a sleep lab and had their eye movements, brain waves, and muscular tension monitored over the course of a night, researchers found that the lonely really did take longer to fall asleep. They also spent more time in a deep sleep before entering the REM phase (a sign of greater overall fatigue), spent less time asleep, and woke up more often.

The discovery of sleep disturbances represented a crucial step in understanding loneliness, because it provided some explanation for the vague illnesses and physical complaints the lonely tend to suffer from. My own loneliness saw me experiencing the headaches I told my naturopath about, as well as slight but persistent migraine symptoms such as blurred vision and a sensitivity to noise and light. Since my doctor didn't know what was wrong, and since some of my complaints could be indicative of neurological disease, I wound up in an MRI lab at four in the morning, being flooded with radio waves that really should have been directed at someone more deserving. Because no one ever found anything wrong with me, and I think now that the source of my ill health was simply loneliness itself.

When lonely people are surveyed, they report symptoms similar to those I was having. They'll describe headaches and digestive problems, as well as chest pains and heart disease. The state, in other words, seems to go hand in hand with a sense of being slightly or significantly *off*.

"A few years ago, I read a short story by W. Somerset Maugham," says Anne, the Illinois social worker, thinking of the health problems that have plagued her over a lifetime of loneliness. "The characters are in a health-care setting, and one is a doctor, and one of his statements is, 'Some people just aren't *made* as well as others.' They tend to become ill more often, they tend to have more things go wrong with their bodies, and no matter how well they try to take care of themselves, that's just going to happen. I kind of lived with that feeling for many years—that I was just one of those people."

Anne's sense of being physically undermined is empirically normal. Researchers in Scotland, who were trying to understand the extent to which loneliness might affect the demand for health care, polled hundreds of lonely and nonlonely adults in Glasgow. They found that lonely adults were twice as likely to report symptoms of ill health. When the researchers asked about doctor visits, they found that the lonely were more likely to have been to their general practitioners. Specifically, the nonlonely Scots had been to their doctors' offices roughly four times in the previous year. The lonely had been there almost ten times a year.

For a long time, no one took the ill health of the lonely particularly seriously. In a stereotype about lonely people that's almost too depressing to think about, it was assumed that lonely people were showing up at doctors' offices simply because they wanted to corner someone into talking to them. When researchers began to probe what was politely called the "listening ear" theory, however, they found that doctors admitted to providing less complete and less attentive care to those who seemed alone. With the doctors essentially zoning out, it began to seem unlikely that the lonely were there just to chat.

An alternative explanation—namely, that the lonely were at their doctors' offices because something was really wrong— began to gain ground in the 1990s, when a Swedish study emerged showing that the lonely were, quite simply, dying earlier than the nonlonely. The Swedish research team, curious about the relationship between quality of life and the ability to rebound from invasive surgery, followed 1,250 patients who had undergone heart surgery between 1988 and 1991. Before the operation, researchers asked each subject about whether or not they felt lonely, and they repeated this question at the three-month, one-year, and two-year marks. Five years after each patient's surgery, the researchers correlated their data on loneliness and mortality. They quickly realized that the lonely—at both the one-month and the five-year marks—were more likely to have died than the nonlonely. In fact, the ratio of deaths between the lonely and the nonlonely subjects was approximately 2:1.

The researchers, surprised by their results, were quick to add that they did not know what was causing the higher death rate among the lonely, and they stressed that—while their findings certainly seemed robust among patients having undergone heart surgery—the ratio might not persist in a broader population. As such, the Swedish finding—that loneliness was a risk factor for mortality following heart surgery—was both alarming and reassuring. While the researchers had certainly found a link between loneliness and a specific medical procedure, their results didn't generalize. It wasn't possible, on the basis of the heart surgery results, to say that loneliness was a risk factor for early mortality *in general*.

Or, more precisely, it wasn't possible to say this until a Dutch team based at Vrije University in Amsterdam released the results of a larger and more unnerving study. The Dutch researchers—who wanted a clearer picture of the relationship between mortality and social support—interviewed 2,900 ordinary Amsterdam residents between 1992 and 1993. All of the participants were between the ages of fifty-five and eighty-five, and none—at the time of the interview—were hospitalized or living in assisted care facilities. During the course of the interview, the subjects were asked about how lonely they felt, how often they felt abandoned, how often they wished they had a close friend or confidant, and how often they felt rejected. Their scores were tallied into a single figure ranging from 0 (indicating low loneliness) to 11 (indicating high loneliness). With these scores in place, the researchers essentially sat back and, over the course of the next twenty-nine months, waited to see who would die.

Obligingly, 202 of the study participants passed on during the follow-up period. As expected, age, the preexistence of chronic disease, self-rated health, and drinking proved to be significant predictors of mortality. Less expectedly, loneliness also emerged as a strong predictor. A higher loneliness score at the time of the original interview translated into a higher likelihood of death twenty-nine months later. More specifically, 5.4 percent of the nonlonely participants died during the follow-up period, compared to 10.4 percent of the lonely subjects. Since the participants had been drawn from a general population, and since none had been hospitalized or institutionalized at the time of the initial interview, the researchers were able to make the more general claim that loneliness—through pathways that were not then well understood—increased the risk of death from a wide variety of causes.

For decades, ever since Robert Weiss began writing in the 1970s, loneliness researchers had been saying that loneliness was really *present*, that it could affect the lonely person and evidence itself in specific ways. What the mortality findings did was bear this argument out in a disturbing, shocking way. The pathways through which loneliness affects the body are now closer to being understood, but discovery of these pathways hasn't worked like an advance in cancer or diabetes. It's possible for researchers to tease out the mechanisms that loneliness uses to undermine the body, but—so long as the individual remains lonely—this information can't be used to offset the physical toll the state is taking.

Policy analysts working today are beginning to insist that loneliness reduction needs to be recognized as a broad-scale public health goal. Their argument is that, in order to ensure longevity, we need to start focusing on ways of making people feel more connected, in much the same way that we've settled on plans to encourage people to stop smoking and to exercise more. While some public health plans have identified loneliness as a specific target, it's still the case that loneliness is most often seen as an individual problem, and—worse—as an individual problem that's somehow nonproblematic. Epidemiologists know that the lonely face significant health risks, but the lonely themselves are likely to hear that their state is a mood, something unconnected to anything significant.

It's worth pointing out that I had to find the papers on mortality myself. In 2006, as my research on loneliness was becoming much more intense and very personal, I found a footnote in a study on isolation. The footnote led me to the med school library, where I ran database searches and pulled gigantic bound volumes off high metal shelves. The first thing I did, when I found the papers on mortality, was take note of the dates. The Swedish study had been published in 1998; the Dutch study in 1997. This meant that both papers had been in existence before my social circle began to shrink in 2001, and before I visited my doctor and naturopath in the spring of 2004. But I hadn't heard about either of the studies. I'd heard about all sorts of other things, such as the risks of trans fats, the problems with hormone replacement therapy, and the possibility of coffee lowering the risk of Alzheimer's disease. But there was nothing readily available in pop culture talking about the risks associated with loneliness, even though the state is a problem for a significant number of people, and even though the number of people struggling with the state is likely growing.

I'm not sure how I would have felt if my doctor or naturopath had diagnosed me with loneliness and then told me that the state was increasing my risk of early death. It would not have been happy news. But there's power in *knowing* something, in understanding just what it is you're facing. When I presented with feelings of stress, threat, exhaustion, headache, nausea, distraction, and anxiety, someone, somewhere along the line, should have asked about my sense of connectedness. Because it was this—not multiple sclerosis, not an overworked adrenal system—that was the problem. And if the problem had been identified, I could have turned my attention to it more closely, and sooner.

As it was, I continued to drift, with no real sense of the risks my state entailed. When I think about that period now—

about my struggles with sleeplessness, my strange headaches and inexplicable feelings of nausea—what comes to mind are memories of the public health nurses who used to visit my high school. They used to arrive with slides showing lungs growing blacker and sootier as an unnamed individual—presumably dead—continued to smoke year after year. And I wonder if my loneliness hasn't worked on me in a roughly similar way, gradually undermining my health and leaving me more physiologically vulnerable than I was before. I have to wonder as well about reversing its effects. Some researchers, such as John Cacioppo, have suggested that the physiological impact of loneliness can likely be offset if secure emotional connections are found, but there haven't been any long-term studies following individuals from a lonely to a nonlonely state. This means that the toll that loneliness took on me might have reversed itself, or it might persist. Despite the fact that the worst of my loneliness is over—or at least changed—I might still be carrying a physiological load that could affect my future. And what bothers me most about this situation is the fact that no one bothered to tell me about the risks. No one saw my loneliness as anything worth mentioning.

Chapter Four

HEART AND SOUL

How loneliness weaves its way into us

Duringthe summer of 2004—almost two years after my loneliness set in, and about two years before I found the mortality papers—I began to engage with the question of *why* I felt so lonely. In the hefty journal I was keeping, I started to ask myself, point-blank, why I couldn't have people in my life the way that others seemed to. My inability to understand what was happening triggered what I now see as my season of lists. I've always liked lists, and—in an attempt to sort out cause and effect—I drew up lists about my shortcomings ("I'm too demanding"), my looks ("perhaps contacts?"), my clothes ("buy sexier underwear"), my body ("lose weight"), and even my shoes ("less sensible").

I must, in the summer of that second year, have itemized just about every aspect of my personality and appearance in an attempt to discern what was triggering my loneliness. Because much of the time, I saw my behavior—or my looks, or my needs, or my shoes—as being fundamentally to blame. This perspective is not necessarily as self-defeating as it sounds.

In some ways, if you see yourself as the cause of a problem, it means it's within your purview to correct that problem. If I could only spot the culpable attitude or garment, I reasoned, I'd be able to isolate it, eliminate it, and in this way end my loneliness.

The odd thing about my lists—I mean, aside from the fact that I was writing them down at all—is that every now and then I'd break down and write "fate." To be honest, I wrote it a bit more hysterically, like this: "FATE!!" Even as I was cataloging the more external aspects of my personality, I often had the sense that loneliness had nothing to do with externalities. Rather than skimming the surface of my life, the state felt ingrained into me, as though it were wound up in my blood and cells and veins. My father had once told me, near the end of his life, that I could ask him anything I wanted about the divorce, and I was astonished to find myself stumped. Even though I had no information about why my parents split up, I couldn't seem to frame an intelligent question. With the divorce having shaped me and turned me into who I was, I couldn't get enough distance from the event to analyze and ask about it in a neutral, curious way.

And this was how my loneliness struck me, as though there was no separation between me and it, as though it *was* me. My worries about loneliness, throughout my teens and early twenties, had always been about something *waiting* to happen. It was if I'd been told I had a hereditary illness and that onset would begin in my early thirties. Thinking about loneliness was like thinking about my nearsightedness, or my wavy hair, or my allergic reaction to golden retrievers. The state felt like something I'd come into the world with, something that had just been waiting for the right mix of time and circumstance to fully make itself known.

Many of the lonely people I spoke to conceptualized loneliness in precisely this way. The state, they suggested, was written right into them. It carried more than a hint of inevitability. "I've often felt as though I have a gene for loneliness," says Trevor, a fifty-something businessman from Minnesota. Even though Trevor thinks that an early move might be partly accountable for his feelings of long-term loneliness—he tells me about his parents settling in a neighborhood where they didn't fit in—he adds, "It's as if it wouldn't have mattered what my beginning roots were. That no matter where I'd lived, I would have suffered from this loneliness."

Part of the reason many lonely people saw their loneliness as inevitable was that they'd grown up with a lonely parent. "I think of my dad," says Adam, the Rhode Island illustrator, when I ask him about lonely relatives. "He's been alone for the last thirty years, he's never had a close friend, and he's lonely."

"At home the phone doesn't stop ringing," says Katherine, a thirty-year-old policy analyst from Nova Scotia. "My mother's always talking to someone or another." Comparing her mother's gregariousness to her own lack of a social circle, Katherine adds, with a bit of a laugh, "I was thinking, 'My mom has way more friends than I do.' But then we had this chat one night, and she said, 'I don't feel like I really have any real friends. People call, but they're just calling to get the gossip.' So my mom feels lonely too."

"My mother was lonely," echoes Rachel, the homemaker from Florida, matter-of-factly. She notes that one of the things that pleases her about having sons instead of daughters is that the difference in gender seems poised to stop loneliness in its tracks. "My sons will obviously get things from me," she says. "But I don't think they'll get this predisposition for loneliness.

And that's an absolute relief, because I would never want my children to feel this way."

Lonely people aren't wrong in intuiting a genetic link to loneliness. The haunting quality that loneliness possesses, the way it seems to lurk on the edges of a life, has actually been borne out by recent scientific research.

The idea of an inherited basis for loneliness was first advanced almost a quarter century ago, when Canadian psychologists studying mother-daughter pairs noticed that UCLA Loneliness Scale scores had a tendency to reproduce themselves. Lonely mothers tended to have lonely daughters, while mothers who described themselves as lacking friends had daughters who perceived a similar shortfall. The psychologists, Judith Lobdell and Daniel Perlman, suggested that child-rearing practices could provide a partial explanation for the repetition, but they left open the possibility of a genetic link, of a trait being carried in the DNA that left the carrier more vulnerable to loneliness.

The idea that loneliness might be carried in the genes—a very scientific idea that somehow feels poetic—was buttressed early this century when two American researchers, Shirley McGuire and Jeanie Clifford, noted that in a small group of twin children, loneliness rates tended to mirror each other. The closer the twins were genetically, the more likely they were to have similar loneliness scores. Although the researchers noted that their study was a small one, and that it needed to be followed up with a larger, adult population, they stressed that their findings provided some evidence of a genetic contribution to loneliness.

The large-scale work advocated by McGuire and Clifford was ultimately undertaken by a combined U.S.-Dutch team that set out to study over 8,000 adult twins in the Netherlands. The somewhat epic study—which spanned ten years—saw each twin being asked how often they felt lonely, how often they felt unloved, how much they liked to be alone, and how often they felt withdrawn around others. The questions were repeated at approximately two-year intervals between 1991 and 2002, and the answers to each question from each testing period were compiled into a loneliness profile for each twin, a sort of snapshot of the role of loneliness within that twin's life.

The results showed that among identical twins—who have identical DNA—the loneliness profiles matched 50 percent of the time. Among fraternal twins, the loneliness scores still corresponded, but only 25 percent of the time. In other words, and just as was the case in the original U.S. study, the closer the twins were genetically, the more likely it was for their experience of loneliness to be the same.

"There is an inborn vulnerability to loneliness in children and adults," wrote Dorret Boomsma, a Dutch genetics expert and the study's lead author. I'd e-mailed her a flurry of questions about her work, and she'd responded quickly and succinctly. "Just as some people are taller, heavier, more prone to depression, or more intelligent, some people will be more susceptible to loneliness." An event—such as a move or breakup—that leaves one person feeling fine could leave someone else, with a different genetic makeup, feeling utterly alone. "Environmental triggers will more easily lead to loneliness in susceptible people," Boomsma told me, confirming what I'd suspected, "while other people are buffered against such feelings."

The Dutch work has been criticized as reductive, as yet another example of the modern tendency to collapse emotional phenomena to genetic cause and effect. John Cacioppo, however, one of the twin studies' main authors, knows that genetic analyses can promote a lot of misperceptions, and he's precise about what the findings do and do not mean. "It's not the case that you have these genes and you're going to be lonely," he insists. "This is *not* genetic determinism. This is what I think it means. Knowing that it's half heritable means treat it the same way you would if you found out you were salt sensitive. If you're salt sensitive, don't eat a lot of salt, and you'll never have cardiovascular problems as a result of taking in a lot of salt. If you're not salt sensitive, enjoy salt. It's good to know your sensitivity to salt, so you know whether you can salt your food or not. And with loneliness—let's say I get this promotion. The promotion requires that I go across the country to where I know no one. If I'm not genetically at risk for loneliness, then do it—it's a professional advancement. If I'm really sensitive, I'm not sure that promotion makes it worth the cost.

"We have the power to select our environments," Cacioppo continues, stressing what lonely people really need to take away from the genetics research. "So if I'm genetically susceptible, it's relevant to the environments I select." I like this idea of scanning an environment to try to calculate its loneliness-promoting properties. It makes sense to me, and sounds like a good loneliness-reduction strategy. At the same time, the idea seems to assume that I'm the driver, loneliness is the passenger, and we're going to go wherever I wish. And I'm not sure, when I really think about it, who has their hands on the wheel.

When I think back to the onset of my loneliness, I can see that one of the main problems I faced was that I was working at a very small firm. Viewed from a certain perspective, I can see my choice to work at a boutique as sensible. I wanted, after all, to save wetlands and forests, and I could only do this by working out of a small office—large firms don't house environmental protection practices. Conceptualized this way, I can see myself making a reasonable decision, and then—for reasons that are almost accidental—finding myself isolated.

But there's a different way of looking at things. I often wonder whether my loneliness, in a sense, propelled me toward the small office, so that it would have an easier time asserting itself. This sounds slightly fantastic—as though my state were possessed of near-human attributes such as foresight and agency—but in some ways, it's the interpretation that makes the most sense to me. I could, after my clerkship, have gone to any firm I wished. But, for reasons that I think are genetic in nature, I selected, from a huge array of choices, the work environment most likely to leave me lonely. It was as though I had a sense of what my genetic inheritance was pointing me toward, and I selected the environment in which it could flourish.

And when I say "inheritance," I'm being entirely literal. The sense I had, in my teens and early adulthood, of being destined for loneliness arose largely from the experience of witnessing my mother's isolation. The sight of her asleep alone in the kitchen filled me not just with sadness but with a sense of instruction, as though I were being given the opportunity to observe a situation before I found myself inhabiting it. Many women worry about turning into their mothers; my worry was much more specific.

"I've been so lonely here," my mother once told me, in her wide, unhurried accent. I can't remember what could have prompted this admission. I know that I was still in university at the time, and that I was living at home for the summer, taking courses at a campus up the road. I might have said something about missing my friends, or about feeling isolated from my fellow students, most of whom attended the college I was registered at only for the summer.

I can't remember what I said in response to her comment.

What I do remember, as though the exchange had taken place yesterday, instead of eighteen years ago, was the powerful urge I had to cover my ears, and duck, and somehow *blot out* what she'd just said. To hear her say the word *lonely* felt like a curse, as though she'd just released an incantation that would bind my future to her past. I think I might have tried to leave the table—I remember that she was standing against the dining room wall, while I was seated and working on an assignment—but even as I did so, it felt as though I'd taken action too late, as though the damage were done.

My reaction was a childish one, of course. My mother wasn't casting a spell on me, and I—at twenty-one—should have had the maturity to ask about her experience with loneliness and to empathize with what she'd gone through. I should also have had the presence of mind to ask about specific difficulties she'd had, and about experiences that had made her loneliness worse, if for no other reason than to face my own loneliness with more insight and awareness. But all I'd wanted to do was hide. If my mother hadn't dropped the subject—and she did—I think I might actually have crawled out of the room in an attempt to bring our talk to a close.

What strikes me as odd now was the fact that my mother was referring to loneliness at all. That summer must have been a particularly lonely time for her—perhaps a friendship had ended, or a love affair had broken off. Since I spent the academic year in a different city, it was hard for me to keep track of the ins and outs of her social life. I do know that our exchange in the dining room was probably the only time either of us had mentioned loneliness in the presence of the other, and this was despite the fact that I recognized the state in her, and she likely recognized it in me. We talked about other things we shared. My mother had been a good writer, and she was delighted to see her skills manifesting themselves in one of her daughters. I was the only one of my sisters who, like my mother, loved to swim; the only one who took long walks; the only one able to tolerate more than two cats in a house. There were all sorts of ways in which we resembled each other, and my mother usually praised the ways in which she saw her own traits appearing in me.

But when it came to loneliness, the overall tone was one of regretful silence. It was not a topic my mother raised with me, nor I with her. I think the basis of my silence in childhood was a basic conversational inexperience—I simply didn't *know* how to mention it. As I grew older, however, and became perfectly capable of communicating the problem, something else took over.

"You hide your loneliness instead of blaming your mother for it," Genevieve once said, in an uncharacteristically blunt fashion. Perhaps she thought I was being rather obtuse and not catching the hints she'd been trying to drop. "Pretending it doesn't exist is a way of protecting her from your anger."

Genevieve's reasoning went like this: my mother, having to support my two sisters and me after the divorce, had gone into survival overdrive—scrambling for work and attending night school—and in so doing, she'd been unable to meet my emotional needs. To make the divorce work, and to keep my mother from going completely over the edge, I'd learned to hide my needs for her and for other people. Admitting the existence of these needs in adulthood would amount to a psychological attack on my mother that my younger self didn't want to mount. Hence I was caught between an adult awareness of my loneliness and a childlike inability to tell my mother about it.

There might have been something to this analysis. It's cer-

tainly true that I had to engage in a lot of emotional management and self-reliance in the years that followed the divorce.
But what Genevieve didn't know—what I hadn't bothered to
tell her, because it was so rarely mentioned in my family—
was the fact that my mother was an orphan. Her own mother,
Anna, had died of tuberculosis in a sanatorium at the age of
twenty-one, when my mother was four. After Anna's death, my
mother had been farmed out to a foster family, and this happened because all of Anna's relatives had disappeared. Since the
unplanned pregnancy had been out of step with the family's
religious beliefs, Anna had been ostracized, and the father—
my grandfather—had flown the coop. The various departures
and absences meant that my grandmother had died alone,
not knowing what was going to happen to her only child. My
mother, in turn, had been set adrift among strangers.

If I was lonely, it was because my mother had been raised in
lonely circumstances, and my grandmother had likely died in a
flood of aloneness. I was, in some respects, a third-generation
lonely person. Through a mix of circumstance and genetics, I
had, unlike my sisters, come to embody an unwelcome family
trait, and it did not surprise me that my mother preferred to
keep the precise nature of our curious heritage unnamed.

My mother was the one person in my circle of friends and
family who lived in the north end, relatively close to me, and
this meant that she saw more of me than almost anyone else as
my loneliness wore on. Our proximity was problematic, since it
allowed her to witness some of the changes and developments I
was beginning to experience.

"I've never seen you so heavy," she said as I sat on her porch
during that second summer in oversized shorts and a shapeless

sweatshirt. I pinched the admittedly doughy flesh behind my knee and muttered that it was my desk job, that I was spending too much time sitting and not getting out enough.

"What are you eating?" my mother persisted. She was sitting on a small wooden bench that seemed to emphasize her fine bones. The thin slats of pine rising up behind her seemed like extensions of her birdlike shoulders and narrow neck. The slight weight she'd carried in middle age was gone, and she looked light and fine in her summer robe and slippers.

"I'm eating normally," I lied, feeling and sounding defensive. Because one thing that had undergone a fairly radical change, as my loneliness deepened, was my appetite. Almost every loneliness researcher I've spoken to has described loneliness as a form of metaphorical hunger. The lonely, says Northwestern University's Wendi Gardner, "are like people who are kind of starving." In my case, my body went literal on me. As my loneliness became more of a problem, I began making furtive early-morning trips to the kitchen, where I'd station myself at the table and snack on sugary cereal bars and fat slices of bread and jam. At work, I made quiet visits to the office's makeshift kitchen, reaching for the boxes of brownies and doughnut holes that sat innocently atop the water cooler. I mixed up food with people, and people with food. When it came to relationships, I described good visits as "nourishing," and limited acts of friendship as "crumbs." When it came to food, I became weirdly preoccupied not with calories—which I perhaps should have been keeping an eye on—but with the quasi-moral properties of food itself. I wanted everything at home to be locally grown, fairly traded, and humanely raised. When my weekly organic produce box arrived, I fixated on the sweet-smelling strawberries and blemished apples, thinking of them not in terms of nutrition but in terms of traits that were nearly human. The apples weren't just edible, they were "good," "safe," "fair," "close."

"You've just *expanded*," my mother added, looking at the undeniably new heft of my hips. Her comment left me feeling stressed. I had a sense that, in seeing my weight shoot up, my mother might intuit the emotional emptiness of my life, and—with loneliness taboo between us—this was something I didn't want her to recognize.

"I'll exercise more," I muttered, telling myself I would not wear shorts in my mother's presence again until I had dropped some weight. And I did exercise. I jogged through the ravine behind my house, stopping to pull up wild carrots in the wide, white patches of Queen Anne's lace, and I kept up my nightly walks near the dog parks of my quiet and humid neighborhood.

My determined attempts to keep fit, however, didn't put much of a dent in my weight, and they didn't seem to counter the other strange physical changes that were coming over me. Because it wasn't just headaches and nausea that presented themselves as my loneliness intensified. At thirty-four, I felt as though loneliness were leaving me less physically sound, creakier. "Middle-aged" was how I angrily described myself in my journal, after coming home from my friend Simon's house, where his wife was setting out flagstones in the garden, and their big mutt was running indoors and out. Compared to the concentrated bustle of his place—where the phone, over the noise of his children laughing, seemed to ring almost constantly—my life felt empty, barren, and quiet. "You're turning into an old woman," I wrote somewhat meanly to myself. "You're too old for anything to change."

Even though I honestly felt this way—as though something crucial and sustaining had passed me by, as though I'd taken a shortcut into a more sterile stage of life—I didn't expect my body to start taking me literally. But after two years of intense loneliness, I began having painful periods, as well as muscle weakness, acne, and night sweats that left my hair and neck soaked, as though someone had just wrung a towel out over my head.

"Do you think she could be perimenopausal?" a middle-aged nurse whispered to my family doctor as I sat in the consulting chair, confused about what seemed to be a case of premature aging. The nurse seemed like more of an authority on the subject than my doctor, and there was a moment where he deferred to her judgment and they both just sat and considered me.

"I'm too young for that, right?" I asked. I hadn't given any thought to menopause. It was like thinking of hip fractures or arthritis—infirmities that might affect me years down the road but which I should be safely insulated from in the present.

"Yes," my doctor said uncertainly. He was a patient man. As my visits became routine, and as my symptoms—sleeplessness, anxiety, migraines—became more diffuse, he maintained a steady and unflappable demeanor, as though he wouldn't have been surprised if I spontaneously combusted on the spot.

"Let's just monitor it," he said finally, adding that I might want to think about keeping a journal as a means of charting my growing list of complaints.

I didn't tell my doctor that I was already all over the symptom log thing, but I did book a second appointment with my naturopath, who I hoped would offer an alternative account of what seemed to be my female problems. I wanted to hear that my doctor was way off in his thinking, that my problems flowed from my disrupted adrenal system, or too little vitamin D. I wanted the sorts of cures that naturopaths tend to prescribe— acupuncture, vitamins, or six drops of mallow essence in a glass of purified water. Instead, Gabriella surprised me by closing ranks with her mainstream colleagues and agreeing with the nurse.

"You have the symptoms of a menopausal woman," she said gently, as though there was a bright side to menopause that she was about to explain to me.

"What does that mean? Does that mean I'm actually entering menopause?"

"No," she said, shaking her head slowly. She was wearing the same expression—furrowed eyebrows and curious eyes over a puzzled little mouth—that had crept across the face of the nurse. "I don't know if that's what it means. You shouldn't think you're entering menopause. You might not be. I just mean you have the symptoms."

This Delphic statement mystified me. My mother had had me at forty, and both of my sisters had had children in their mid- to late thirties, so I knew early menopause didn't run in my family. And I didn't think I *was* menopausal. I was, after all, still getting my period. What troubled me about the diagnosis was the way it seemed to align with my sense of aging, of turning—in my early thirties—into someone slight and brittle with loneliness.

I was unsettled by this turn of events. In the unconscious bargain I thought I'd made with loneliness, I'd been careful to set out the main terms: the state could have my thoughts and feelings, but I was to retain ownership of my body. This was, after all, the agreement I was used to hammering out with depression. When depressions had hit, I'd swum, run, and biked my way out of them, using my body to ground me when my mind was out to sea. In fact, during my work term in the Arctic, it was depression—and the accompanying urge to *out-*

walk something—that had fueled my long nightly hikes across the tundra.

Although it took me some time to notice it, I began to realize that the deal I'd struck with depression—mind for it, body for me—simply wasn't carrying over to loneliness. Between the weight gain that overcame me and the strangely painful periods, I sensed that loneliness had jumped the dividing line between mind and body. Standing at the kitchen counter, stuffing myself with warm bread and melted cheese, I understood that any agreement I thought I'd signed with loneliness was null and void. Not only was the state latent within me, rising up from my genes, it was manifesting itself only to extend its grip outward and take hold of me as a whole.

Clinicians who study the health effects of loneliness are clear that the outcomes they're uncovering flow from loneliness, not related states. "There are a lot of other constructs that people assume loneliness is related to, that it's just another word for," says Louise Hawkley, Cacioppo's associate at the University of Chicago. Since the late 1990s, Hawkley has been looking at the relationship between loneliness and physiology, and I'd wanted to talk to her about the ways in which loneliness could affect us physically. At the start of our conversation, Hawkley emphasized that what she was focusing on was loneliness itself. "We control for and look at other psychological variables," she says, "to make sure we're not talking about something that's already known." In studying the relationship between loneliness and health, Hawkley and her colleagues aren't inadvertently picking up on the effects of depression, hostility, or distrust. Rather, the outcomes they're finding have to do with loneliness alone.

One of the ways in which loneliness is able to exert its effects on the body is through something known as total peripheral resistance. TPR represents the overall resistance to blood flow offered by all the arteries and capillaries of the body. As vessels tighten, resistance to blood flow increases, and overall levels of TPR rise. Hawkley, working with John Cacioppo at Ohio State University in 1999, noticed something about TPR in lonely people right away. Hawkley and Cacioppo had invited lonely and nonlonely students to their lab for stress tests: the students were to count backward by three, pretend to ask someone out on a date, and defend themselves against a false charge of shoplifting. The tasks were standard ones, designed to let the researchers explore differences in heart rate and blood pressure. And while there were some differences in these areas—quite poignantly, the hearts of the lonely, as though underexercised, beat more slowly than the hearts of the nonlonely—the stress reactions were not, in themselves, nearly as interesting as baseline levels of activity. "The lonely were just sitting there, quietly," Hawkley says, referring to their cardiovascular profiles, "and they were *looking* different."

Hawkley was struck by the fact that the lonely students, even when they weren't engaged in any of the stress tasks, had higher TPR levels than the nonlonely students. Thinking that perhaps the lonely students were simply finding the lab setting intimidating, Hawkley and Cacioppo strapped the students up with cardiovascular monitors and sent them out to attend to the tasks of an ordinary day. Even in more comfortable surroundings, however, TPR didn't budge. "Across a day," says Hawkley, "regardless of what they were doing—and, by the way, they didn't differ in what they were doing—the lonely still looked like they had in the lab, with this chronically higher level of TPR."

Heightened TPR is not, in itself, an objectively bad thing. But it's an interesting marker to find in young people for a few reasons. First, TPR tends to rise with age, but there weren't any age differences between the lonely and nonlonely groups. This means that, even though the lonely were the same age as the nonlonely students, they were starting to look physiologically older—a change that my doctor and naturopath, although they couldn't quite delineate it, were picking up on. Second, heightened TPR is usually associated with threat perceptions. If you take students—as researchers at the State University of New York did—and tell them to quickly start subtracting 7 from 1,528, the students who can't do math and who feel overwhelmed by the challenge will display elevated TPR. The lonely students being studied by Hawkley, however, weren't being asked to do anything psychologically stressful or threatening. "We weren't seeing these TPR differences as related to anything event-related," she says. "There's nothing in their lives that's driving it. It's sort of an underlying, chronic sense that life is more than they can handle and they're going to succumb at any moment." Buffeted by pervasive feelings of threat, the lonely students were behaving as though they were trapped in an endless lab experiment. As their sense of being overwhelmed persisted, so did their chronically high levels of TPR.

Last, and most significantly, high TPR—if it's maintained over time—can lead to serious problems with blood pressure regulation. The lonely and nonlonely students studied by Hawkley all had similar blood pressure readings, but this was because they were young. Even though the lonely had higher TPR levels, they could rely on other physiological systems, such as the kidneys, to keep overall blood pressure low. As we age, however, compensatory systems such as the kidneys aren't as efficient in offsetting blood pressure increases. As compensatory systems fail, the heightened blood pressure cued by elevated TPR is likely to simply remain high. This means that a fairly idiosyncratic physiological response in young people—high TPR—could, over time, amount to consistently elevated blood pressure levels in middle-aged or elderly adults.

And in fact, when Hawkley and Cacioppo switched their focus from lonely young students to lonely older individuals, increased blood pressure was what they found. In a study of 255 Chicago residents aged between fifty-three and seventy-eight, blood pressure levels were 10–30 mm higher among the lonely, with each 10-point increase on the UCLA Loneliness Scale cuing a neat 5 mm increase in blood pressure. Since weight gain tends to raise blood pressure by only 5–10 mm, and inactivity tends to lead to 5 mm gains, the effects exerted by loneliness were actually stronger than those associated with behaviors we typically classify as risky. And since it takes only a 20 mm increase in blood pressure to double the risk of death from stroke and heart disease, the lonely seniors being studied by Hawkley were at significantly greater risk of illness and mortality, simply by virtue of being lonely.

"We *have* to have our social needs met," says Hawkley. "Social connectedness is a pretty core facet of who we are as human beings. So to lack that, or to feel as though one lacks the kind of connectedness or the depth of connectedness that one needs, would be expected to have some pretty profound effects." Hawkley is a relatively soft-spoken and modest researcher. She doesn't come across as someone eager to overturn decades of conventional wisdom. But the idea she's trying to get across—namely, that the perception of isolation can manifest itself in physical outcomes—is one that people have been roundly dismissing for years.

The poor physical health of the lonely might seem like a difficult fact to gloss over, but there are a couple of ways it can be done. First, physical symptoms can be recast as psychological ones, with lonely people's health complaints being reduced to, in the words of one 1970s psychiatrist, "nothing more than disguised cries of self-pity from unhappy souls." Alternatively, the complaints can be accepted as valid, but then explained away in terms of lifestyle choices made by individual lonely people themselves. According to this viewpoint, the lonely really do get sick more often, but that's because they're drinking, smoking, eating junk food, and—as one self-help writer puts it— "subconsciously courting death."

To say that the lonely are subconsciously courting anything is nonsense, and the characterization of the lonely as unhealthy has the whiff of stereotype about it. The lonely are the ones who (for reasons that are never entirely explained) can't cook, who live off TV dinners and hang out with Johnnie Walker. Not only does this portrayal contain a strong element of blame— the lonely get sick because they bring it on themselves—it's largely at odds with how the lonely actually behave. The lonely people I was speaking to were working out, walking instead of taking the bus, fine-tuning their cooking skills, and generally taking care of themselves. Some of my respondents had trouble with the bottle—"When I was all by myself, it was just there, and I'd find myself drinking a lot because I had nothing else to do," says Frances, a twenty-nine-year-old physiotherapist from Missouri—but many others, including me, were completely dry. I'd drank in the early days of my loneliness, sipping red wine and reading old diaries for a sense of connection, but then I remembered a little piece of advice my psychiatrist had given me about alcohol.

"Someone like you can't drink," he'd said flatly, referring

to the viciousness of the depressions that had overtaken me in the past. "Every time you take a drink, you should think about holding a loaded gun. Alcohol's a depressant. That drink might be a blank, or it might be the one that blows you away."

With this subtle message serving as a reminder, I'd poured all the booze in my apartment down the sink. Ever since then, all of my experiences with loneliness, and all of my efforts in trying to overcome it, have taken place against a backdrop of sobriety.

In general, attempts to link loneliness to adverse health behaviors have been inconclusive. In virtually every study that's been done, the lonely have been shown to smoke, drink, and consume caffeine to no greater extent than the nonlonely. The lonely are just as likely to be exercising, and just as likely to be abiding by doctors' orders. Even in Britain, where researchers took unsuspecting civil servants and measured their waist-to-hip ratios, there were no significant differences between the lonely and nonlonely groups. It wasn't the case that the lonely were round and apple-shaped, while the nonlonely were healthier pears. The two groups simply looked and weighed the same.

But the fact that the lonely and the nonlonely have similar health behaviors doesn't mean that they have the same health outcomes. In a recent survey of 2,400 individuals in rural and urban Holland, researchers found that 37 percent of lonely individuals described their own health as either poor or very poor. That's simply too high a figure to explain away in terms of displacement or lifestyle, and since none of the people in the Dutch study were physically isolated, the number suggests that something other than objective isolation has to be at work.

A different explanation for the physical complaints of the lonely was offered as early as the 1980s, when researchers at

Ohio State University noticed that the lonely tend to have slightly underperforming immune systems. In one study of lonely medical students, conducted in 1984, the immunologist Janice Kiecolt-Glaser found that levels of NK cells—the cells we need to hunt down viruses and stop tumor growth—were approximately half those of what they were in the nonlonely.

Kiecolt-Glaser suggested that loneliness might be undermining immune function, but she couldn't come to a firm conclusion, largely because she was just drawing blood from lonely people and conducting cell counts—she wasn't measuring immune response over the long term in people's everyday lives. This was something that doctoral student Sarah Pressman decided to do in 2001. Pressman told me that, because she'd been feeling slightly lonely herself after a move from Ottawa to Pittsburgh, she decided to look at how loneliness might affect our bodies' ability to resist disease. Instead of simply counting markers such as NK cells or T-lymphocytes, Pressman set out to follow antibody response in students who had just received their first flu vaccinations. The goal was to assess the interaction between loneliness and antibody production, and the nice thing about the experiment, explained Pressman, was that "what's happening is real. It's the actual body. So it's a measure of how well the immune system is functioning."

Pressman gave the students PalmPilots and—for two weeks immediately following the vaccinations—paged the students four times a day. Each time they were paged, the students had to fill out a short version of the UCLA Loneliness Scale. After this intense two-week monitoring period, the students were called or e-mailed every two weeks and asked about their loneliness levels.

At the end of four months, Pressman was able to compare antibody levels with loneliness levels. Since she'd drawn blood samples at the start of the experiment, she was able to determine the extent to which antibody levels had increased over the course of the study. By month four, the difference between the lonely and nonlonely groups in terms of antibody production was striking. Students who scored high in loneliness produced 20 percent fewer antibodies than those who scored low in loneliness, with antibody levels falling as loneliness scores increased. In fact, in 6–7 percent of the lonely students, antibody levels were so low that they amounted to almost no defense at all. "We never know exactly how much antibody your body has to produce to protect yourself, because we're not allowed to run studies where we give you a vaccination and then expose you to a virus," says Pressman with a laugh. "But you can see that with the people who were lonely and isolated, it's a poignant difference in how much antibody they were producing."

And while Pressman was testing just one component of a person's immune response—antibodies are just one contingent in an overall immune army of NK cells, T- and B-lymphocytes, and phagocytes—it's possible that the lower antibody production was actually a sign of a weaker overall immune reaction. Whether or not the antibody response generalizes for every immune measure that exists, explains Pressman, is uncertain. "Whether they'd be worse at fighting colds, we don't really know that. But our best estimate would be perhaps, it's possible, that the immune systems of the lonely would be compromised in other ways besides just this one."

One of the reasons that overall immune function might be weakened in the lonely is that the lonely seem to be producing slightly more cortisol than the nonlonely. "We don't know exactly what does it," says Pressman, "but we know that feelings of social isolation have an effect on your body through cortisol, which is an immune-dampening hormone. As cortisol goes up, immune system function tends to go down, because cortisol suppresses it. It's sort of a general stress response. You can imagine that, if you were experiencing a brief stressor and had to, say, run away from a lion, then it would be helpful to have your immune system not operating optimally because you need that energy to run."

Lonely people are not, however, running from lions. Their cortisol levels are going up because they seem to experience events as more stressful than the nonlonely. "There are times," says Katherine, the policy analyst from Nova Scotia, "where probably to any outside observer, they'd say, 'Her life looks really peaceful and happy.' But at those times, I can fly off the handle at nothing at all. Somebody will look at me sideways and I'll burst into tears."

One of the main ideas in social epidemiology is something known as "stress buffering." This means that other people can run interference between you and the difficulties you might be facing. They can offer practical support—such as loaning you money or lending you the car—and they can help mute the physiological effects of stress through their mere presence. In an experiment at the University of Pittsburgh, for instance, researchers had students subtract aloud by seventeen from a number in the thousands. Half of the students in the study did the math while standing alone, while half did the subtraction in the presence of a close friend. Heart rate and blood pressure went up in both groups, but it went up significantly less among people who were with friends—and this was the case even though the friend was doing nothing more than standing silently with one hand on the subject's wrist.

It's precisely this form of quiet support that lonely people seem to lack. Even if there is someone on hand to offer practical assistance—such as helping with the shopping or babysitting on occasion—there's often no one in the picture to lean on psychologically. "You can sit alone at home for so long that you kind of start to get a case of cabin fever," says Ray, the fundraiser from Philadelphia, as he describes the stress of living alone. "You don't really have anyone around for positive reinforcement." It's this lack of emotional support that researchers are beginning to hone in on as crucial in the development of adverse health outcomes. Without the certainty of emotional support, lonely people are likely to have a more acute response to stress than the nonlonely, and this heightened stress response could, over time, be linked to illness.

To test the stress reactions of lonely people, Andrew Steptoe, the psychologist at University College London, decided to have civil servants complete two basic tasks. The bureaucrats were to try to trace a star in a mirror (which, if you've ever done it, is completely maddening), and to identify the names of colors written in the wrong shade (the word *blue*, for example, would be written in red, creating a cognitive mismatch that's hard to quickly overcome).

Steptoe found that, even though the lonely and nonlonely were completing the same tasks—and even though the lonely didn't say that they felt more stressed—lonely individuals had a stronger physiological reaction than the nonlonely. Across the board, lonely participants displayed larger increases in blood pressure, more marked decreases in NK cell production, and larger spikes in fibrinogen—a clotting agent that's been linked to heart disease.

The magnitude of the changes was not, in itself, overly significant. "We weren't," Steptoe says wryly, "trying to cause our participants any difficulty in that respect." The results were telling not because they showed major changes but because they provided a glimpse of how lonely people respond to basic stressors. And if this heightened response were maintained over time, the lonely could—down the road—be confronting serious health problems. "Think," says Steptoe, "of an analogy with a cigarette. A cigarette produces a small biological response acutely. About half an hour later, blood pressure is back to normal again, and everything's back to normal. But a cigarette every half hour, every day, every week, every month, every year, for fifteen years generates a very large difference in biological responses. And so in a sense it's the same kind thing. What one is trying to model is the kind of experiences that people will be confronting in their everyday lives. And these small differences may accumulate over time to generate a genuine difference in health outcomes."

And differences in health outcomes are precisely what loneliness researchers are beginning to uncover. Researchers at the University of California have found that lonely senior citizens are three times more likely than the nonlonely to develop a heart condition. Researchers in Indiana have discovered that—at least in one study—women with higher UCLA Loneliness Scale scores were more likely to be diagnosed with breast cancer. And researchers in Holland have concluded that lonely people are three times more likely than the nonlonely to develop symptoms debilitating enough to leave them housebound.

Longitudinal studies—surveys that follow lonely people over years or decades—are still needed, but research seems to suggest that chronic loneliness mounts a quiet war of attrition on the body, gradually unsettling immune function, blood pressure, sleep patterns, and cortisol levels until the body breaks down and illness sets in. "We're thinking that people who are chronically lonely," says Hawkley, "are building up—you might say the opposite of a reserve—they're just wearing and tearing their bodies by virtue of this ongoing physiological effect. And it may vary over time. The physiological effect in a young adult may look a certain way that's different from what it looks like in an older adult, and maybe that's because these effects accrue over time. And so what looks like a fairly innocuous effect in young adults gets worse and worse and worse, until the point where, in older adulthood, the chronically lonely people are going to show up with objective, medical diagnoses. They're going to have *disease*, not just preclinical symptoms of something going on."

To date, most of the illnesses and clinical markers associated with loneliness have concerned the body. This makes sense, since most complaints from lonely people have involved *feeling* unwell. But other, subtler effects of loneliness are just now coming to clinical attention. One of the things it took me some time to notice about my loneliness was that it was leaving me slightly spacey. I've gone through life, from grade school to grad school, as a natural teacher's pet, effortlessly collecting Best Student and Faculty Scholar awards. By the end of my second year of chronic loneliness, however, I was having trouble following strands of discussion in ordinary conversations. My vocabulary collapsed, my memory became untrustworthy, and my intelligence as a whole started to seem lightly shredded. I'd stare at a *New York Review of Books* article and realize I had no idea what the author was talking about; I mixed up Paul Wolfowitz with Donald Rumsfeld, and then forgot when Wolfowitz left, and why. I tried to channel my loneliness by writing short stories about it—I tended to create a lot of lonely female characters, women suspiciously like myself—but while the plots came relatively easily, I found it hard to believe in myself as a writer.

"You have the talent," an editor wrote to me, and I accidentally read it as "You had the talent." My creativity, that little spark of certainty and skill I'd been aware of all my life, seemed to diminish in the face of loneliness. In some ways, losing my hold on it left me doubly lonely. It was as though, in addition to seeing my relationships winnow themselves down, I'd lost a way of communicating with myself, as though a window within me had just slammed shut.

There's an argument among psychologists who study belonging that we need our intelligence in order to navigate the social world, that we need to be smart to be able to communicate, share ideas, pass along information, and monitor others in a constantly changing environment. If our social world begins to shrink—if we find ourselves actively excluded or simply unable to connect with others—then there's less of a need for this sort of nuanced, flexible, and responsive sort of thought. Researchers have noted that, due to ethical considerations, it's not really possible to permanently ostracize someone and then monitor decrements in their ability to think and reason. It is possible, however, to cue short-term feelings of loneliness and isolation in subjects, and then assess whether those subjects are thinking and learning as quickly as people who aren't exposed to such manipulations.

At Case Western University, researchers wanting to explore the links between feelings of isolation and intelligence gave undergraduates a personality test and then one of two scenarios. Students who received the first scenario were told that they'd likely have rewarding relationships all through life, including a long and stable marriage, and friendships that would last into old age. Students who received the second scenario were told that:

> You're the type who will end up alone later in life. You may have friends and relationships now, but by your mid-20s most of these will have drifted away. You may marry or have several marriages, but these are likely to be short-lived and not continue into your 30s. Relationships don't last, and when you're past the age where people are constantly forming new relationships, the odds are you'll end up being more and more alone.

With half of the students cued to feel alone, the researchers administered a short IQ test, a reading comprehension test, and various GRE analytical problems. Almost without exception, students who'd been cued to feel lonely underperformed their embedded peers. On the IQ test, the isolated students answered only 69 percent of the questions correctly (compared to 82 percent for the embedded group), they were significantly less able to remember what they'd read, and they could solve only a fraction of the analytical problems. And the results couldn't be attributed to anxiety. As a control (and possibly just for fun), the researchers had conducted the same tests on a group of students who'd been told that they'd likely become severely accident-prone as they aged, and these students— facing a possible future of cuts and car wrecks—didn't display the same cognitive shortcomings.

The Case Western experiments are just snapshots of the effects that aloneness might have on cognitive function. The feelings cued in the experiment, though, weren't long-lasting. As soon as the tests were over, the students were debriefed and told to snap back into their normal lives. In the real world outside of a researcher's office however, some people find themselves caught up in lives of isolation that aren't make-believe. There's no white-coated experimenter leaning against the wall; there's no door for them to exit from. And, in looking at these people, it's possible to draw more alarming conclusions about the effects of loneliness on our mental abilities.

The links between loneliness and cognitive decline began to be uncovered in 2000, when Dr. Robert Wilson and his colleagues at Rush University Medical Center began a study of 823 older individuals in the Chicago area. At the start of the study, each participant underwent a complete medical exam, a complete neurological exam, and extensive cognitive testing. The subjects agreed that any who died before 2005 would donate their brains for postmortem examination, and they all also agreed to annual assessments of their loneliness levels and cognitive abilities.

Every year, for the next four years, the subjects told Wilson how lonely they felt. Specifically, they indicated how strongly they agreed with statements such as "I feel like I don't have enough friends," "I often feel abandoned," "I miss having people around," and "I miss having a really good friend."

The average age of the subjects at the start of the study was eighty, so—as the years went by—cognitive skills began to decline. Among some members of the group, Alzheimer's disease began to set in. The incidence of Alzheimer's disease, however, wasn't at all random. The loneliness scale Wilson was using had five points, with 1 indicating low loneliness and 5 indicating high loneliness. Combining the annual scores into a single measure, Wilson found that the risk of Alzheimer's increased by 50 percent for each point on the final loneliness score. Overall, subjects with high loneliness scores were twice as likely to develop the disease. Even among those who didn't develop Alzheimer's, the lonely participants displayed a more rapid overall decline in cognitive function, growing progressively less able than their nonlonely counterparts to remember events, recall words, and compare numbers.

Wilson thought that cause and effect might be counterintuitive. That is, instead of loneliness causing neurological decline, neurological decline might be causing loneliness. The thinking here is that as a person develops more physical signs of Alzheimer's in her brain, she's going to become increasingly isolated and so feel lonely. When Wilson conducted autopsies on the brains of the 106 individuals who died during the study period, however, he didn't find more physical traces of Alzheimer's in the lonely. Pathology couldn't be driving the loneliness, because the nonlonely individuals had just as many nerve plaques and tangles in their brain as the lonely. Wilson concluded that it was through other pathways—pathways that seem ghostly and aren't yet understood—that loneliness was leading to dementia and cognitive decline.

"We need to be aware," Wilson has said, summarizing his findings, "that loneliness doesn't just have an emotional impact but a physical impact." Glimmerings of this idea sometimes appear as tiny items in the popular press. "Be socially active!" a small newspaper notice put out by the Alzheimer's Society tells me. "Connecting socially helps you stay connected mentally." In much the same way, my favorite high-gloss women's magazine has—with all the richness that a bullet point allows— attempted to convey the results of Pressman's work on antibody production. "Hey ladies," the item purrs, "isolated people tend to have weakened immune systems. A regular night out with your pals is always healthy!"

The problem with these notices is not just that they're short, a little vague, and easy to miss, it's that they don't name loneliness as the central difficulty. Our culture has a collective stutter when it comes to talking about the state. We need to start putting loneliness front and center. We need to start naming it. Here are some sample headlines that could run, ideally, as part of a public education campaign about the state: "Loneliness Triggers High Blood Pressure." "Loneliness Causes Dementia." "Loneliness Undermines the Immune System." Naming loneliness focuses the lens. It gives lonely people a sense of what they're up against, and—if zeroed in on time and time again—it might help shift the static notion that the state is trivial and its effects imaginary.

In some ways, we need to accept that loneliness affects the body because the idea is a primer, a stepping-stone to a more complex and more radical notion, which is this: loneliness doesn't just have an impact on our body, it can act on and undermine aspects of what we're used to thinking of as the self. The state, once it's made itself at home, can not only weaken us but turn us into someone we didn't used to be. Paradoxically, the state might change us in ways that make it harder to ward off. Even as we crave companionship, we might find ourselves pulling away from it, and falling deeper into loneliness.

Chapter Five

PARADOX

Loneliness and the mystery of the changing self

In early May 2005, as my loneliness was approaching its third anniversary, I signed up for a four-day cycling trip in northern Ontario. May is not a particularly welcoming time in the north. I knew the weather might be cold and possibly rainy, with the grass still flat and matted and the buds barely out on the trees. But the prospect of dim days and muted scenery didn't really bother me, since I wasn't going to sightsee.

What I was going for was company. I'd learned about the all-women's outfitting company from my eldest sister, Christine, who—by this point in my loneliness—had begun to adopt a slightly managerial attitude toward my social life. Given the ten years between us, as well as the fact that she'd moved out when I was eight, leaving us with little in the way of shared experiences, it didn't seem practical for her to step into the role of companion herself. What she could do—and what she and others in my family were increasingly trying to do—was track down opportunities for me to socialize with others.

"You should *go*," Christine said over brunch one weekend,

slipping a news clipping across the table to me as my nieces looked on. "You could meet someone." Thinking that perhaps the emphasis on my lack of a someone might prove embarrassing, she'd added, rather neutrally, "And the cycling is forty kilometers a day. That's a good workout."

I nodded, and quickly pocketed the clipping, adopting the demeanor that was becoming my default in these exchanges: I stifled the anxiety I was feeling about being alone, and tried to seem upbeat and resourceful. If my family was going to focus on my dating status and not mention my loneliness, I was more than prepared to play along. The state always seemed particularly clunky and messy at these family gatherings: the optics, as a marketing rep might say, were all wrong. If I'd been a TV child, perhaps someone like Laura from *Little House on the Prairie*, my sisters would have been my closest companions. I knew why they weren't—not only were they much older than me, they'd grown up in a different sort of family—but the fact that I could rationalize the distance between us didn't make it less awkward. My need for connection was sometimes strongest at these family gatherings, and when they ended, when I headed back to my apartment alone, I sometimes felt bereft and slightly confused, as though I'd just blown a first date or said something off-color to drive the others away.

It was with these feelings of loss that I'd opened the news clipping that Christine had given me. The photo was alluring— two women standing on a beach and hoisting a canoe up over their shoulders—and I soon found my way to the Web site, where the message of easy sociability was hammered home. I knew I was being sold on something—the cycling trip cost a cool $550—but the images entranced me. I liked the way they looked—all those headscarfed women with matching smiles and synchronized postures—but most of all I liked the way they made me feel. The pictures of sociability reminded me of what I thought of as my best self, my social self. When I saw two women checking the air in each other's tires, I could imagine myself doing the same thing, and this imaginary act of friendship cued memories of real friendship: laughing with girlfriends on the lawn behind my high school; rushing to Martin's house with a huge care package after I learned of his father's death; sitting dreamily and slightly drunk with Simon at our favorite Italian café. The fact that I wasn't doing these things anymore didn't matter as much as the fact that I had done them. The trip seemed to promise a shortcut back to the person I used to be. As I sat alone at the computer, this other version of myself—trusting, confident, open—seemed almost within arm's reach. And the site made it easy. All I had to do was enter my credit card information. I did so in a rush, and the matter was settled: I was going.

It didn't entirely escape my notice, as I sat daydreaming about a social self, that the engaged person I was imagining had receded from view. Thinking of myself as social was like staring at a passport photo taken five years earlier: I knew the person in the picture was me, but in some key ways that former self seemed distant and unreachable. Because when I thought about my sociability in the present, I had to admit that certain changes had taken place.

I'd developed, for instance, an emotionally fraught relationship with the phone. I'd be sitting in my kitchen, writing in my diary about my need to make friends—I simply don't have enough of them, I'd be thinking—and then the phone would ring. I'd consider it warily. I knew, intellectually, that I was supposed to answer it, and I also knew that conversation might dislodge my feelings of isolation. But the sheer strength of these feelings made answering seem like something of a gamble. Superficial conversations—a request for cat-sitting, or a newspaper calling to tell me I could win a prize if I took out a subscription—would leave me feeling doubly alone. Even talks with friends, if the conversation delved too far into the details of their romantic relationships or child-care problems, could make me feel unnecessary and obscure. I wouldn't be able to connect with what they were telling me, and the gap between my experiences and theirs would heighten my sense of aloneness. These concerns meant that, as the phone continued to ring, I'd be engaged in a sort of emotional fortune-telling, trying to predict who was on the line, what we might talk about, and how the conversation might affect me. These considerations were so complex that the phone usually stopped ringing before I decided on a course of action, meaning I'd go back to my diary with a sort of relief, happy to have ducked the turbulence a ringing phone seemed to portend.

And it wasn't just the phone that became problematic. One of the strangest aspects of my loneliness was that my reaction to it began to seem illogical. As my need for others intensified, I began to retreat from them. Throughout the winter of 2005, I'd started to turn down invitations, and did so broadly and indiscriminately. I said no to baby showers, to hikes in the ravine, and to brunch with my stepmother. Even when I forced myself to join an online meet-up group, I arrived at the selected location only to beetle away from the people I'd set out to meet. The plan had been to convene at the museum for a tour of a Korean art exhibit, and as soon as I saw the group of strangers clustered near the base of a pillar, I scurried toward First Nations Arts & Culture, where I remained huddled near beadwork until the others had moved on. *You're being ridiculous*, I told myself, pretending to study a moccasin. *You came here to meet people, and now you're playing a solo game of hide-and-seek*. But even though I could see that my behavior was self-defeating, I couldn't seem to change it.

It's worth noting that this wasn't because I was socially anxious. "Loneliness and social anxiety are separate," says the Northwestern University social psychologist Wendi Gardner. Gardner is interested in the psychology of belonging—how we feel within and outside of social groups—and I'd wanted to speak to her about her findings on the lonely. "It's not unusual for socially anxious people to be lonely," she says, "but lonely people are not, by and large, suffering from social anxiety." The whole time that I was steering away from others, failing to answer the phone, and peeking out from behind glass display cases, I was actually taking on new social roles. I'd started teaching law at a community college in the suburbs, and I was doubling up on my volunteer shifts at the soup kitchen. And in these situations—where I was required to be voluble, slightly aggressive, and empathic—I was fine. It was when the situation was more personal, when an interaction seemed to touch on my emotional self, that anxiety began to set in.

I tried to understand why this was happening, but the explanations I hit on were only partial. If I took my uneasiness and parceled it out, I could see that about a quarter of it came from the stress of having to hide my loneliness, having to assume a relaxed look and tamp down my need for others. Another quarter likely flowed from the dissonance that sometimes arose when companionship didn't offset my sense of isolation. A third quarter could probably be attributed to my diminished sense of self, to my growing conviction that, in becoming lonelier, I was taking up less space and somehow beginning to disappear. Yet the fourth explanation—the pie wedge I needed to make the circle whole and come to terms with my behavior—was missing. When it came right down to it, I didn't *know* why I was avoiding others. I just knew that, as I became lonelier, feelings of comfort and threat had become live and cross-wired. Isolation had started to feel safer than togetherness, and the more time I spent alone, the riskier social interactions began to seem.

In some ways, my behavior was depressive: I was shying away from others and anticipating negative outcomes. But depression wasn't really the problem. The bouts of depression I've had in my life have seen me detach in a straightforward way. Even when I've been lucky enough to have someone holding me and trying to comfort me, I often wanted nothing more than for them to get off the bed, so that I could get on with my self-lacerations in peace. Depression has, at least in my experience, been internally consistent: it's seen me avoiding others because I've lost interest in them. Within the context of acute emotional distress, my sociability hasn't really mattered one way or the other.

My loneliness differed from depression in that the retreat it signaled was occurring within a context of not just heightened need but heightened awareness. Because even as I was declining invitations, I was becoming increasingly preoccupied with people in the abstract. On my way home from work, I sometimes made my way to the library, where I sat in the cheerful, windowed reading room and flipped through photography books, spending a long time staring at portraits of faces, torsos, and hands. Any given day would see me seeking out places where I could glean a sense of connection without actually connecting. After my swim, I'd sit in the bleachers beside the pool, breathing in the sharp smell of chlorine and letting the sight of the varsity swim team—its members all doing the front crawl in tandem—soothe and calm me. At lunch, I perched on one of the tiny stools beside the Italian deli counter, eating my eggplant sandwich beside someone tackling a big plate of veal. In the mornings, I waited patiently for the 8:30 downtown express bus I'd started taking as a means of avoiding the subway. The other commuters struck me as community of sorts, and their overheard strands of conversation sometimes became my own. "We talked it over, and I think everything's going to be all right," I heard a woman saying, and this statement—evocative of a boyfriend and reconciliation—was so rich with togetherness that I recorded it in my own diary, as though it were something I'd said, or wished I'd had the chance to say.

My loneliness, in other words, didn't let me tune out. Depression is like a blindfold: you can walk down a street and notice nothing and no one except your own despair. Loneliness is like a set of binoculars that's trained on the social world. This has actually been proven. Psychologists have long theorized that, when the need to belong is unmet, people automatically start to pay more attention to the social world around them. "It's like when you're hungry, and you notice all the food signs on the highway," says Gardner. "When you've been left out, or when you feel unconnected, you notice social cues."

Gardner became interested in lonely people because they were struggling with long-term feelings of social deprivation—feelings she couldn't ethically trigger in the lab. To test her intuition that the lonely would be advantaged in social processing, Gardner conducted two main studies: she asked lonely and nonlonely people to read a blog describing someone's social life, and she exposed both groups to photographs depicting different facial expressions. After reading the blog, the subjects were asked to list as many of the social events as they could remember; after seeing each photo, the subjects were asked to identify the mood—anger, fear, happiness—being expressed.

Gardner found that, across the board, the lonely were better at recalling social information, and more accurate in reading strangers' faces. "When it's a perceptual task," says Gardner, "the lonely are rocking out. They're doing so much better than the nonlonely." Because of their need for other people, the lonely become skilled at what's known as "social decoding"—that is, reading other people, and reading social situations, quickly and accurately. "I'm always hyperaware of other people's feelings," notes Rachel, the homemaker from Florida, "and of what's going on, and thinking, How can I help you?" When I ask Rachel what the end of loneliness might look like for her, she immediately identifies a toning down of perception. "I'd be a person who wouldn't care as much," she says. "I think I would just lack as much insight into other people."

The problem with loneliness is that the enhanced ability to process social information isn't twinned with an increased drive toward social interaction. "The lonely tend to tune in," says the University of Arizona's Chris Segrin. "But these same people are not always as active expressively. In other words, they're not talking, they're not participating as much. You can almost imagine someone standing back in the corner of a party and just observing, that kind of phenomenon." Researchers are just now starting to understand why this withdrawal occurs. The reasons they've hit on are complex, but one source of the withdrawal is likely increased social awareness itself. That is, it's hard to be trained on the social world and not start to adopt an external perspective toward *yourself.* "Lonely people are focused outward," says Gardner, "which is why they do so well on all these social cue and social memory tasks. But that means they can become overly aware of how others are perceiving them. It's almost an excess of perspective-taking, if you will. Instead of just being focused on the other person, they become focused on themselves through the other person. So it's not just that I'm listening to you," she says, as we talk on the phone, "it's that I'm listening to you, and at the same time I'm really thinking about how you're perceiving what I'm saying and what you're thinking about me."

It's partly because social awareness cues self-consciousness that loneliness can begin to feel so awkward and unmanageable. If social attentiveness is heightened, but the desire to interact declines, the emotional floor the lonely person is standing upon can start to seem warped and off-kilter. If turning down the volume on social processing isn't an option, and if real interactions are anxiety-provoking, it might seem as though the lonely person is truly caught, with no options to draw on to help bring interests and inclinations into line. But, interestingly, this isn't the case.

In the first year of my loneliness, I'd experienced "mild highs," when my sense of isolation would simply vanish, as though it had never been. This automatic soothing of my sense of aloneness had disappeared when my loneliness became chronic. Without it, I had to put something more purposive and planned in its place. Increasingly, throughout 2004 and 2005, my lonely nights saw me *doing* things. I'd sketch the fruit bowl on the kitchen table, or I'd sort out the story drafts that littered the floor of my office. But these activities—the ones I consciously settled on—were smoke screens. I understood that their real purpose was to divert me while my mind got busy. Because as I sat there, sketching or sorting, my imagination would begin to unfurl. I'd imagine a move to Ottawa, a move that might see me settling in with a small and closely knit group of crunchy environmentalists. I'd start to wonder about graduate work, about falling in with a cohort of like-minded students at a leafy campus out east. Or I'd fantasize about calling up the foxy fisherman I used to date, and embarking, somewhat improbably, on a new life as a cook on a long-liner off the Alaskan coast.

And as the daydreams gained steam, I'd start to feel better, lighter. An imaginary embeddedness would see me feeling more optimistic, more gregarious, more confident and secure. Unlike depression, which tended to latch itself into me with hooks, my loneliness was, as a psychiatrist would say, "labile." If I thought closely enough about togetherness—if I really let go of the reins and pictured myself laughing in the grad lounge, or serving up stew to a group of hungry fishermen—I could alter my mood. The sense of unfocused anxiety and restlessness I was struggling with would fade, and in its place would be an odd sense of social engagement and ease.

"Sometimes when I talk to myself," says Rachel, describing her daydreams, "I don't feel as alone, I don't feel as lonely." She pauses to tell me that she's not crazy, and I assure her I know she's not. "It's so hard to explain, to tell someone this, because I've never told anyone this before, but I'll have these talks when I'm walking down the street. I'll have a whole scenario up, and then suddenly it doesn't feel as lonely."

In the past, when researchers have asked lonely people to solve social problems, they've uncovered signs of magical thinking. At Stanford University, for instance, psychologists have staged mini creative-writing workshops and asked lonely people to sketch out the steps between an isolated present and a populated future. "Candace has just moved in and doesn't know anyone," one vignette begins:

*She wants to have friends in the neighborhood. The story ends
with Candace having many good friends and feeling at home
in the neighborhood. Begin the story with Candace in her room
immediately after arriving in the neighborhood. Describe how
Candace manages to solve the problem of making friends.*

When nonlonely people are surveyed, they'll cite commonsense solutions: clubs, intramural sports teams, invitations to
coworkers, and coffee dates with acquaintances. When lonely
people are surveyed, the whole process starts to read like something out of *The Blue Fairy Book*. Gone are the coffee shops and
photography clubs. In their place are chance meetings, blind
luck, and unlikely encounters, such as Candace discovering her
soul mate in the seat beside her on a domestic flight.

The fantasy findings have been interpreted as proof that the
lonely are unable to think practically about social outcomes,
and that they're unable to hit on the effective social strategies
the nonlonely devise. I don't think these conclusions are correct. Many of the lonely people I spoke to were trying to end
their loneliness in completely ordinary ways: Katherine knew
she had to sign up for an art class; Sonia had started begin-
ners' pottery; several others were doing volunteer work; and
I'd signed up for my bike trip. The difficulty with these approaches was that they didn't possess the efficiency of fantasy;
they weren't instantaneous.

"I'll think about having people I can call up and depend on
and be around," says Sonia, somewhat wistfully. "They can
impose on me, and I can impose on them, and we're just able
to have a good time. But that's the daydream, that's the thing I
make up in my head. In situations when I am with people, I find
it tiresome, and uncomfortable."

It's likely because fantasy offers an express route to feelings of connection—one that bypasses the difficulties attaching to real relationships—that lonely people tend to rely on it when asked about forming connections. It's not that the lonely don't know how to meet other people, it's that the sense of embeddedness being asked about is one they correctly associate with daydreams. What the researchers who conducted the social outcome experiments in the 1980s didn't seem to realize was that the emotional shifts cued by fantasy and magical thinking are real. We're so used to thinking about the dead weight of depression that we don't recognize the queer lightness that sometimes attaches to loneliness. More recent social science research has shown that the state is responsive to "impractical" strategies, such as praying to God, or walking a pet collie. Our need for others is so strong, sociologists suggest, that we've learned how to satisfy it—at least temporarily—through abstractions and substitutions. And if prayer, fantasy, and quality pet time can truly, if briefly, lift feelings of isolation, then these approaches can't be described, as the original researchers suggested, as misguided.

Of course, if a lonely person can temporarily assuage her loneliness by conjuring up images of togetherness, it's probably also true that the lonely are particularly vulnerable to and hungry for such images. There are many factors playing a role in the popularity of magazines with such team-based names as *Us* and *People*, but their ability to cater to lonely people and provide easy, immediate images of intimacy is surely part of the reason for their success. The problem with representations of togetherness is that they're consequence-free; divorced from real sociability, they can promote a sort of risk-taking that's not particularly well thought out. When I logged onto the cycling outfitter's Web site and was presented with representations of sociability, the commonsense considerations a nonlonely person might have reached for were beyond my grasp. I didn't stop to wonder whether embeddedness could really be so easily achieved; I didn't ask whether real and imaginary relationships might cue two entirely different sets of reactions. I didn't, in short, stop to wonder whether I might be making a mistake.

I drove to the base camp with a friendly ER nurse who made triply sure that our bikes were correctly fastened to the back of her car. Julie was calm and soft-spoken, with the mildly distant air of someone who works with people in crisis. We drank coffee out of paper cups and talked about soaring property values in our north-end neighborhood. She sheepishly asked if she could play Anne Murray, and as "Snowbird" filled the car, I felt as though I'd made the right decision, as though the sociability I was after might be within reach. It was only when we arrived at the camp—a twenty-acre stretch of pine and spruce dominated by a few cabins and the main house—that I started to feel uncomfortable.

"We'll head in first," Julie said, "and then get the bikes."

"I'll take the bikes down," I said. We were the first to arrive, and the idea of having to mingle in an unstructured way with the trip leaders was making me shy.

"Don't be silly. Let's get some tea."

The house was exactly as I expected it. An old A-frame on the outside, it was kitted out within to resemble an almost novelistic idea of what a farmhouse should look like. There were lace curtains over chipped cream window frames; mismatched chairs; a tomcat in the corner; thick plank flooring; and a fat-handled kettle on the stove. Our guides—sporty young women in bandanas and tight Lycra T-shirts—were scattered around the room, sorting out emergency medical supplies. I gravitated toward the corner and leaned down to pat the cat, who seemed mercifully uninterested in me. The others were more attentive, peppering me with questions about my cycling experience and general outdoorsiness. No, I'd never biked so far before. Yes, I liked to camp. No to bringing my own air-pressure gauge, and yes to a question about seeing the grounds.

"There's lots of women here for the first time," said Susan, our trip guide. She was standing up, preparing to give me a tour of the place. She was heavyset and almost aggressively confident, in a way that made me feel, when I stood in front of her, that I was about to be pushed backward. "But after the first day or two it's like they've known each other for years."

I had an inkling that this might not happen for me. Julie— my one contact—was already deep in conversation with one of the guides who she knew from a previous trip, and I felt awkwardly alone. Susan was leading me out the front door, and for the first time I noticed that the cabins stopped at the tree line, and that there were only four of them.

"Will there be roommates?" I asked, trying to sound cheerful. There were eight of us on the trip, and I was telling myself, somewhat unrealistically, that some of the women must be planning to camp. The itinerary hadn't said anything about shared quarters, and the prospect of losing my aloneness altogether made me feel unexpectedly tense.

"Tonight, here at the camp," Susan said, nodding. "And then a night or two out on the trip. It depends on who ends up where, and how many single rooms we have. You'll get a room to yourself at some point, but not tonight. Why?" she asked, stopping to look at me. "Is it a problem?"

"No," I said hurriedly. I was running some numbers through

my head. Seven strangers. Four days. Two to a room. It was the companionship I'd been looking for, the vigorous break from isolation that I'd signed up for. Yet the emotions presenting themselves weren't the ones I'd planned on. The levity that was so much a part of my daydreams had vanished. I could feel my breath start to quicken. I began to feel surrounded. Scanning the grounds, I saw a fifth building, one that looked older and more neglected than the others, and I asked what it was.

"The boathouse," replied Susan. "Where the canoes sleep."

As soon as Susan said this, I began to imagine the interior—the dry smell of wood and sawdust, the relative darkness, the stillness that would have built up over months of disuse. The mere idea of the place seemed comforting; its quiet emptiness seemed to offer the aloneness I was beginning to crave. I had to physically stop myself from heading toward the building, because Susan was opening the door to the nearest cabin. Inside was a small, wallpapered room with a nightstand between two single beds. Susan was saying I was lucky—I had first dibs.

About thirty years ago, social psychologists began studying the behavior of lonely and nonlonely people, often using techniques that bore a closer resemblance to police investigations than to social science research. The lonely were filmed behind mirrored glass while talking to their nonlonely counterparts; researchers bugged their conversations. The lonely were called and asked to volunteer time for bogus experiments; they were seated across from strangers, given a stopwatch, and asked to pick conversation topics from a random list of subjects. They were asked how often they shared secrets with friends and siblings, they were quizzed after conversations to see how much they remembered, and they were asked to present themselves to potential dating partners while researchers caught them on videotape.

The driving force behind these ideas was that the lonely somehow lacked key social skills, that they didn't possess, as the theory put it, basic "social-communicative competencies." "The social skills deficit model of loneliness," explains Chris Segrin, the behavioral scientist from the University of Arizona, "says that, for some reason, Person A did not develop a full repertoire of social skills—and there's a million different reasons why that could be the case. They then go out into the world armed with these sublevel social skills, they encounter difficulties forming relationships, and loneliness follows from that."

The skills deficit approach to loneliness is really a heightened encapsulation of lay thought. It suggests that there's something wrong with lonely people, and that their loneliness flows from their own personal shortcomings. The idea seems so rife with stereotype that it should be easily dismissed, but researchers actually began to uncover behaviors that seemed deficient. When the conversations of lonely people were assessed for what's called "talk time proportion," it was found that they were saying less than the nonlonely; when they did talk, they were more likely to be changing the subject, and less likely to be asking questions of their partners. When lonely people were asked to volunteer time, they offered up fewer hours than the nonlonely; when asked to pick topics for conversation, they steered toward the impersonal. The lonely described themselves as being uncomfortable with disclosure—failing to cough up the secrets that nonlonely people divulged—and when interaction partners were asked how well they'd gotten to know their lonely counterparts, the answer was usually, "She's still a stranger." The lonely were the least likely to want to publish something they'd written, and the least likely to offer up personal information when asking someone for a date. Most damningly, when lonely people were surveyed, they said they were socially inhibited, telling researchers that they had trouble introducing themselves at parties, entertaining in their homes, and calling people up to initiate social activities.

As far as proof went, the evidence against the lonely looked, as young lawyers like to say, bulletproof. The lonely said less, they disclosed less, and they were the ones with a grimace on their face at parties. The skills deficit approach—at least until the late 1980s—seemed conclusive and watertight: the lonely were lonely because they lacked the skills the nonlonely took for granted. In 1987, however, researchers at Stanford University arrived at an interesting finding. If lonely people were assigned roles (rather than being asked to simply "interact"), and told to help devise solutions to a social problem, they actually talked for *longer* than the nonlonely. They generated more answers, they were seen as just as sociable, and their solutions were just as good. The researchers, John Vitkus and Leonard Horowitz, noted that their results were anomalous, in that the lonely people in the experiment weren't showing any skill deficits. Vitkus and Horowitz, who were then in a firm minority position when it came to loneliness theorizing, stressed that perhaps the lonely didn't possess any skill deficits at all, but were rather caught up in a situation in which loneliness was cuing passivity.

The idea of loneliness driving behavior gained ground in the 1990s, when a team of Finnish researchers showed that long-term feelings of loneliness could predict the ways in which a person might behave a year or two down the road. The Finnish researchers, Jari-Erik Nurmi and Katariina Salmela-Aro, followed hundreds of students at the University of Helsinki over a four-year period. The interesting thing about the experiment is that Nurmi and Salmela-Aro were able to assess both loneliness levels and activity levels in year one, and then measure how each variable influenced the other over time. On one hand, the researchers found some support for the skills deficit theory of loneliness: the more likely a student was to report feeling uncomfortable in groups, the more likely that student was to become lonely. Much more strikingly, however, the reverse was also true: the lonelier a student was in year one, the more likely he or she would be to gradually begin avoiding social situations, stop discussing problems with others, and start spending more time alone. The authors, who were writing in *Personality and Individual Differences*, a highly specialized journal, came to a conclusion that buttressed what the Stanford researchers had said: loneliness could trigger certain behaviors, with socially skilled individuals becoming more socially inhibited the longer loneliness lasted.

The nice thing about the Finnish results is that they align with how lonely people often experience their lives and their social interactions. "My social skills are *fine*," emphasizes Sonia, the copywriter from the West Coast, who is well aware of the stereotype of the lonely person as social klutz. "I don't think the reason I'm lonely is because I lack the *ability* to socialize." Anne, the Illinois social worker who's been lonely for years, agrees. Interviewing for a job several years ago, she told her interviewers that she was sometimes nervous in front of people. "And my bosses started cracking up," she says. "They said I was the most interesting conversationalist they'd ever interviewed."

Many lonely people who contacted me—especially those who wrote in trying to communicate some sense of what their lives were like—stressed that they had good social skills in place. "I'm not a loser," one person wrote. "I'm popular." Or, "No one, knowing me, would think I had a problem with loneliness." What seemed to bother lonely people was not that they lacked social skills, but rather that they had good skills but found themselves cut off from using them. Presented with social opportunities—opportunities they knew they needed in order to fend off their loneliness—they found themselves retreating, and becoming less likely to accept invitations or join group outings.

"There'll be a mixer announced for after work," says Katherine, the Nova Scotia policy analyst. "And I'll think to myself the whole day, 'I should go to this, I should go to this, I should really go and meet some people.' And then I don't go, because I feel weird about it." Katherine stresses that she knows how to socialize—on the phone, she's funny and cheery—but says that she's become inhibited, and more likely to withdraw than spend time with others.

"I find I've become uncomfortable dealing with people," says Sonia. "I feel a *lot* more comfortable on my own." When I ask if this preference for solitude gets in the way of socializing, she laughs. "I've skipped *tons* of things. I've managed to find a way to get out of engagement parties, bridal showers, weddings, and just get-togethers. I don't go to things. I don't show up."

It would be easy enough to argue that Katherine's and Sonia's social inhibitions come first, and that ipso facto, that's why they're lonely. But when I asked about the dynamic between withdrawal and loneliness, many of my respondents stressed that the loneliness was at the forefront: they hadn't been shy, but their loneliness had left them that way; inhibition once hadn't defined their social lives, but now it did.

"I don't do things as much as I used to," says Frank, the

freelance journalist from Seattle. "There was a period where I used to go out a lot. I mean, I've cut down on drinking, and that isn't so much because I don't like it or because I've wanted to, but just because I don't go out anymore. And I think I've just found it easier and easier to isolate myself, it's just more and more convenient to do so. Which is sort of a vicious cycle—it ends up making me feel worse, but I think I've consciously isolated myself more. Even when there are opportunities, I tend not to take them up as much as I used to."

Some of the lonely people I spoke to had been able to hide their withdrawal. "Most people don't understand it," says James, the engineer from Quebec, referring to the urge to retreat, "so you kind of glaze over it. Someone will say, 'I couldn't get ahold of you,' and I'll say, 'Oh, I was probably out,' when really I'd turned the phone off, or unplugged it or something." For other lonely people, their tendency to retreat had become so pronounced that others had noticed it. "I have a friend," says Anne, "who mentioned to me that there were times when I certainly preferred to be alone, and where I was, to her, obviously avoiding social contacts. And yet she also said, 'But when you do that, it's not like you *can't* socialize, you just don't *choose* to.'"

Almost all of the lonely people I spoke to could spot the relationship between their loneliness and withdrawal, but most of them explained the connection in terms of their own ineptness and poor decision-making.

"You're making a stupid decision consciously," says Frank, somewhat harshly, describing his tendency to spend time alone instead of socializing. "I say 'stupid' because very often there's no real reason to stay in, nothing happens to make me want to stay home, but I do, and that's why I say 'stupid.'"

"It's a choice I make," emphasizes Sonia, telling me why she blames herself for her own loneliness. "Every time I decide not to go out, *I'm* the one deciding those things. I know that."

If I'd been on the phone with someone whose main problem was depression, and who said that the reason they were alone was because they were unlikable, I could chirp, "Reality check!! That's the mood driving that perception. It has nothing to do with you or your attractiveness." Many of us know, when talking about depression, to take note of its overwhelming ability to cue distortions—to change the way a depressed person thinks and feels about the facts of his or her life. With loneliness, however, there's no buffer zone. If the lonely person is declining social contact, the reasoning goes, it's because they really *are* socially hopeless. They're *right* in thinking they're incompetent; there's nothing about the state itself that might be driving their perceptions or altering their behavior. Within this schema, depression emerges as a state capable of changing thoughts and behavior, while loneliness remains—somewhat incoherently—a powerful state that has no real effect on how a lonely person might be leading her life.

There are at least two major problems with the portrayal of loneliness as inconsequential. The first is that it can leave lonely people convinced that they're engineering their own isolation, a belief that's bound to further undermine their sense of self-worth. "I'd be frustrated with myself," says Frances, the physiotherapist from Missouri, referring to her tendency to keep her distance from what she calls the "party circuit" operating in her small town. "It exacerbated my feelings of inadequacy and incompetence, and left me feeling sort of hopeless." Casting yourself as the source of the problem can make social difficulties seem doubly troubling: not only do you have to deal with isolation, you have to endlessly analyze why you seem to be self-sabotaging.

The second major problem is that, if we fail to assign a certain degree of agency to loneliness, we're losing sight of the full power and extent of the state. The Finnish research findings, which appeared in 1997, suggested that loneliness could cue changes in behavior, with lonely people gradually becoming more inhibited, isolated, and withdrawn the longer the state lasted. These findings, however, were Finnish, and results that seemed true in a small socialist country didn't seem to apply in North America, where the prevailing wisdom was still that lonely people lacked the skills necessary for socializing.

That, at least, was the situation until 2000, when John Cacioppo, curious about the Stanford data showing that the lonely actually had good social skills, decided to test our standard notions of cause and effect. To assess the relationship between loneliness and behavior, Cacioppo and his colleagues did something deceptively simple: they took twenty students and hypnotized them, cuing them to feel first lonely and then socially embedded. To cue feelings of loneliness, the researchers asked students to think of a time when they'd felt isolated and friendless. To cue embeddedness, the students were told to think about being a member of a close-knit group, or to remember the feelings associated with having a best friend. After each mood change, and before the students were led out of the hypnotic state, the subjects completed a battery of surveys designed to test how anxious, optimistic, shy, and sociable they felt.

What Cacioppo found was that students cued to feel lonely rated themselves as more anxious and less social than their nonlonely counterparts. "When the students were made to feel lonely," Cacioppo told me, "they felt more hostile, they felt more negative, they feared negative evaluations, they were shyer, and they felt like they had poorer social skills. And when we made them feel less lonely, they went the other direction—

all these variables went the other way." A key aspect of Cacioppo's findings is that traits such as shyness and inhibition rose and fell in keeping with levels of loneliness: they weren't characteristics of the students themselves. This means that a nonlonely subject could be made to feel withdrawn and inhibited if he was made to feel lonely, and this change would occur regardless of the personality traits and social skills of the individual in question. Loneliness also had a uniform effect on all of the subjects, suggesting that that the state was acting *on* a personality, not flowing from it.

Cacioppo is well aware of the difference between loneliness and depression, and he stresses he's not simply cuing negative affect in subjects. "We're not moving them in and out of depression," he explains. What he's doing is something he describes as "more profound" than just triggering the blues. One of Cacioppo's main arguments is that sociability is key to who we are as human beings, with tendencies toward bonding, care, and attachment being part of our genetic heritage. Since our brains are, as Cacioppo puts it, "fundamentally driven by sociability and driven for sociability," the absence of connection is going to cue a host of cascading reactions within the psyche of the lonely person, in much the same way that oxygen deprivation will cue profound physiological shifts. It's not possible, in a sense, to become chronically lonely and remain the person you thought you were. "It changes a *lot* of things," says Cacioppo. "Your feeling of social support, your feeling of hostility, your feeling of negativity, your shyness, your social skills—all those features change. Your emotional stability is affected, your agreeableness, your extroversion—all of those aspects change."

The prospect of loneliness changing a person sounded immediately right to many of the lonely people I spoke to. "It *does* change you," says Frank, the freelance journalist, emphatically. "It certainly does. I mean, a large part of the way I am now I guess I've always been. But I definitely know and remember periods of my life when there were things I could get over and things I could just move on with that I don't feel able to do anymore. I think in that sense it changes you as a person, and how you think about and look at situations around you."

The ability of loneliness to cue significant changes is best understood through the prism of evolution. "Don't think about downtown Chicago," says Cacioppo. "Think about the middle of Australia, or some hostile environment." Someone alone in this environment is going to have an increased sense of threat, and one of the biggest threats imaginable is other people. "If you've been rejected," Cacioppo notes, "and the reason the disconnection has occurred is because of something within a group, and you've been ostracized, then it's dangerous for you to push your way back onto that team." It's simply safer, after our initial desire to connect with others has been rebuffed, to shy away rather than to continue to try to interact. "If a new group comes up, they're more likely to be foe than friend," says Cacioppo. "If you go out in some area that's hostile, where people are struggling to live, and now you're looking for resources too—I'm not sure you want to run into a new group, and embrace them."

It's because loneliness can cue what Cacioppo calls a "prevention focus" rather than a "promotion focus" in social interactions that it can become unmanageable. If other people are perceived as risky, it can start to seem reasonable to try to reduce that risk by retreating from them. The lonely person who does this will start displaying the supposed "skill deficits" that earlier research was picking up—she will say less, disclose less, and end interactions more quickly. These behaviors are actually effective and sensible in the short term, since they insulate the lonely person from potential threats and rejection. But in the long term, the behaviors can become self-defeating. As isolation becomes more entrenched, threat perceptions will become more acute, and it will be harder for someone to pursue the relationships she needs to fend off loneliness.

It's hard to emphasize just how dramatically Cacioppo's theory departs from mainstream thinking about loneliness. The popular portrayal of loneliness casts it as a mood that's easy to fend off and one that, if it does settle, doesn't have much of an effect on the lonely person directly. Cacioppo is saying something completely different: the state, once it descends, can wrap itself around lonely people like a net, altering their perceptions and levels of sociability, and ultimately—as it makes them feel shyer and more uncomfortable around others—becoming queerly self-perpetuating. Cacioppo has effectively nailed down the difference between short-term and chronic loneliness. A person suffering from short-term feelings of loneliness hasn't become enmeshed in a web of self-consciousness and withdrawal. Something fortuitous—a good friendship, a new romantic connection—has deflected the loneliness and triggered renewed feelings of sociability and extroversion. When this doesn't happen, however, when there's no lucky break from feelings of isolation, chronic loneliness can overtake a personality, leaving the lonely person stuck with feelings of inhibition and social discomfort that may have been adaptive thirty thousand years ago but are confusing and counterproductive today.

It's also worth noting that Cacioppo's theory applies to everyone. We all share the same evolutionary heritage. Each of us is wired for togetherness and vulnerable to emotional absence. And while it's true that some people are genetically predisposed to loneliness, this just means they feel lonely more quickly and in a more diverse set of circumstances. It doesn't mean that they differ from the nonlonely in terms of skills or personality traits. In fact, Cacioppo's reasoning makes the whole category of "nonlonely individuals"—a staple of social psychology research—seem porous and unguarded. Since we all need social connection, and since we're all likely to start to retreat when faced with protracted aloneness, anyone confronting a long period of isolation might start to develop self-protective perceptions and behaviors. The pivotal point in Cacioppo's work isn't personality but isolation: it's a sense of dangerous aloneness that works on and changes a personality, rather than the personality engendering its own isolation. And since anyone can become isolated—and this is especially true now that isolation is becoming more common, as I'll discuss in chapter 7—anyone might get caught in the loop that Cacioppo has mapped out.

The perceptual and behavioral shifts that occur in the course of loneliness are real. We like to offer lonely people the sort of advice that got handed to depressed people twenty or thirty years ago: Snap out of it. Pull yourself together. Can't you see that you're your own worst enemy? But it's very hard, when you're swamped with vague feelings of threat, to go out and embrace sociability, and it's almost impossible to do this when you're not aware that loneliness is capable of cuing changes. This means that one's own behavior, when chronically lonely, can become a source of shame and confusion, with messages to the effect that one should simply "get it together" reinforcing the idea that loneliness is entirely the lonely person's fault.

Cacioppo notes that it is possible for lonely people to exert some control over tendencies toward withdrawal. They can do this, he says, through "careful self-regulation." That is, lonely people can monitor their reactions and ask themselves whether their sense of threat is appropriate; they can examine their urge to retreat and remind themselves that the impulse to withdraw is an atavistic one, not one that's necessary for safety in the present day. But while this sort of self-monitoring isn't impossible to do, it's hard to do. It's difficult to unconsciously perceive other people as threats and not react by withdrawing from them; it's tricky to see the world as a risky place and not try to mitigate that risk by retreating to a state of protective isolation. I know this because I tried to follow the pop culture advice: I tried to "snap out of it." Embracing a sort of exposure therapy—in which the thing you fear most is the thing you force yourself to confront—I decided to get out there and socialize. Buoyed by my daydreams of sociability, I was going to *become* the person of my imaginings. I was going to be gregarious, embedded, fearless. And I was going to do this regardless of the cost.

The third night of the cycling trip saw me on the skinny top bunk of a big, drafty cabin, every muscle in my body hurting from that day's long bike ride and my hair and skin still feeling damp from hours in the pouring rain. It wasn't late, but I was alone. There were three others assigned to the cabin that night, but my roommates, along with the trip guides, the other cyclists, and the local woman who had appeared out of nowhere to cook for us, were all over in the next cabin, singing. I could hear bursts of laughter and tremulous little solos emerging from next door, and every high note made me burrow even more deeply into my sleeping bag, which I had pulled up over my head.

The trip hadn't gone entirely according to plan. At least, it hadn't for me. The other women were behaving as though they'd just stepped off the Web page: they were sharing secrets, riding side by side along dirt roads, and eating off each other's plates at lunch. I, by contrast, had become almost hypnotically withdrawn. When our little convoy stopped for meals, I sat toward the far end of the table, grinning slightly but remaining oddly silent. When the cycling started up again, I hung toward the back, so that I could bike along on my own. When the other women pried into my romantic history—the big question on the trip was who was or wasn't gay—I seemed to intimate that I'd never dated anyone in my life. I didn't share secrets, I tensed up when someone tried to pat my back, and my smile started to feel tense and horrid, as though I had a spectacular toothache.

"Beautiful, isn't it?" asked Gertie, an agreeable German girl who, like me, tended to bike toward the back of the pack. We were standing at the base of a small waterfall, watching the water pool around the rocks. There was something about our matching physical appearance—Gertie and I were both tall and blond, with our hair up in ponytails and our helmets tucked under our arms—that made me feel as though conversation should flow naturally, as though we were sisters. Gertie radiated friendliness; I could *see* that she was nice. But I still found myself growing uncomfortable. Even with something as obvious and unusual as a waterfall cheerfully serving the role of conversation piece, I found myself choking on my words.

"Pretty, yes," I said, sounding as though I were the one for whom English was a second language. "Maybe we should get back to the group," I added, looking at the rest of the women, who were sitting and talking around a couple of picnic tables. I didn't particularly want to head over—I'd booked off to the waterfall for a bit of privacy—but standing alone with Gertie was making me uneasy. I knew I was *supposed* to be talking, and my inability to do so made me want to lose myself in a crowd.

By the third night of the trip, I was developing something of a reputation: I was the standoffish one, the weird one, the one whose absence at the sing-along would not be particularly missed.

And as I lay on the bed, I couldn't figure out why any of this was happening. Out of everyone on the trip, I was probably the one who needed sociability the most. I'd craved it and day-dreamed about it; I'd hatched plans and spent money to try to achieve it. Yet when confronted with strangers who wanted to get close to me, I retreated into a stiff and stammering version of myself, and became oddly resentful of the people who were trying to befriend me. And this protracted self-sabotage—which I could see developing but could do nothing to stop—left me feeling shipwrecked, as though I'd been thrown alone on a deserted island and would never again reach a friendlier shore.

It would have been helpful, as I lay there trying to deal with the migraine that seemed to be developing, for a social scientist to have bounded into the cabin superhero style, his lab coat hung like a cape around his neck and his little clipboard carried up front like a shield. He could have told me that cognitive shifts were under way, and that my loneliness was altering my behavior and my perceptions of others in ways that pre-dated me. But of course no such figure presented himself, and I was left struggling with feelings of withdrawal and with a longing for aloneness so powerful I thought it was going to roll me right off the bunk.

When I finally, two days later, made it back to my apartment, I kissed the ground and told myself I'd never do something so out of character again. My foray into intense sociability, in other words, had been counterproductive. The unnatural stretch of togetherness had left me anxious to the point of nearly fainting, and to ease the anxiety I became even more dedicated to my aloneness.

This was the dynamic that kept reproducing itself during my years of chronic loneliness: I'd tell myself I needed sociability, sociability would present itself, I'd become stressed at the prospect of interacting, and to assuage the sense of stress I'd spend more time alone. The more challenging real interactions started to seem, the more I relied on my daydreams; the more rich and satisfying my daydreams became, the more unruly and draining real interactions began to appear.

And what was most troubling about this situation was the fact that I couldn't gain an external perspective on what was happening. I couldn't catch loneliness doing its work. Although by May of 2005 I was well into reading about loneliness, I hadn't yet discovered Cacioppo's work on perceptions. I was still two years away from talking to him. This meant that I had nothing to draw on in trying to understand my skewed reactions. I couldn't engage in the self-regulation that Cacioppo has described because I didn't know what there was to regulate. Ignorant of the cognitive shifts that loneliness could cue, I became easy prey to them, letting them turn me into someone more introverted, more withdrawn, and—until someone walked into my life and grabbed the wheel to stop its spinning—much, much lonelier.

Part III

CONTEXT

Chapter Six

HANDLES

Thinking about a state that feels so unwieldy

One of the difficulties I faced in understanding my loneliness was that I wasn't, initially, able to identify the ways in which it was skewering my perceptions and promoting a situation in which withdrawal seemed welcome. But this lack of insight was only part of the problem. Another major difficulty had to do, in a sense, with language. When I thought about depression, a whole vocabulary snapped to attention. I knew the mood could be clinical or subclinical, and reactive or endogenous. I knew it could present as nothing but the blues (in which case it was unipolar), that it could be mixed with dangerous highs (in which case it was bipolar), or that it could run along at low tide without ever fully cresting (in which case it was dysthymic).

I had a sort of geeky affection for these terms. I always spent a long time, when depressed, rifling through Web sites and books, thinking, Yes, that's it, or, No, that doesn't sound like what I'm feeling. As a lawyer, I was used to aggressively close terminology, to the careful parceling out of meaning so that it was one thing to rescind a contract and another to revoke it; one thing to defame someone and a different thing to libel them. I always had trouble with the more conservative aspects of the law—the lockstep thinking on certain issues, the difficulty of introducing change, and the sort of heads-down deference that required everyone to stand, as though at church, whenever a judge entered a courtroom. But I was a sucker for the law's meticulousness, for the unabashed pleasure it took in distinguishing between void (not in force) and voidable (capable of not being in force), between frustration (the inability to complete something) and impossibility (the inability of something to be completed).

This line drawing was a natural extension of how my mind worked. In some important ways, I had to name something in order to really see it. There was a whole universe of vegetation in the ravine between my house that simply remained green and lumpy for me. Since I didn't know what certain trees and flowers were called, my attention tended to skip right over them. It was only when I could apply a label and recognize something as forsythia, hyacinth, or wild rose that the object in question seemed to solidify and become real.

The problem with loneliness was that it didn't seem to align with this quirk in the way that I thought, and needed to think. And this meant that some of the problems attaching to the state weren't emotional so much as verbal. When I first starting thinking about loneliness, in 2003, I came up with lazy terms such as *big, foggy, shapeless*. The lack of definition troubled me. It made it seem as though there was nothing to define, that the reason I couldn't reach for a more precise vocabulary was that there was nothing in particular need of vocalizing.

There's an idea in pop culture that the last thing you want to do with a problem is overanalyze it. The idea flows partly from mindfulness and partly from a larger tradition of anti-intellectualism, in which to think too closely about something is a sort of un-American activity. The fashionable approach is to be purposively hands-off, an idea that's often captured, with a sort of furry Buddhism, in the instruction to give a troublesome cow a large field. "The more you pen it in," my mindfulness instructor liked to remind us, "the more it's going to kick."

I could see the logic in what my instructor was saying, and I knew that refusing to do battle with the anxiety that sometimes accompanied my loneliness often had the effect of disarming it. But passivity took me only so far. I *liked* analytical arguments, and I didn't see why analysis was being encouraged in the largely male world of work, and discouraged in the largely female realm of mindfulness meditation (where only one man, a brave and quiet soul, made it through all eight of the training classes). Although I would never have said so out loud, I wanted to pen my cow in. I wanted to see that particular creature divvyed up and quartered like the side of beef it was likely to become.

"I don't know how you can do battle with something that's nondescript and nontangible," says James, the engineer from Quebec, who refers to his sense of loneliness as being, as he carefully puts it, "very nonspecific." This, in large part, was what drove me crazy about the state. If I couldn't name what was happening to me, how was I ever going to respond to it?

When I first saw terms being applied to loneliness, I was back in the psychology section at the University of Toronto library. This was in the spring of 2005, after my visits to the library had passed the point of becoming routine and had begun to border on obsessive. I'd started scouring the shelves in the areas of social psychology, stigma, and self-blame, and I'd often return to stare at the small loneliness section, thinking it desperately needed a more modern and personal addition. It was on one of these evenings, with undergraduates scattered at the tables nearby, that I returned to a book I'd spotted earlier in my research. It was a 1989 text entitled *Loneliness*, edited by two American psychologists, Mohammadreza Hojat and Rick Crandall. I settled at one of the big wooden tables, dropped my bag to the floor, and began flipping through the pages. I'd gone through them before, of course, but that reading had been introductory, and I hadn't noticed something significant.

The book was actually a collection of papers written by different researchers, and I began to realize they were addressing different themes. Some psychologists were writing about what they called "emotional isolation"; others were addressing "social isolation." One author was splitting loneliness into "situational" and "trait." Another was concerned with the difference between "objective" and "subjective" isolation. As I sat reading, trying to tune out the whispered cell-phone calls around me and trying to ignore the rather odd fact that I was spending all of my free time holed up in an undergraduate library, I began to feel my loneliness separate into the columns and categories I so dearly loved. The state, I realized, could be broken down just as neatly as depression. I felt like grabbing the shoulder of one of the earbudded twenty-year-olds next to me and shouting, "Look, I told you it had substance!" Not wanting to shock anyone, however, and not wanting to be removed from the library for behavioral reasons, I simply closed the book and smiled. I had the tools I'd been looking for.

The most important distinction researchers have hit on to date is the difference between emotional and social isolation. We tend to talk about loneliness as a single thing, as what researchers call a unidimensional state, such as nervousness or embarrassment. As soon as loneliness research began, however, psychologists knew that they needed more than one term to describe the state. There might be a common core to all loneliness experiences—feelings of threat, insecurity, aloneness, and frustration likely characterize the state in all cases—but researchers insisted there had to be a way of distinguishing between the widower who missed his longtime spouse and the lonely twenty-something who had a casual girlfriend but no circle of friends.

It was Robert Weiss, working in the late 1960s and early 1970s, who advanced the notion that there were at least two distinct types of loneliness. A sociologist, Weiss was working with lonely housewives in the Boston area, and with the Boston chapter of a Parents Without Partners group. Weiss knew he needed to distinguish between the loneliness of the wives, which was presenting itself despite the fact that they had good marriages, and the loneliness of the recent divorcees, who had good friends but lacked an intimate attachment. Ultimately, Weiss hit on a way of explaining the difference. The isolated housewives, he decided, were struggling with what he called "social loneliness": they may have had a spouse in place, but they lacked access to a broader network of friends and colleagues. The singletons, on the other hand, were struggling with what he called "emotional loneliness": even though they had close friends, they lacked an "attachment figure," or an individual who could provide them with a strong feeling of secure intimacy.

"I think I overstructured the field," says Weiss, thinking back to the categories he developed more than thirty years ago. I'd called him at his home, and because of a glitch on my part in calculating time zones, had gotten him from the table in the middle of dinner. He was kind, however, and happy to talk about the state he'd been so instrumental in bringing to attention. "I think it's possible to find companionship in intimacy," he says. "So the lining up of community relationships—the friendships and kinships and work relationships—on the one side, and the attachments of family relationships on the other, I think it's about eighty percent right, but you don't want to believe it one hundred percent."

Even if the categories aren't as cordoned off as Weiss originally thought, the two groupings have proved extremely workable as ways of conceptualizing loneliness, and researchers active in the field today continue to use the categories as a sort of shorthand to describe a lonely person's individual situation.

"Emotional loneliness deals with the more intimate difficulties one may have," says Enrico DiTommaso, a psychologist at the University of New Brunswick who's followed up on Weiss's original typology, "for example, with your family or romantic partner. And that's a different kind of loneliness from the loneliness you may have in regard to your network of friends. Emotional loneliness means your emotions are internalized, and you keep them to yourself. You don't engage in sharing those emotions with others, and they don't share with you. And with social loneliness, you're not participating in broader social events."

With two broad categories of loneliness identified, one of the main puzzles about loneliness became clear. It had long been noted that loneliness often persists despite companionship. It can be, in Weiss's nice turn of phrase, an "eerie affliction of the spirit," one that seems to persist for no apparent reason. With a distinction drawn between emotional and social loneliness, however, Weiss was able to explain why the state sometimes lasts. Weiss had a theory called "provisions," which meant he saw different types of relationships as providing us with different emotional satisfactions. If different relationships respond to different needs, then a person can't use a friendship to satisfy the need for attachment; conversely, an attachment figure can't meet our need for collegiality and social embeddedness. It follows that, to avoid feelings of loneliness, most people need both a social circle and an intimate attachment. While Weiss is now saying that some people can find companionship in intimacy, it's still the case that most people who lack a specific tie will, at one point or another, feel socially or emotionally isolated. If they try to mend their isolation by substituting a friend for a lover, or a lover for a friend, the loneliness will persist.

The interesting thing about seeing loneliness as comprising two different states—emotional and social—is that they can be tracked back to different antecedents. One of the most interesting and intuitively right results that emerged from early loneliness research was that adult loneliness is linked to the experience of having had your parents divorce during your childhood. When the New York–based psychologists Carin Rubenstein and Phillip Shaver surveyed thousands of lonely people in the late 1970s, they found that individuals whose parents had divorced before they were eighteen were more likely to describe themselves as lonely, and that an inverse relationship existed between loneliness and the age at which the divorce had occurred—the younger the child, the more severe the adult loneliness, with the worst loneliness presenting itself among those whose parents divorced before they were six. While this research hasn't been updated for the new millennium, and while the relationship between loneliness and divorce might have eased somewhat as divorce has become more common, it's still the case that a child whose sense of security is disrupted might be more vulnerable to emotional loneliness as she enters adulthood.

"It's going to depend on the child and their psychological makeup," explains DiTommaso when I ask him about the relationship between loneliness and childhood loss, "but if someone is faced with a disrupted situation, whereby they start to question their ability to engage with other people—because all around them they see that things are failing—they can develop a cognitive model of the world as one with no consistency, where they can't really trust things to stay the same. And if you have those kinds of views, it's less likely that you'll connect or want to connect with people, because you'll fear they're going to let you down again."

"I think I'm probably afraid," agrees Sonia, the West Coast copywriter, whose childhood saw major disruptions. When she tries to explain—to me and to herself—why she lacks emotional connections, she notes, "There's just fear there, of the dependency it would involve." With a remarkable degree of insight, she admits, "I'm alone because I'm afraid not to be. I'm afraid to reach out, really."

If your childhood has been a lesson in the fact that relationships are risky, it can be difficult, in adulthood, to take the steps necessary to form close emotional ties. The word that Sonia used to describe her loneliness—which she describes as having lasted her entire adult life—was *secure*. "I don't know if I've ever *not* felt lonely," she says, without a hint of self-pity. "I don't know if I've ever felt emotionally connected to anyone, ever. And I think feeling that might take away the security I have now."

There was a sort of déjà vu aspect to Sonia's use of the term *security*. The word is one that bobs to the surface whenever the subject is loneliness. For Cacioppo, it's feelings of threat and security that get skewed by the mood, driving the lonely person toward a state of protective isolation. My therapist, Genevieve, who was relatively uninterested in evolutionary psychology, advanced the same terms, only she set them on a different stage.

"You associate relationships with risk," she said quietly one afternoon, trying not to sound as though she were passing judgment on me, "and aloneness with safety."

It was surprising, in my talks with lonely people, how many of them referred to disrupted childhoods—not in the sense of pitched battles or abuse, but rather the quieter hardships of cross-country relocations, the departure of a parent, or the experience of watching a mother or father stay but take to the bottle. "She drank," notes Anne, simply, referring to her mother. "We moved about ten times when I was growing up," says Claire, rather calmly, "and I think the ability to feel a strong sense of security was never really well established." Adam, whose parents divorced when he was twelve, stresses, "My adolescence was *extremely* unstable. From the time I was twelve to the time I was twenty-five, I never lived in the same place for longer than six months."

To a certain extent, loneliness seems to be a learned behavior, in the sense that a person learns that reliance on others is hazardous, and that the self is the only person who can be truly counted on. And once this dynamic—whether you want to frame it in terms of our evolutionary heritage or a disrupted attachment system—is in place, loneliness can become something of a haven, a state associated not only with feelings of stress and isolation but, paradoxically, with a sense of calm and control.

"When I think of loneliness," says Anne, "I think of a person being alone and it being *peaceful*, and maybe you'd want it to go away, but maybe not."

It's because loneliness can become twinned with a sense of surety and command that ending the state can become so complex. "It's possible to feel safe within a relationship," Genevieve suggested, after she'd assessed my inverted perceptions of risk and reward. I'd nodded, as though to indicate "of course," but I really had little idea of what she was talking about. My parents' divorce, which occurred when I was four, had left me with a sense of doubt in others that had never culminated in anything dramatic, but at the same time had never really gone away. Throughout my years of loneliness, I dreamed, at least once a month, of abandonment. Each dream featured the same tired scenario, one that—if I'd seen it crop up in a novel—would have made me crinkle my nose and think, Isn't that a bit trite? I'd be in a restaurant, or a hotel room, or standing in my real apartment, and I'd be grasping at someone's arm or hand, trying to keep them from heading to the door, all the while trying to plead and reason with them to stay. Until the worse part of my loneliness ended—until I went through the long, difficult, and I think unending process of having to learn new behaviors and beliefs—the person in question never stayed. The dream would end with me standing alone in a room, and I'd awaken with a sense of sick familiarity, frustrated with myself for having had the same, almost fetishistic dream *again*.

Loneliness interventions can take different forms: lonely people can be brought together in conversation groups; they might be offered hands-on help in restoring or maintaining relationships; or they might be provided with information about loneliness itself. Such interventions have been under way in various countries for about the past ten years, and one thing that's been noticed about the most effective ones is that they allow lonely participants to reassess their expectations of safety in relationships. "What's come out quite strongly in our most recent study," says Mima Cattan, a UK-based health promotion researcher who is at the forefront of looking at responses to loneliness, and who has worked extensively on visiting and befriending projects, "is that people say, 'We can *trust* that person.' When they say they're going to phone, they *always* phone. Or when they say they're going to come round and see them, they *know* they're going to come and see them. What they're actually saying is that having someone you can trust, who makes contact, who doesn't always hone in on your problems, but who talks about day-to-day things, like the weather, the flowers, your dog—for them, that's an important part in giving them more self-confidence to then go and do other things. I mean, some of the people we talked to were absolutely convinced that this had broken the chain of their loneliness."

Overcoming loneliness seems to be, in no small part, a process of revising trust beliefs, replacing disrupted notions of trust with models in which other people can be safely relied on, and learning—as Genevieve put it—that you can be safe in relationships as well as outside of them. I don't think this is an easy lesson to learn, or a quick one, or one, like tying a shoelace, that's ever fully mastered. But I do think it's possible, and I think the best loneliness intervention programs—and, interventions aside, the best strokes of luck—are those that present us with the opportunity to revise our trust beliefs, and come to see others as safe and reliable.

If emotional loneliness seems somewhat complex, rooted as it is in feelings of threat and safety, social loneliness is somewhat easier to grasp. Social loneliness—the absence of a network

of friends, colleagues, neighbors, or fellow faith members—
is something we hear more about, largely because the socially
lonely are more willing to name and discuss their problem.
Discussion of social loneliness is easier because social isolation is generally judged less harshly than emotional isolation.
When Ken Rotenberg, a psychologist at Keele University in
England who is the leading authority on loneliness and stigma,
asked college students to rate a fictional person who was either
lacking a group of friends or lacking a close relationship, he
found that it was the emotionally lonely person who received
the harshest judgments. The fictional person who was socially
lonely was let off relatively easily.

We're more comfortable with social loneliness partly because we see it as something that's slightly out of a person's
control. While it's expected that *everyone* should form a close
emotional tie, it's accepted that some people are simply going
to be better at creating social networks than others. "When we
look at people who are comfortable with social interactions,"
says Niels Christensen, a psychologist at Radford University
in Virginia, "there's a big enduring personality component to
that. If you take a variable like extroversion—how outgoing
and sociable someone is—there's a big chunk of that that's genetic. So people who are really extroverted and social, when
they find themselves in a new situation—perhaps they move to
a new town—they really go out there and they try to establish
those new relationships. It's the people who are not that outgoing, who maybe are a little more socially anxious or maybe
predisposed to being lonely, that when they find themselves in
a new situation, they're not going to be able to establish those
new relationships as fast as they'd like."

It's because social loneliness overlaps with ideas such as extroversion and introversion that we can explain the phenome-

non to ourselves and so become less likely to blame the socially
lonely for their predicament. It's also the case that social loneliness is often seen as less important than emotional loneliness.
We tend to pity the person who's single, but we don't worry
overmuch about the married person who lacks a group of
friends. But Robert Weiss, who settled on the category of social
loneliness over a quarter century ago, notes that this assump-
tion is misguided, and he stresses that social integration is crucial in allowing us to feel confident and at ease in the world.

"If you can imagine yourself walking into an office where
you have a job, and everyone knows you and likes you, and
more than anything else accepts you. You walk in the front
door, and the secretary looks up, smiles, says Hi, looks back.
You're not anybody who has to be dealt with. It's rather that
when you show up, you have a right to be there, and that sense
of acceptance and affirmation is reassuring. The sense of belonging—you're part of something that's trustworthy, and that
helps you feel secure. You don't think about it very much, but
you feel it. And you feel like you're likely to be accepted in the
next encounter that you have. And if you feel good about yourself, and feel that you're acceptable—which is one of the things
that membership provides you—you communicate that."

It's because networks provide us with a sense of self-worth
and confidence that people who lack membership in a larger
group are likely to feel not just lonely but insecure, self-
conscious, and unsure of themselves. When Leanne, a thirty-
nine-year-old woman, moved from Austin to New York with
her husband only to find herself suddenly friendless, she realized that her lack of a social circle had an impact on everything.
"It got so frustrating," she says, referring to the seven years she
spent without close friends. "I got so sad, and so down. It was
unbelievable—like, 'What am I doing here? If I wasn't mar-

ried, would I still be here?' And 'Maybe this isn't right for me,' and on and on and on."

The experience of being outside of a social circle was, for Leanne, bewildering. "I always had a lot of friends in grammar school and then high school and college. I've *never* had a problem making friends, *ever*. I don't have a problem talking to anybody about anything. So I think I just assumed I'd come to New York and it would all be groovy, and I'd meet people. And the first year, I thought, Well, the first year's kind of tough." By year seven, she says, she was talking to the cat when her husband was away, and her loneliness was like "when you have a dull ache in your leg, or you're sort of depressed or something—you don't realize it's not necessarily the norm." It was only in making a fast friend again, Leanne notes, that she's found renewed energy and confidence that filters out toward other areas of her life. "We're just pushing each other," she says, "to think about what else is out there, and I think that translates into a bigger picture of what's possible. I feel like I'm exploring things more."

It's not just that our social circle gives us the confidence we need to branch out. It's also the case that we define ourselves in relation to others. When our social networks thin out or crumble, we have fewer points of reference available to us in thinking about who we are and who we'd like to be. "When I was younger and going to conferences and things like that," says Katherine, the policy analyst from Nova Scotia, describing her busy late teen and early adult years, "I'd always be with these go-getter kids. They were all, like, I'm going to do *this*, or I'm going to get my doctorate. And at that time it was easier for me to talk about, and imagine, all the things I could do." Now that she finds herself lacking a close network of friends, Katherine describes a situation in which, she says, "I've kind of stopped planning, and hoping, and imagining what things will be like. I don't have a picture of what my life will be like in five years' time, or ten years' time. Somewhere along the way, I stopped thinking about what I want to be when I grow up."

One of the things that social networks do is flesh us out. When they're lacking, it can start to feel as though there's less to us, less clarity and definition. A major issue I struggled with when lonely was the prospect of coming out. During my years with Martin, I used to scuttle into gay bookstores and read guiltily in the stacks. In law school, I'd briefly dated a beautiful and powerful corporate lawyer, and a vivacious radio producer with a perfect bob. After my short affair with Ron, the professor, ended, I told myself it was time to, in a sense, straighten things out. The women's bookstore had a poster up for a collection called *Go the Way Your Blood Beats*, and I thought, turning from the poster to a dishy brunette, *My blood beats thataway.*

When I started working on this book, the director of a literary agency asked me if the whole reason I was lonely was because I was in the closet. It was a reasonable question, but it wasn't one—even after years of experiencing and thinking about loneliness—that had ever occurred to me. I've talked to some lonely people, such as Adam, the illustrator from Rhode Island, who do link homosexuality to loneliness. "I think a lot of gay people," he notes, "don't go through a normal adolescence, with dating and rejection and all that, and so we wind up with these backwards dating skills" that interfere with romance in adulthood.

I could see Adam's point, but it wasn't my problem. My dating skills, though I wasn't exercising them much, were fine. The difficulty was that my loneliness was making it hard for me to engage in self-definition. What I didn't say to the agent then—but what I would say now—is that my homosexuality didn't lead to loneliness. It was my loneliness that was preventing me from claiming my homosexuality. I didn't have anyone, during the years that I was trying to come out, to define myself against. It was as though, as I spent less and less time with others, I was beginning to disappear. And this dizzying sense of not being fully *there* made it hard for me to claim any identity at all. My plants didn't care if I was gay or not, and—with so many evenings and weekends spent with nothing but their company—I had to ask if even *I* cared.

Many of the lonely people I spoke to specifically emphasized that the end of their loneliness would help them expand emotionally. It would see them turn into different and more solid selves. "I was reading something about friendship at one point," says Sonia, the copywriter, "and it mentioned that with almost everyone you meet, or with people you make connections with, you discover a new part of you. So I feel like if I could just make more connections with people, there'd probably be more about myself that I would realize, or understand, or feel. There'd just be *more* to me, just more to things I don't even know about."

To say that I needed other people to help me forge my own identity makes me sound like the least self-actualized person on the planet. But the fact is that loneliness left me feeling stunted. Just like Sonia, I knew that a different, more solid self would emerge if only I felt connected. It was my inability to reach this other self that was so frustrating. A good deal of the envy I began to feel in the course of my loneliness was linked to the intuition that others weren't just *happier* than I was, they were more fully present. Other people had spouses and colleagues to provide them with information about who they were, what they liked, and what they should aim for. I had to struggle with all of these issues solo, and the work involved was exhausting, demoralizing, and—in a sense—unfair. Nonlonely people had help with the extraordinarily difficult task of becoming themselves. As a lonely person, I had to face every hurdle alone, and every challenge that arose seemed more daunting as a result.

If the difference between emotional and social isolation constitutes one distinction, the difference between trait and situational loneliness marks another. Trait loneliness is the sort of aloneness you feel you've been born with, the kind you feel you can't escape. The trait can even be part of how you mentally describe yourself, with *lonely* ranking high on an imaginary list of attributes, alongside *athletic*, *stubborn*, and *attractive*.

For other people, loneliness is a more accidental event. When loneliness has not been lifelong but has been triggered by something specific, it's referred to as "situational." (It was situational loneliness I was trying to claim in 2003, when I was thinking about my state as being linked to my city, or my dating status—to anything but my genes and learned behaviors.) The notion that situational loneliness might differ from chronic or trait loneliness was tested in the late 1970s by Daniel Perlman, who asked both chronically and situationally lonely people to view slides, and to nonverbally communicate to observers whether the slide they were viewing depicted a scene of violence, happiness, or peace. What Perlman found was that the situationally lonely subjects were better communicators—they were more alert, more avid, more engaged. They were trying harder than the chronically lonely to get their point across.

When I spoke to people who were situationally lonely—who had fallen into loneliness by virtue of their circumstances—I was struck by their willingness to engage with the state. They didn't see it as a necessarily unchanging feature of their lives. Even when the loneliness was extreme, they hadn't entered into that paradoxical state in which social relations had begun to seem threatening rather than welcoming. Stephanie, for instance, a thirty-eight-year-old teacher from Wyoming, hadn't had much experience with loneliness before a divorce ended her decade-old marriage. After the divorce, however, her loneliness went from being a relatively minor issue to something she describes as "an overriding concern." "I feel the need to fill my days with things to get rid of it," she says. "I've taken on a whole bunch of extra jobs at work, and nothing really seems to fill the void. It's just something I struggle with every second of the day."

While Stephanie's loneliness is intense, it doesn't seem to pose the problems of self-censure and secrecy that trait loneliness presents. Although most of her acquaintances ask about depression—which, she stresses, isn't really the problem—she's able to talk to close friends and family members about her sense of isolation. It's also the case that *being* with these people helps to offset the state. "It definitely helps," she notes, referring to time with friends. "And spending time with my family is a big help as well." When the people close to her suggest proactive measures such as joining clubs, or becoming involved with alumni activities, Stephanie doesn't necessarily see these responses as missing the point. While she recognizes that reunion dinners might not touch her pervasive loneliness, she's not shying away from sociability. When I ask her how she wants people to respond to her loneliness, she quickly says that she wants a dinner invitation, or tickets for two to the movies. The state, in other words, hasn't turned her social world into something she's retreating from. Rather, her situational loneliness is animating her to pursue social connections.

A willingness to seek out interpersonal connection can persist even if the situational loneliness seems overwhelming.

Maggie, for instance, a New Zealander from Auckland, hadn't had trouble with loneliness before illness hit. "About seven years ago," she says, "I was working really hard, socializing really hard, and trying to do different things." With a wedding planned and a wide circle of friends in place, loneliness wasn't part of Maggie's world. That changed when she was diagnosed with a severe form of multiple sclerosis. Within a year, she'd lost mobility, her balance was gone, and she was exhausted a great deal of the time. Her engagement was called off, she had to leave her work as an actor, and her social circle began to shrink. Now, seven years after her diagnosis, Maggie lives at home with her parents and confronts a social world so small it's striking. Most of her friends have thrown themselves into lives filled with work, husbands, and kids, and Maggie's parents' house is far from the downtown location where she used to live, meaning that social interactions are few and far between. "There are two friends I see maybe three times a year," she says, running through an inventory of connections as we talk. "Then I have another two friends where I'm lucky if I see them once a year. They've got babies and husbands and things. Then I have another friend who lives far away—I might see her once a year. So it evens out that I see friends about eight times a year or something."

Loneliness, of course, has become a problem for her, especially when she's feeling sick, or when her medication throws her off her sleep and she finds herself up alone late at night. But what's striking about Maggie is how she's responded to her state. When I e-mailed her a question about whether she'd tried ways of countering her loneliness, she sent me back a list of about fifteen different things—volunteering, games groups, school reunions. "I'll search for things like the community section of the local council to see if there are any groups," she says, referring to her time alone late at night. "Or I might type in 'women's friendship groups Auckland' to see if there's something that interests me." Despite being largely housebound, Maggie is still marked by the resourcefulness of someone for whom loneliness isn't a chronic problem. I felt almost ashamed in talking to her. Healthy as I was, it seemed as though our circumstances should be reversed, as though she should be the one writing the book about loneliness, and me the one actively surfing the Net for groups to join. Why this isn't the case—why she's determined and optimistic, while my loneliness is chronic and entrenched—is a complex question, but it's one that surely refers to the experience of loneliness in early life. For Maggie, loneliness hadn't been a problem before her illness set in, and with an explanation in place for the state, it likely seems like a more manageable thing to battle.

The ability to put loneliness in perspective also seems key for Beatrice, who's found herself confronting a relatively empty social life after throwing herself into a grueling work schedule. Working thirteen-hour days as a lawyer in Washington, Beatrice says, "I just barely keep in touch with a few of my colleagues and friends by e-mail. I'm usually so exhausted that I don't even have time to eat when I get back home, let alone socialize. I'd like to get a pet, but I'm not really doing too well with plants." What Beatrice is able to do—and what the chronically lonely people I spoke to couldn't do—is normalize her loneliness into something a great number of her peers are experiencing as well. "I know my female friends, the ones who are unmarried or who got divorced, they're kind of going through this on their own, saying, 'You know, my job is really great, but how can I be more social?' They're just trying to focus on how to get more active and how to meet people."

With her loneliness being mirrored back to her by her similarly overworked colleagues, Beatrice seems able to step away from the state and imagine life without it. "I've been thinking back to what I really enjoyed in life before all of this came on," she says, "and I really enjoyed times when I was volunteering—with the food bank, or the literacy group, or nonprofits. And I haven't had time to do that in so long." As her long hours start to seem more and more unusual, and as a life marked by little more than e-mails starts to seem unsatisfying, Beatrice can think about rearranging her life in such a way that the loneliness doesn't come to the fore—in fact, her last note to me said that she was thinking of leaving the corporate world for part-time work with a legal aid firm.

Make no mistake about it, situational loneliness can be intense. As Stephanie puts it, "It's like there's something missing. It's like there's something everyone else has that I don't. And there's sort of a jealousy of looking at other people and seeing what they have, and thinking—what's wrong with me?" What's notable about situational loneliness is that it doesn't seem to wall the sufferer off. Stephanie can talk to people about the state, Beatrice can think about changing her work life in ways that make it less of an issue, and Maggie can throw herself into online discussion groups and chats. All three women seem aware of the fact that their loneliness might simply last, but the state hasn't yet slipped its bounds and become chronic. It hasn't turned into something that has overwhelmed them.

"You've got to be in it to win it," says Maggie, describing the attitude she takes toward finding connections. "You've got to try all these things, because if you don't try it, you can't say you've put in the effort to try to help yourself." It was this sense of agency that seemed to be missing from my talks with chronically lonely people. The state, for them and for me, didn't seem like something one could throw the gauntlet down against. But

Stephanie, Maggie, and Beatrice were *doing* things to keep their loneliness at bay—they were talking about it, making changes in their lives, and seeking out connections. In so doing, they were likely keeping the cognitive shifts that Cacioppo has identified at a distance, and my strong hope for them is that they're successful in keeping the state from becoming a dominant theme in their lives.

Last, loneliness can reflect an objective or a subjective reality. This means that a lonely person might be literally alone, or they might feel alone even when they're with others. The former point may seem obvious, but it's one that's often overlooked. For a long time, until about the mid-1960s, loneliness was conceptualized as a correlate of objective isolation. That is, the lonely person was seen as someone who was often literally alone, either living on a distant farm or cut off from others by virtue of a disability. Our tendency to describe isolated places as lonely—as in, "That's a pretty lonely spot they've got there in the woods"—flows from this idea of loneliness being rooted in a largely depopulated reality.

In the 1960s and '70s, however, something curious happened. Between 1960 and 1980, the number of people living alone soared. At the same time, no-fault divorce became the norm in most provinces and states, leading—in some jurisdictions—to a quadrupling of the divorce rate. Just as more people were finding themselves objectively alone, however, our concept of what loneliness involved began to change. A state that seemed to refer to an external reality moved "indoors," taking up lodging in the lonely person's evaluation of his social networks. It's this idea of loneliness as a purely subjective phenomenon that finds expression in all sorts of pop culture vehicles, such as the high-hustle British Web site SelfEsteem4Women, which insists that "feeling lonely is largely created by your own *perception* of not being connected to the people around you. The great thing about this perception is that it can be changed. And the even better news is that YOU can change it once we show you how!"

While it's true that loneliness is often a subjective experience—one that presents itself when companionship is available—the modern tendency to see the state as a purely internal event skips over the extent to which lonely people are often literally alone, and this omission is highly convenient. Saying that loneliness flows from a problem with "perception" means we don't have to imagine what it's like to spend days on end with nothing but your own company. It means we don't have to ask tough questions about whether ending isolation should become a broader public policy goal. Instead, we can take comfort in the idea of loneliness as a sort of figment of the lonely person's imagination, something that doesn't involve the rest of us in any way.

The reality of loneliness is much more complex, and doesn't align itself neatly with the idea of the state being an entirely subjective phenomenon. In virtually every study that's been done, the lonely report simply being alone more often than the nonlonely. They're more likely to be eating dinner alone, more likely to be spending weekend evenings alone, and more likely to be living alone. To put it bluntly, they're more likely to be confronted with stretches of real isolation they haven't chosen and from which they can't escape.

"For the entire past year, just because of the way my work is," says Frank, whose job as a freelancer means he often finds himself between projects, "I'd have minimum contact with people for work. There would be entire days where I'd go without speaking to a single person. At home, I'd just keep looking at the phone, thinking, 'I haven't spoken to anyone in days.' And it would seem unreal to me. I couldn't figure out why I was paying a phone bill."

"I work by myself, at home," says Adam, the illustrator. "And it's very individual, the work. You can just focus on your drawing board and work all day. And if I don't plan to do something in the evening, if I don't have dinner plans, or running plans, or whatever plans, and I'm still here at six or seven o'clock, I just feel like shooting myself, because I can't *take it*, because it's so quiet here, and I'm so by myself, perched at the dining room table, reading the newspaper, defrosting something from Trader Joe's, and it's like, *this* is gloomy."

Just fifty years ago, the anthropologist Margaret Mead joked that North Americans needed a "solitude day" to help them over their collective anxiety about being alone (Mead suggested Wednesdays). It's hard to imagine someone making this joke today, largely because solitude has become rather cool. As objective isolation grows, the ability to dabble in isolation— to completely control the extent to which you're alone—has become something of a status symbol. Months in ashrams have become popular, as has living off-grid and hiking alone through the few remaining parts of the world that haven't been crammed into a Lonely Planet guidebook. This sort of aloneness is the stuff of laudatory magazine articles. It's an aloneness that people who come back from ashrams and solo voyages tend to describe as "intense" and "enriching."

A different sort of dialogue attaches to aloneness that hasn't been chosen. Someone sitting alone in a tent at the foot of Everest blogs about his experience; someone alone in her living room keeps the fact of her aloneness to herself. "When I'd be cooped up by myself," says Claire, the financial analyst, who describes long periods of time spent on her own, "if someone would call, I'd just say, 'I'm planning on going out.' I'd not let people know what was going on. Even if someone asked, I wouldn't really offer up what I was doing or how much time I was spending alone. I would just avoid it completely." Adam is more hands-on when it comes to obscuring the extent of his isolation. "I close the shades when I'm here at night, having dinner alone, because I don't want anyone to *see* me having dinner alone."

It's because younger lonely people are able to devise strategies for hiding their aloneness that we tend to see objective isolation as a problem that besets only older people. While it's true that many senior citizens struggle with aloneness—one British study found that a fifth of seniors could go at least a week without any contact with friends, neighbors, or family—we need to accept that social isolation is a problem for people in younger age groups as well. When I'd taken a long vacation from work to focus on my writing, I found that I could go days on end without seeing anyone but a few hikers in the ravine and the librarians at my local branch. At the grocery store, my exchanges with clerks started to sound glassy and shrill. I realized that I'd gotten out of the habit of talking to other people. My anxiety—which was already ticking along pretty nicely—became even more pronounced, and I scrambled to find an excuse that would allow me to go back to the office a week early.

During this period of what began as a vacation and wound up feeling like a field trial on the effects of isolation, I couldn't ignore what struck me as a dogma of sociability. In starting to research loneliness, I inevitably found myself fascinated by its opposite. If I was chronically lonely, I became intrigued by people who didn't have any problems with the state. It was for this reason that, as I sat alone in my apartment, I was flipping through *Urban Tribes*, a book dedicated to the notion that young singletons—people like me—are not isolated but are enmeshed in dense, rich social networks. "In an average week," writes the author, Ethan Watters, "among my group of 25 friends, there were hundreds of one-to-one emails, a dozen group emails, and perhaps 50 phone calls exchanged." I read this description after having had no social interaction at all for several days. I wondered, briefly, if Watters and I were from the same planet. I also wondered how Watters would respond to an isolation so complete he was forced to rely on his own journals and the radio for a sense of engagement. To make light of my situation, I daydreamed about a scenario in which both of us were washed up alone on separate deserted islands. I would, I realized, be way ahead of him in terms of survival. Watters would be calling out to *me* for tips on how to handle aloneness. (Whether or not I'd provide him with these tips would depend on my mood.)

It's important to note what objective isolation isn't. It's not solitude. A lot of lonely people tell themselves—or have other people tell them—that they're supposed to see their time alone as a period of meditation. "My friend gave me this cheesy self-help book that had a chapter in it on loneliness and solitude," says Frances, the physiotherapist from Missouri, with a laugh. "And that was where I got the idea that I should think of my aloneness as a time of freedom or enrichment, or that sort of thing. And so I kept trying to see it as solitude, as a time to commune with myself or whatever. But I never really felt like that. I was sort of *irritated* to be all by myself."

The difference between loneliness and solitude can best be seen as a function of choice. If you're purposefully choosing to be on your own, aloneness can indeed be immensely curative and delightful, and lonely people can enjoy it as much as anyone else. "A lot of the time I'm just more interested in doing things by myself," says Frank, the freelancer, "just simple everyday things like thinking or writing or walking around. It's not all bad," he says contentedly, referring to time spent alone. But then he adds, rather reasonably, "It's a question of whether you *want* it. There are people who don't want to be by themselves, and for them to see aloneness as a period of growth, they'd have to make something out of it, which is basically like saying, 'You don't have any friends, so why don't you work *harder?*' "

I tried to do this work when I was alone. I tried to commute my loneliness into what Frances jokingly refers to as "an extra-long meditation." My guidebook in this endeavor was a monograph by the Oxford psychiatrist Anthony Storr, who—in his book *Solitude*—stresses that the modern age has come to overvalue personal relationships, and that "many of the world's greatest thinkers have not reared families or formed close personal ties." I especially liked this passage. I pictured a row of busts—Storr had mentioned Isaac Newton, Immanuel Kant, and Søren Kierkegaard—and tried to tack my own image to the end of the line. But not only was I young, female, and really bad at math, I had a hard time seeing my aloneness in terms of creativity and inspiration.

"Sometimes aloneness is on purpose," says James, the engineer, who describes himself as often experiencing "days and days without even speaking, let alone seeing anyone." He notes that sometimes aloneness is "for good things—it's a positive aloneness." This is the sort of aloneness that Storr is describing, and which Newton presumably experienced. But then there's another kind of aloneness, the kind that doesn't get written about in books decorated with images of men sitting contemplatively in rowboats. "Sometimes you're alone," remarks James rather dryly, "and you haven't left the apartment for three days other than to take the garbage out and go downstairs to the store for a bottle of Coke."

It might be argued that the people I was interviewing weren't really as alone as they told me they were. That is, even if someone like James could go, as he says, "days and days" without speaking to anyone, he could still "connect" with others through the Internet. The Internet has emerged as *the* fallback argument in any debate about social connectedness and isolation. The idea is that, even if we don't have anyone to talk to, we can still send messages via e-mail, or update our Facebook page, or Twitter away to anyone who wants to listen.

What I found most interesting about my talks with lonely people was that the Internet simply didn't play a large role in most of their lives. I don't mean they weren't online. After all, everyone I spoke to had contacted me after seeing my ad on Craigslist. I'd scheduled all of my interviews over e-mail, and potential respondents had to find and review my blog, so a high degree of comfort with the Internet was basically a prerequisite for becoming involved with my study. But, with a few exceptions, the lonely people I was speaking to weren't using the Internet to offset their loneliness.

"Someone would have to pay me a huge sum of money to show up on Facebook," says Frank, only minutes after telling me that he struggles with extended periods of isolation. His response didn't surprise me. After all, I'd experienced years of loneliness without setting up a Facebook or MySpace page (I still don't have one, and have no intention of getting one). It might seem odd for the lonely to "fail" to take advantage of social networking sites, but the challenges posed by those sites need to be recognized. People who struggle with chronic loneliness are already highly sensitized to representations of sociability, and less able to tune out social information. To participate in a trend like Facebook, you have to be able to read about someone else having 50, or 80, or 350 friends, and not be bothered by it. This is not something most chronically lonely people are able or willing to do. The chronically lonely are already beset with a profound sense of having fallen socially behind. The last thing they need are minute-by-minute updates of other people's rich social lives. Facebook has always struck me as a sort of playground bully, a device dedicated to telling everyone what their social lives should look like, and belittling those who don't fit the prescribed pattern. Steering clear of it is, I think, a defensible strategy.

I mentioned that there were exceptions to the general trend of not using the Internet as a substitute for missing social ties. One exception was for people, like Ray, the fundraiser from Philadelphia, who played online games. "I had a character that I loved playing all the time," he says, "and I tended to play the game when I was lonely. The character was very entertaining, very jovial, and whenever I'd go online and play him, someone would eventually just see me and yell out, 'Ray!' And I'd feel less lonely, I'd feel part of a community. It was different from Facebook. The people were strangers, but there was still a sense of community, and less loneliness, because the others were familiar with my character and knew who he was."

I have to admit to not being overly familiar with online games, but—when I was speaking to Ray—I knew right away what he was talking about. He was describing a fictional world, a world that was manageable and nurturing precisely because it was make-believe. The sense of connection that Ray took from online gaming sounded just like the experience I took from reading novels. Ray and I had both found a way of making our real selves invisible, and losing ourselves in worlds that gave us the chance to experience different aspects of our personalities. To the extent that online games open up imaginary communities to people who might not be bookish, they can probably be seen as a reasonable short-term response to loneliness.

It's also the case, of course, that the Internet offers truly new ways for people to band together regardless of geographic location. Maggie, who was housebound in New Zealand, used the Internet to link up with people from around the world who were suffering with MS. "I used to get a lot less lonely when I'd spend time and energy having a lot of online interaction," she says. "I'm not talking about chats. I'm talking about being part of an online e-mail group. I'd end up treating the group as I would a friend. If something medical happened, I'd right away think, 'I'm just going to post this online.'"

Like Maggie, I'd used the Internet for a specific purpose. I'd wanted to create a site where loneliness could be openly discussed. If it weren't for the anonymity and geographic irrelevance created by the Internet, it would have been very difficult for me to have reached out to others and learned about their experiences. To this end, I would say that the Internet was useful, and I'll admit that, when I was blogging about loneliness, I'd temporarily feel less alone. But it's one thing to say that the Internet is useful, and that it lets us connect in new ways, and a different thing to say that it can solve problems of loneliness and isolation. As I'll discuss in the next chapter, we're becoming more isolated, and the Internet is repeatedly being held out to us as a development that makes this growing isolation less relevant. Of course we might be seeing less of friends and family, this message tends to run, but we can read their blogs every day!

We need to be aware of the limits of the Internet. For some

people, like Maggie and Ray, it will provide a way of briefly sidestepping feelings of isolation. It will certainly provide a new way for like-minded people to get in touch. But a computer can't provide company. What I needed, during the vacation I'd taken from work—a break that had found me utterly and relentlessly alone—was a sense of belonging and intimacy. I had a laptop at home at the time, and it was wired to anything I might have wanted to connect to, but I didn't turn it on much. In fact I tended to shy away from it, since when I did turn it on, it communicated way too much information about sociability. There were ads for online dating sites that popped up whenever I opened my Hotmail account, "news" items about celebrity relationships, and faux-journalistic pieces from MSN about "How to Connect in Your New City!" This glut of information was bewildering. It left me feeling disoriented, off balance, and out of step.

Perhaps I was being insufficiently modern, but I never felt as though I could cure my loneliness through technology. My computer was just a part of my apartment, less comforting than my fridge, less familiar than my toaster, and I object to the idea that I should have somehow reached out in my loneliness and tried to turn it into a friend.

Objective isolation, of course, whether it's accompanied by technology or not, isn't the only precursor to loneliness. The isolation in question might be subjectively rather than objectively felt. That is, the lonely person might have companionship, but still feel alone. This experience is often captured, culturally, with the expression "lonely in a crowd." This phrase has always sort of bothered me, in part because it cues a silly image of the lonely person drifting forlornly through a train station at rush hour, and this picture misrepresents the experience of subjective isolation in a couple of significant ways.

First, the standard image—head down, crowd swirling—fails to recognize that crowds, for lonely people, can be quite reassuring. Many researchers have noted that loneliness can drive someone to seek out company in any form—at church, on buses, at busy downtown intersections—and lonely people readily admit to doing this. "Sometimes I'll just go and run an errand at the mall," says Claire, the financial analyst, "just to be in a big crowd of people. I like being part of a big, anonymous group. It's sort of comforting. Even though I'm not really having any interactions with these people, just being in their presence, just being around them, it feels sort of communal in a strange way, and it's very soothing at times."

It's also the case, of course, that strangers aren't really the problem when it comes to loneliness. It seems odd to have to state this next point explicitly, but lonely people don't complain about feelings of disconnection in relation to people they don't know. The whole problem is that they feel disconnected around people they *do* know. "Even with close friends," says Frank, the freelance journalist, "even with people I've known for decades, who I still know, it's just sometimes . . . something's not there." It's feelings of distance and disconnection, of not being fully engaged and present, that lonely people highlight when they talk about their loneliness—and these feelings emerge despite the fact that lonely people often have support networks and significant others in place. "When I think about loneliness," says Anne, the social worker, "I think about just feeling like I don't have intimate connections that touch on all the different aspects of myself. And it's not that I don't have intimate relationships. It's that I don't have ones that cover all of who I am."

The whole problem with loneliness is that you can have a social network in place and still, frustratingly, feel quite lonely. "Social networks are things which one can measure by observing the interactions people have, and the number, density, and frequency of those connections," says University College London's Andrew Steptoe. "And that experience is not the same as the psychological experience of being socially connected. You could have someone who has quite a variety of contacts every day, but who still might feel lonely because they don't see the intimate support they're looking for." Contrary to what we're told about the power of online social networks to "connect" us in brave new ways, such networks—regardless of how large they are—might do nothing to touch feelings of isolation. Someone with a hundred "friends" on Facebook might still feel bewildered and alone, and that's because the online relationships in question don't offer us the intimacy we need.

In an early study addressing the difference between breadth and depth of relationships, researchers at the University of Tulsa had lonely and nonlonely people carry a diary for four days. Each time they had a social interaction, the subjects were to record who they were with and what the nature of the interaction was like. The researchers found that, while the lonely were sometimes interacting with more people than the nonlonely, their interactions were more likely to be with impersonal others, such as clerks and acquaintances, and less likely to be marked by warmth and reciprocity. That is, even though the lonely could point to a variety of people with whom they were having at least some degree of contact, they couldn't point to support or intimacy within those connections.

It's easy enough to understand loneliness if you see it as a function of lonely people simply lacking intimate relationships. The situation becomes more complicated if you accept that lonely people can have these relationships in place, and still be troubled by feelings of disconnection. And this persistent, subjective sense of isolation is what researchers are starting to hone in on. "When we look at some objective indexes of whether lonely people have relationships," says the University of Chicago's Louise Hawkley, "namely—are they married, do they have an intimate relationship, is it of good quality, do they have friends—we still see an effect of their perception of loneliness that's independent of these objective measures of having somebody there." Loneliness, in other words, can become something quite complex and unnerving—a state that seems to refer to the absence of social support but which stays in place even when social support is available.

Warren Jones, a pioneering researcher now based in Tennessee, argued early on that feelings of loneliness might persist because they're embedded in "the habitual behaviors and internal processes of the lonely person" him- or herself. Many lonely people would concur that there's something about how they're seeing the world that's predisposing them to loneliness. "I don't think it's anything a relationship can offer," says Frank, referring to the end of loneliness. "Because I've lived in different states, with different groups of people, and I've felt it in every one of those contexts. So I'm sure it has something to do with environment, and how comfortable you feel, but—I don't know. I feel as if it's something inside."

"I got married, and that's like the ultimate," says Rachel, the homemaker from Florida, with a laugh. "You think, 'OK, now I'm legally with someone, they're going to *have* to be around!' And the same with your kids, you think, 'You've got it made now.' But loneliness is a state of mind, and you can become even more lonely when you realize that marriage doesn't take it away."

Loneliness researchers are just beginning to explore what processes might be in place to make people feel persistently alone. It might be the case, suggests Cacioppo, that the lonely simply have higher needs than the nonlonely. "I eat a *lot*," he explains, by way of analogy. "And I see people who are having trouble with their weight, and I feel sorry for them, because they're being very careful, while I'm going, 'Give me your extra food!' Now, instead of food, imagine that was social relationships. If that's how much I required to feel satisfied, I'd be a good candidate for a lonely person. People to whom I felt connected would have to be giving me a *lot*. And many people aren't so willing to do that. Maybe they'd be giving the same amount to you and me, but it doesn't take as much for you to feel really satisfied and connected."

One person might be born with a relatively low threshold for feeling satisfied with relationships—Cacioppo notes that the link could be genetic—while someone else might need a *lot* of contact for feelings of isolation to fade. "I think I'm probably someone who needs to feel a strong sense of connection with people, just connection at a very deep level," says Claire, agreeing with Cacioppo's analysis. "And maybe I need a lot of relationships to feel less lonely, and other people don't."

It's also the case that the lonely might not have higher needs for others, but might simply be more susceptible to social pain and rejection than others. "It might not take any more or less contact for either one of us to feel nurtured," explains Cacioppo, "but when there's a rejection, I might react *really* strongly, while you don't react so strongly." Being badly hurt, the person who feels social pain acutely might become more wary of social relationships, and more prone to loneliness, even when relationships are in place.

Disrupted trust has actually emerged as one of the key elements that might predispose someone to feelings of loneliness. The findings on divorce prompted psychologists to think about the relationship between disrupted trust and childhood experiences fairly early on, and more recent research has expanded on this work. Keele University's Ken Rotenberg has conducted experiments in which subjects have been primed to feel either trusting or distrusting—they've been exposed to sentences containing words such as *safe* and *share*, or *lie*, *risk*, and *cheat*—and he's found that manipulating trust perceptions leads to changes in self-reported loneliness. "The more trusting someone is, the less lonely they are," says Rotenberg, simply. "Or, conversely, the less trusting someone is, the more lonely they become. We've demonstrated that, almost literally, across the lifespan."

An event that disrupts trust can leave you less likely to share intimacies, and more likely to keep a safe emotional distance between yourself and others. "When you believe you can't trust others, and you feel cut off from them," Rotenberg tells me, "then you feel more lonely. Period. It's almost a cognitive mechanism, rather than a social mechanism." What's interesting about Rotenberg's research is that he's experimenting on adults. The feelings of distrust he's priming don't flow from formative experiences but from experiences the subjects are having in the present. This means that it's not just childhood events that affect our odds of being lonely, but current experiences—the betrayal of a secret, the dismissal from the job to which one has devoted oneself—that can lead to loneliness in susceptible people.

What's clear is that loneliness can be cued in one of two ways. The lonely person might actually be alone, or they might feel alone. These factors likely intersect. An extended period of objective isolation can make existing relationships seem distant, while a pronounced sense of subjective aloneness might make actual isolation seem sensible and even welcome. What's important to notice about subjective and objective isolation is that they point to the core of the loneliness experience. If depression is a state of mind marked by feelings of helplessness and failure, loneliness is a state of mind marked by a relentless sense of absence. Whether this absence reflects a real or subjectively felt lack of social ties is partly immaterial. What matters is the mental vision of the self alone in the world. If chronic loneliness is accepted as a unique psychological problem—which is what researchers are trying to impress on us—then the heart of that problem resides within a mind that is unable, for months, for years, or for a lifetime, to admit a sense of companionship. The aloneness in question might be experienced emotionally or socially. The isolation might be objective or subjective. But the sense of being cut off and deprived is the same from case to case, and it's this feeling of isolation that the lonely person has to struggle with, day after day after day.

Chapter Seven

THE COHORT EFFECT

How our culture is leaving us lonelier

It's easy enough, with talk of subjective isolation and disrupted trust, to see loneliness as a purely personal problem, as a shortcoming internal to the lonely person him- or herself. My genetic heritage, my upbringing, and my strong need for connection certainly steered me toward loneliness. I'm hesitant, however, to cast my predispositions as the sole causes of my aloneness. Because what Cacioppo has stressed in the wake of his genetics experiments is the importance of environment. Loneliness is only *half* heritable—the situation you find yourself in is going to be a major determinant of whether your loneliness comes to the fore.

"I've often said, 'Let me play God for a day,' " jokes the University of North Carolina's Daniel Perlman, " 'and I'll make anybody lonely.' " Given the right set of circumstances, anyone—regardless of their genetic endowment or personal predispositions—will succumb to the state. I think I recognized this early on, but it was hard for me to tease out the factors that might be informing my loneliness. And let me be clear: I *wanted* to be able to point to cultural factors. By the middle of 2005, I'd come to understand that framing my loneliness within a broader social context would make my guilt and embarrassment abate somewhat. It was because I wanted to feel less *responsible* for my loneliness that I began looking for clues that would allow me to see it as a societal, rather than a strictly personal, problem.

My first attempt to externalize the isolation I was feeling involved blaming the city I was living in. Even after I'd recognized my urge to flee as somewhat irrational, and had decided to remain in Toronto, I couldn't shake the idea that the place was somehow fueling my loneliness. "Monumental and lonely," was how the Pulitzer Prize–winning author Carol Shields chose to describe Toronto in *Unless*, and I signed on to this description wholeheartedly, thinking that there was something about the city, with its buzzing helicopters, endless roads, and relentless traffic, that was tweaking my sense of aloneness.

I'm not sure now that my quick conflation of Toronto with loneliness was entirely accurate. In various studies that have been done, loneliness rates have tended to be the same in both small and large centers. New Yorkers test just as lonely as those in Billings, Montana, while women in Moscow, Idaho, report the same degree of loneliness as women in San Francisco, California. What cities do seem to do is promote a greater degree of isolation. In a recent study undertaken in part to test the relationship between urban life and loneliness, researchers in the Netherlands compared loneliness and isolation rates in the city of Amsterdam and the rural area of Binnenmaas. What they found was that city dwellers were more likely to have smaller social networks, and were less likely to be able to count on practical support from those outside their households. Literal isolation, in other words, was more likely to be a threat in Amsterdam than in the countryside. For people who weren't socially isolated, however, loneliness rates didn't differ much between the two locations. Twenty-four percent of Amsterdam residents described themselves as lonely, compared to 20 percent of the rural residents.

The Dutch results suggest that, so long as you have a basic network in place (the Dutch researchers defined social isolation as knowing four or fewer people as potential supports), loneliness can be as much of a problem in the countryside as in the city. Many of the lonely people I spoke to had discovered this firsthand. "My boyfriend was from a very small town in the north," says Claire, the financial analyst from Saskatchewan. "We moved there, and the sense of family was so strong there, and the sense that everyone knew everyone. And initially I found that just being part of that strong sense of community did kind of on the surface get rid of the loneliness for a bit. But then, after about six months, it seemed to come back again," she adds. "So it didn't really work in the long run."

Secretly, I think I knew that Toronto wasn't the real cause of my loneliness. After all, I had friends in the same city who seemed to have no problems with the state, and one of the least lonely periods of my life had been spent in Montreal, a city of over a million people. But if I wasn't going to blame Toronto, I wasn't sure where else to turn in my attempt to externalize the state. I'd perk up when I heard encouraging comments, from friends or the media, about ours as a lonely age, but there was always something vague and disembodied about these remarks. Either the statements literally weren't finished— loneliness would be ditched as the speaker moved on to a more general criticism of overwork or corporate greed—or they were weirdly philosophical, concerned with a broad-scale loss of faith or the lack of an overarching common purpose, like imperialism or abolitionism. Allusions to loneliness as a contemporary problem were never twinned with the sort of empirical evidence that accompanies discussions of depression. With depression, for instance, it's possible to flip to peer-reviewed articles in the *Journal of the American Medical Association* and see graphs showing the disorder affecting growing numbers of people at younger ages across a variety of cultures.

This was the sort of thing I wanted to find for loneliness. I wanted numbers, tables, charts. Since I couldn't find anything immediately available, I took it upon myself to simply demonstrate evidence of an increase. Most loneliness studies contain information about the participants' average UCLA Loneliness Scale scores, and I began arranging the studies in chronological order, thinking that if I just set the studies out from 1978 to 2005, I'd uncover proof of an upward climb. I soon realized, however, that there was an error in my reasoning. The scores in question were just providing me with a rough sense of how lonely individual participants might be. They weren't telling me whether more people *overall* were feeling lonely.

To arrive at that conclusion, I needed rates. I needed data on the number of people within a population describing themselves as lonely. Happily (or perhaps unhappily), I found this information rather quickly. The first studies of loneliness had been conducted in the United States in the mid-1960s, and these studies had uncovered a loneliness rate of about 25 percent. Later studies, undertaken in different countries, have shown the rate edging up slightly. When researchers at Central Queensland University surveyed 1,250 Australians in 2002 and asked about feelings of loneliness, 33 percent of the respondents described themselves as being "quite lonely." In 2004, when the British mental health organization Mind asked 1,000 Britons about their experience of isolation, 29 percent of the respondents identified aloneness as a problem in their lives.

The Australian and British surveys point to an increase in the prevalence of loneliness, but I couldn't compare the findings to the original U.S. rate, because the studies all asked different questions. In order to really show an increase in the loneliness rate, I needed a tidier methodology. I wanted to find work concentrating on a single group of people, in a single city, being asked the same question from one decade to the next.

And voilà. After parking myself in front of a library terminal and running the words *loneliness*, *increase*, and *cohort* through PsychInfo about six hundred times, I found a paper that, when it was released, received little in the way of attention. Why would it? It was a study about the elderly, who so rarely make the news, and it was asking about loneliness, which so rarely gets discussed.

But the findings were fascinating. In 2002, researchers at St. George's Hospital in London realized they had four sets of data. Surveys had been conducted in London in 1948, 1957, 1963, and 2001, and each survey asked a question that probed loneliness among the elderly. In 1948, the question was "Are you very lonely, lonely at times, or never lonely?" In 2001, the question was "Do you feel lonely all the time, very often, sometimes, rarely or never?" The fact that the questions were roughly similar meant that the researchers were able to compare response rates across the decades, to determine whether loneliness was emerging as more of a problem over time.

They discovered signs of an increase. In 1948, 6 percent of elderly respondents identified loneliness as a frequent problem. In 2001, 9 percent of the respondents were having trouble with frequent feelings of the state. Even more significantly, the number of respondents who identified themselves as "never lonely" had fallen sharply over fifty years, from 83 percent in 1948 to 67 percent in 2001. These numbers provide the strongest evidence to date that loneliness is becoming more of a problem. In order to really appreciate them, you need to understand that loneliness doesn't increase with age. In virtually every study that's been done, loneliness rates have tended to fall as people get older. In the 2002 Australian survey, for instance, people in the 60–69 age group were less lonely than those in their twenties, thirties, and forties. The fact that older age doesn't lead to greater loneliness means that the higher rates of loneliness uncovered by the British researchers can't be explained in terms of the aging process itself. Rather, something about our society is changing in ways that have left the elderly—and the rest of us—more vulnerable to the state.

Researchers who work in the field of depression often talk about something called a "cohort effect." By this, they mean that a certain emotional experience might become more prevalent from one generation to the next. The best way of thinking about a cohort effect is this: the number of people with a genetic predisposition toward a state might be fixed, but cultural changes can influence the extent to which that predisposition makes itself manifest. Depression researchers point to cultural shifts such as increased urbanization and changed family patterns as influencing the overall depression rate. As life becomes more urbanized, and as more families fracture, depression is going to emerge as a problem among a growing number of people—people who might not have had trouble with the mood in a previous era.

The same sort of framework can be applied to loneliness. In a period marked by increased connectivity and interpersonal meaning, the rate will presumably fall. In an era marked by increased time alone and decreased intimacy, it will undoubtedly rise. Loneliness, perhaps more than any other state, is social in nature. It's an indication of how embedded we feel not just in our immediate relationships but within the community at large. And if there are trends toward increased isolation and decreased meaning within that community, loneliness will inevitably become more widely felt. A person with a genetic predisposition toward loneliness will simply, in an era marked by disconnection, have a harder time avoiding the state.

To say that culture and context matter isn't to say that personality plays no role—my decision to retreat from sociability when lonely, for instance, was a strictly private one. But I didn't make that decision in a vacuum. The culture I was living in helped me reach the point at which the decision was being made at all. What people with a tendency toward loneliness need is connection and heightened intimacy, and what they're finding today is decreased contact, a greater risk of isolation, and a steep falloff in companionship. These factors can interact with innate tendencies in such a way as to simply trigger loneliness. Someone who might not have had a problem with the state in the past might, today, find themselves struggling with it.

The priming and readying role played by culture is an important one to recognize. It's very easy for loneliness, especially since it's not generally spoken of, to begin to seem like the ultimate private problem, a state unconnected to the larger world. But the culture we live in can greatly affect our chances of becoming lonely. Certain changes can give the state the leg up it needs to become settled. And once loneliness is in place, the lonely person might respond by feeling unique and unusual, unaware that growing numbers of people are feeling the same way, and that the difficulty they're all facing is one that's partly cultural.

Absences are, in some respects, hard things to measure. It's
easier to sketch out a map of who is there than who isn't. But
social scientists working today have devised a host of measures
and techniques that track the extent to which we're involved
and present in each other's lives.

One way of assessing togetherness is quite simple: researchers simply focus on the extent to which we're alone. Some of
the earliest data on aloneness came out of the University of
Chicago in the late 1970s, when the sociologist Reed Larson—
who had equipped 180 teens and adults with beepers, as well as
with instructions to record who they were with each time they
were beeped—estimated that the average North American was
spending about 26 percent of his or her waking hours alone.

What time-budget researchers have been doing in the inter-
vening years is monitoring how this time alone has increased.
Glenn Stalker, a sociologist at Brock University in Ontario,
studied time-use data from the Canadian General Social Survey
between 1986 and 1998. He found that in the mid-1980s, time
alone clocked in at 28 percent of waking hours—fairly close to
Larson's 26 percent finding. By 1998, however, time alone had
risen to 34 percent of waking hours. This finding, like many
others concerning isolation, hasn't been widely reported. I'd
come across Stalker's research because we'd both gone to the
University of Toronto, and I'd seen a short write-up about his
work in the alumni magazine. I tracked him down over the Internet, and—when I got him on the phone—asked if he'd been
surprised by his 34 percent figure.

"Not really," he replied. "That's a pretty consistent finding.
This time-based data is collected by most Western nations because it's the best way to capture micro-level daily life. And

people who are doing this type of work have all found that there's been a really big increase in the amount of time people are spending alone in a lot of different contexts."

Stalker stresses that his numbers aren't being spiked by a certain group—that is, he's not just catching a rise in aloneness among the elderly, or among graduate students delaying marriage until they finish their MSc. "I looked at whether this was a trend that was particular to a specific cohort, or whether it was occurring throughout the life course," he notes. "And it was actually occurring throughout the life course." In other words, we're all—regardless of our age group—likely to be faced with more time alone today than we were twenty or twenty-five years ago.

As time alone has increased, time with others has, necessarily, gone down. If you want to know whether or not isolation is becoming more of a problem, you can—like Stalker—investigate the extent to which time alone is on the rise. Alternatively, you can flip the focus of your analysis and ask how much time someone is spending with family and friends. When investigators trace visiting patterns back to the 1970s, what they find is evidence of a falloff in time spent with those close to us.

For instance, when the Yale University political scientist Robert Lane analyzed U.S. companionship data between 1974 and 1994, he uncovered signs of what he calls a "sharp and continuous" decline in socializing. Between the mid-1970s and mid-1990s, visits with neighbors fell by almost 10 percent. During the same period, visits with family members fell by 6 percent. Lane found some evidence that the "friends generation" was replacing visits with family with visits to friends— the number of people who said that they saw their friends frequently increased by about 2 percent over the twenty-year period—but this increase wasn't enough to offset the larger decrease in socializing. "I think the data shows that you're more likely to be at home with your TV set than you are to be visiting with someone," Lane tells me, rather bluntly. "And when we replace companionship with aloneness," he adds, "we lose the unconscious validation that we're all right, that what we do and think is the right thing to do. The data show that Americans are more anxious than anybody, and I think that's because they feel as though they don't belong."

A similar picture of decreased social contact has been uncovered in the United Kingdom. The British Social Attitudes Survey samples approximately 4,000 Brits, Scots, and Welshmen annually. Part of the survey asks how often the respondent visits with his or her mother, father, sibling, and best friend. When researchers with the survey compared responses from 1986 and 1995, they found signs of social erosion. Weekly visits with parents had fallen by 10 percent, visits with siblings and other relatives had fallen by between 3 and 7 percent, and visits with friends had fallen by 6 percent. The results showed that one type of contact (such as visits with family) wasn't being replaced with another (such as visits with friends). Rather, as the report authors concluded, "people have generally become less likely to visit, or be visited by, anyone at all."

When I asked one of the researchers with the British Social Attitudes Survey why time with others had dropped, the first thing she cited was work. "One of the factors," explains Ceridwen Roberts, an Oxford-based sociologist, "is that, in a household with two partners, and both of them working—and increasingly, that's the model, even if they're only working part-time—there appears to be less time available to create social networks in the first place, and then to maintain them in the second place."

"If we send an e-mail," notes Beatrice, the lawyer from

Washington, describing what her social life has become in the midst of seventy-hour workweeks, "people will usually get it the same day, and there'll be a short response or whatnot, just something to say, 'I'm thinking of you, and I'm here.' But if we were to set up a lunch date or something, we'd usually have to reschedule two or three times to actually get a date." She adds that one of the things that's gone missing in her life is the time and energy needed to nourish old and new relationships. "You have to foster friendships," she says, "and if you have to reschedule two or three times even with your good friends to get a date, there's something really not ideal about that."

Economists see time as a fixed commodity. You can spend it socializing with friends and family, or you can spend it at work, but you can't do both. As work hours increase, they'll necessarily crowd out time available for friends and family. Not only do people wind up with less time for creating relationships, but—with the average work year having increased by approximately 150 hours, or an entire *month*, since the early 1970s—many people are simply too tired to sustain the ties they have. "If I have a long shift at work," says Ray, the fundraiser from Philadelphia, "I'll almost be to the point, when I get home, of telling people who phone just to piss off. I'll be thinking, 'I want to be alone, I want to be alone.' I just won't want to talk to anybody, and I'll kind of shut myself off from everyone."

What spending more time at work does is shift the emphasis of your socializing from the home to the workplace. As work hours have increased, so has time spent with coworkers and colleagues. This is not necessarily a bad thing. Anyone who's ever held a job they've liked can testify to the good humor and support the folks at the office can lend to a day. The problem with socializing at work is that the ties in question are often temporary. At the law firm where I clerked, the founding partner,

who was approaching ninety, used to still wander the halls—
he'd spent his life at the firm, and was planning on dying at his
desk. My fellow clerks and I had other ideas. We were taking
off—for other firms, foreign trips, or grad school. The idea of
working for life at a single job has become an anachronism, and
this is as true in manufacturing as it is in accounting. People
lucky enough to have secure careers are encouraged to "transition" to more fulfilling work; many people are caught in the
trap of "perma-temping," in which they work one contract
after another for a shifting range of employers; and millions of
individuals are simply being fired, and left with no work at all.

What the shift toward longer workdays did was signal a
transition away from the private ties of friends and family and
toward the more commercial ties of coworkers. But the very
nature of the commercial world, with its emphasis on change
and instability, means the ties in question can't be counted on
over the long term. Work relationships today can't provide us
with the constancy and durability we associate with our more
personal links. Instead, as time with family and friends has
dropped, we've become more reliant on relationships whose
duration is controlled by someone else.

It might be argued that people have always treated work ties
lightly, and that the coming and going of colleagues shouldn't
be seen as a source of concern. For this argument to work,
however, there have to be permanent ties in place *outside* of
the workplace. That is, short-term and market-based relationships are unproblematic only if other, longer-term connections
are available. And for increasing numbers of people today, the
world of work, with its tenuous links, is emerging as the sole
source of sociability.

When my naturopath, Gabriella, diagnosed me with chronic
stress in 2004 and told me that I was spending too much time at

the office, she was trading in outdated notions that cast home as the heart of sociability. My own home—until my situation changed in late 2006—didn't provide sociability or companionship at all. It was *work*, with its coffee runs and casual back-office chats, that gave me a sense of connection. When I quit my job in the summer of 2005 to write full-time, I became, against my will, almost hermitlike. I was still teaching, but that work was only part-time, and the fall term hadn't yet begun. This meant I was faced with long stretches of days in which I saw almost no one at all. And I was lucky. I knew how to offset my aloneness by writing stories that let me conjure up feelings of connection and intimacy. I was also in the highly unusual position of researching and writing about loneliness, a stance that allowed me to convert my isolation from problem to subject. I'm quite sure that, if loneliness hadn't been my topic, I probably wouldn't have been able to make the transition from lawyer to writer. Isolation, rather than skill or desire, would have determined the course of the following years. Aloneness would have pushed me back into another law firm—not because I wanted to practice law, but because I needed the sociability of an office. It was only because I'd become intrigued by loneliness that I was able to see my isolation as raw material, and in this way turn it into something that, while unwelcome, served as a strange source of drive and inspiration.

Other people, whose talents and interests rest in other areas, aren't so fortunate. Jamie Oliver, the United Kingdom's "Naked Chef," recently remarked that ours is the first generation to face an economic downturn without knowing how to cook. To this overall sense of unpreparedness, I'd add that we're probably the first generation that's had to face a recession without having anyone else at home with us. Hundreds of thousands of people across North America have, in the time that I've been writing, been "let go." What I haven't seen noted, in the many columns that have been written about the recession, is the fact that, when these people lose their jobs, many of them are losing their main source of companionship.

The average household size in North America and the UK at the start of the last century used to be five or more people. Beginning in the 1970s, however, and due in large part to increases in divorce, single parenting, extended life spans, and the growing independence of women, household size began to drop. By 2000, 26 percent of all households in the United States were composed of just one person, up from just 17 percent in 1970. A quarter of households in Canada are now, as in the United States, composed of a single individual; in the United Kingdom, people living alone account for at least 32 percent of all households.

Many people who look at these numbers assume that the increase is accounted for by widows and widowers—according to this line of reasoning, there are more single-person households today because the elderly are living longer, losing their spouses, and being left to carry on alone. When statisticians crunch the data on aloneness, however, they find that the bulk of the increase is made up of people younger than sixty-five. In the UK, the number of people between twenty-five and forty-four living alone has tripled in the past twenty years. In the States, it's the baby boomers—the ones who are now in their forties and fifties—who are driving the rate up: people under sixty-five now account for 65 percent of single-person households in America. And the interesting thing about living alone earlier in life is that the state is more likely to persist; it's a different sort of aloneness. When we think about the elderly becoming single, we tend to think of married individuals losing a spouse—they're moving from a lifetime of companionship to a shorter period of aloneness. If it's a forty-year-old who's alone, however, it's more likely that he's been that way for some time, and that he'll stay that way in the future. When the UK's Joseph Rowntree Foundation looked at the persistence of aloneness among men in their thirties, for instance, it found that 30 percent of the sample group had been alone for more than ten years, and that less than half were likely to start living with another person again.

The shift toward single-person households has been described as the most significant demographic trend of the twentieth century, and the change has been so marked that it's given rise to its own mini-industries in publishing and legal advocacy. On one hand, how-to manuals such as *Living Alone and Loving It* and *Living the Good Life Alone* have emerged to champion the state of the "ever-single," stressing that those who live alone have the luxury of complete control over their personal lives. On the other hand, singles' rights advocates have appeared to argue that being single is so fraught with discrimination that the state ought to be seen as analogous to being black or being gay.

These ideas are rather contradictory, and they capture the ambivalence we feel about the shift toward single living. The how-to manuals are all about completeness, about the fact that solo living doesn't constitute a state of emotional deprivation. "My friends see me as a family," states the author of an article about facing life crises, such as cancer diagnoses, while living alone. The word *family*—whether applied to people or to the classification of plants—means "more than one," and the fact that the term is being stretched to cover those who are on their own shows how much spadework is being done to make aloneness seem like an agreeable, familiar state. While there's no doubt that many people flourish alone—Anita Brookner's beautiful *Hotel du Lac*, which features an imaginative woman turning down an offer of marriage so that she can keep on with the writing and solitude she loves, is probably the finest testament to the single life ever created—the majority of people can be said to "choose" to live alone only in the sense of having adapted to it. In 2005, Unilever—a corporation that needs to understand social patterns in order to effectively develop and market its products—commissioned a study looking at why people were living alone. Its findings showed that only 27 percent of the people surveyed had actively chosen aloneness over other options. The majority of people in the study had been forced into aloneness through divorce, bereavement, a shortage of friends, or the departure of a child.

The singles' rights movement, with its emphasis on generalized unfairness, comes closer to matching how many single dwellers actually feel about their situation. Singles' rights advocates such as Bella DePaulo have devoted entire books to the supposed prejudice, stereotyping, and discrimination attaching to the state of singleness, calling it "singlism" (to make it rhyme with racism or sexism). The argument about singles being discriminated against is rather confused. It swallows up issues, such as same-sex and common-law rights, that have nothing to do with singleness; it betrays a weird lack of awareness about the real, sometimes life-threatening discrimination faced by blacks and gays; and it's hard to see how legal protection can be extended to a state (unlike gender or race) that people are constantly moving in and out of.

A lot of the concern about the "unfairness" and "stigma" attaching to singleness is really a displaced concern about loneliness. "Something odd happens when people notice someone who is single," writes DePaulo. "Their mind leaps immediately to notions of loneliness. In fact, *alone* is often used as a stand-in for *lonely*." Much of the "rights" work being done today is really a concerted lobby effort against the notion of single individuals as lonely individuals. But studies show that people living alone really are more likely to be lonely than those who live in larger households. In a survey conducted by the National Institute of Mental Health in the late 1970s, for instance, the loneliness rate was roughly 10 to 20 percent higher among those who were living by themselves, and academics working in the field are quick to recognize how hard it can be for people outside of families and partnerships to make and maintain social ties. "If you're someone who's never married," says Oxford's Ceridwen Roberts, "or you're a divorced man, and your children have moved away, and you don't have a good relationship with them anyhow, because of the nature of the divorce, and you're living in a small flat somewhere in a town where you go somewhere else to work—how the *heck* do you make links unless you are very proactive in joining sports clubs, or choirs, or hobby groups of some sort? It does become quite difficult."

Statements such as Roberts's are hard to find in the singles' rights literature, which trips over itself in an effort to stress that aloneness doesn't equal loneliness. While this might be true for some—especially the young—it's certainly not true for others. The oddest thing about the singles' rights movement is that it's emerged at a time when loneliness is becoming more of a problem, only to position itself firmly against the notion that loneliness *is* a problem. Instead of arguing that loneliness should be viewed as a critical issue in people's lives, the movement has premised itself on the notion that loneliness doesn't exist. It's done this out of desire for mainstream acceptance, but in shoving loneliness to the sidelines, it's undercut its own argument. Perhaps the only reason that people living alone need to be treated differently is that their lives really *are* harder than those

with close family ties, but—with loneliness denied—it's hard
to make this argument, and without a foundation, the whole
notion of recognizing singletons as a special class falls apart.

One of the reasons that loneliness is a real problem among
those who live alone—and even among those who live in small
households with only one other person—is that these living ar-
rangements offer little in the way of what sociologists call "passive company." Passive company is something that's hard to
define but easy to recognize. It's the comfortable, quiet state of
cooking as your spouse reads the paper at the kitchen table, or
half-listening from the study while your brother takes a call in
the living room. Passive company provides us with the chance
to simply be with someone else. It's time, as Glenn Stalker puts
it, "when nothing much is being said."

What's emerged over the past few decades, as family size has
whittled itself down to ones and twos, is an increased emphasis
on "active socializing"—scheduling a get-together at a café,
making dinner plans at a restaurant, or attending a sports event
at the local arena. This means that while the number of people
within the home has collapsed, scheduled dates out with others
have actually increased. They've increased *because* we're alone
more often. As we find ourselves increasingly on our own, we
try to offset that aloneness by setting up get-togethers with
others. When Stalker crunched the numbers on Canadians' lei-
sure time, for instance, he found that time out at public meeting
spots such as cafés and restaurants had increased by 4 percent
over ten years.

Active socializing might be perfectly enjoyable—there's
nothing wrong with indulging in a high-fat latte with a
friend—but there are a few problems associated with it. First,
the shift toward active socializing will inevitably exclude those
who don't have any discretionary income, and who can't afford

not just a high-end latte but even a coffee at a greasy spoon. When researchers with the Department for Works and Pensions in the United Kingdom surveyed 7,350 low-income families and asked them whether they could afford outings or meals with friends even once a month, a fifth of the respondents said no. Inevitably, as poverty rates increase, the growing economic disparity will be matched by a growing social disparity. If socializing is moving beyond the home, it's those with disposable incomes who are going to be able to keep up with social contacts. The increasing numbers of people who find themselves in financial straits might discover that their economic problems are compounded by social ones. Individuals facing bankruptcy, especially those who live alone, might find themselves without the resources they need to stay in touch with others.

Second, even if one imagines that finances aren't an issue, the gradual shift toward active socializing isn't going to affect everyone in the same way. Unlike passive socializing—where all you have to do is sit at the kitchen table—the ability to pursue and enjoy active socializing is going to depend on a host of variables. It's going to involve, says Stalker, "people's network structures, and the opportunities they have in their social world, and their own psychological predispositions—how easy it is for them to engage in relationships, and introversion, extroversion—all of those sorts of issues." There's going to be a certain sort of person, in other words, who might have perfectly good social skills but who has a hard time with active socializing—maybe they don't know enough people, or they aren't interested in another coffee date, or they'd just rather stay home.

"I can *meet people*," says James, the engineer, impatiently, thinking of all the times people have told him to join a group or volunteer at the library. What lonely people want isn't yet another cocoa with whipped cream, but rather a sense of connection that's present, lasting, and strong. Many of the lonely people I spoke to didn't want what Beatrice—the lawyer who was already working around the clock—called the "second job" of having to socialize. "When I make plans," says Adam, the illustrator, picking up on the labor theme and explaining the problem, "it's not difficult to do, but it's *work*. You're getting on the phone, arranging things, and it's like, 'How about three weeks from Thursday?' and all of that. And I just want something to be *not work*."

There can also be a strange, Möbius-strip aspect to active socializing. Even though it's supposed to lead to a sense of connection, the limited nature of the outings can create a feeling of dissatisfaction that the lonely person can only respond to by setting up more dates. "There's lots of times I don't want to do it," says Adam, referring to the dinner and coffee dates he goes on. "You're sort of beating your head against the wall. Because I think I'm doing it with this diffuse goal in mind that it's going to lead to *not* having to do it, but it never does."

Part of the reason that active socializing can feel so tiring is that, just as it's become more common, the nature of the companionship we can expect to find when we're out has changed. The U.S. General Social Survey asks people in America who they discuss important matters with. The question is seen as a workable proxy for intimacy and confidence sharing—people named in response to the question tend to be those with whom you have strong, intimate ties. When researchers asked the question in 1985, most of the Americans polled could name three or more people with whom they discussed important matters. When the survey was readministered in 2004, the average number of people named in response to the question was close to *zero*. Twenty-five percent of the respondents reported that they discussed intimate matters with *no one*. Another 19 percent discussed personal matters with only one other person. These findings suggest that almost half of the U.S. population now completely lacks a confidant, or is only one person away from having no one to confide in. The healthy confidant networks that used to exist in the 1980s—when a third of the population had four or more people to share their worries and concerns with—have shrunk to a meager 15 percent, meaning that having a wide confidant network is now less likely than having a high salary.

To make their point about the diminishing depth of people's emotional lives, the sociologists who crunched the 2004 data, Miller McPherson and Lynn Smith-Lovin of Duke University, made up a standard person, someone they described as "a white, married, 25-year-old male high school graduate." In 1985 this person—let's call him Jim—would be "virtually assured of a discussion partner." When they aged Jim by nineteen years, however, they found that "his probability of being an isolate would have quintupled." Twenty-five years ago, we were statistically likely to have close confidants. Today, we're statistically likely not to.

"I was just torn apart today," says Katherine, referring to a fight she'd had with her partner, whom she describes having a slightly distant relationship with. "I was just thinking about all the stuff going on, and feeling like I was about to fall apart, and trying to keep my focus at work, and just thinking, 'God, there is *no one* I can talk to about this.' "

We tend not to hear admissions such as Katherine's very often. This is in part because lonely people hide the fact they don't have confidants. Claire, who had recently moved to a new town, remembers someone asking her directly whether she had close connections in the area. "And at the time I knew a few people," she says. "I didn't know them very well, but I said, 'Oh, sure. I have a couple of close people who I know.' And that wasn't really true. I knew them, but I wouldn't really say we were close. I just sort of overembellished to seem less lonely."

Many of us feel the need to overembellish because the ideal in our society is a whispery one, one in which we all have plenty of opportunities for sharing and support. In fact, ours has been described as a "confessional culture," one in which we've supposedly dropped the tasteful civility that prevails in Jane Austen novels, and have become likely to disclose secrets on national television. The people I went to law school with loved to make fun of these sorts of shows, in which strangers would present their innermost feelings and most formative experiences to the camera. The words my friends used to describe these appearances were *vulgar* and *tacky*, as in, "What sort of person goes on *Oprah* and talks about running over their nephew? That's so unbelievably tacky." It didn't occur to my law school friends, or to me, when I smiled in agreement, that the people appearing on the shows might not have anyone else to confide in, or that the people watching the shows might not be hearing confidences from anyone else. The idea of Oprah Winfrey serving as a sort of multipurpose confidant is distressing, but it's probably wrong to see the popularity of such shows as a sign of creeping moral decay or uniquely modern bad judgment.

My law school friends—the ones who were happy to stop in the middle of a discussion of tort law and gleefully poke fun at talk shows—never seemed to notice that they were, in a sense, doing exactly the same thing as the people they were deriding, only they were doing it in private, and they weren't getting a free trip to Chicago out of the deal. If the people of middle America had Oprah, my relatively upscale classmates had therapists and counselors—people they paid for the chance to confide in and ask for assistance. In some senses, my classmates were on the edge of what sociologists such as Stanford University's Arlie Russell Hochschild call the "commodity frontier," or the edge of the commercial as it begins to slice its way into the personal.

It used to be that we paid for goods—a bar of soap, spiffy new shoes—but what we're increasingly paying for are services, and what those services are increasingly aimed at is the interior of our private life. Throughout my years of loneliness, I found myself constantly shelling out. I paid a massage therapist to touch me, and I paid Genevieve for her undivided attention. I paid for interaction at stores, where clerks had to talk to me, I paid my naturopath, and I even thought about paying a psychic to tell me how long my loneliness might last (though I never actually did this).

I sometimes got angry about the fact that sociability was being linked to cash. In the summer of 2005, after I'd left my job and found myself swamped with aloneness, I decided I needed a break. Reading and writing about loneliness could only take me so far. I needed sociability in *some* form. To this end, I decided to head to a huge bookstore about a mile from my house. Once I was out in the shopping district, I went to a record store, and a natural food store, and a hair supply place. I bought a book, an Emmylou Harris CD, and a new supply of jojoba oil. As I walked home, I noticed that the conversations I'd had with cashiers had eased my loneliness somewhat, but I also began to feel oddly stressed. When I got back to my apartment, I put my bags down and picked up one of the light wooden chairs that circled my kitchen table. Without thinking, I threw the chair as hard as I could against the opposite wall. Partly, I was overheated—the temperature in my apartment must have been close to 90 degrees—but I was also enraged by the fact that all the interaction I'd had access to had been commercial in nature. I felt used, as though the stores had somehow taken advantage of a terrible vulnerability on my part. Too humiliated to unpack my things, or listen to my new CD, I sat cross-legged in the empty spot where the chair should have been, and then tried to calm down by lying flat on my back and focusing on the coolness of the floor against my bare legs and arms.

Researchers such as Hochschild stress that whole areas of our lives have become open to commercial intervention. Not only are we increasingly paying for the privilege of interaction, but private functions—such as organizing birthday parties, taking care of the elderly, removing clutter, and babysitting children—are being partly or largely taken over by the market. As the market begins to intrude on what sociologists call the home or "moral" economy, we're left with less that's strictly personal. The less we're left with, the more likely we are to turn to the market in an attempt to fill the gap. Smart marketers already understand the symbiotic relationship between loneliness and the commercial sphere. In a recent issue of *Psychology & Marketing*, two authors remind store owners that many people at malls are there because they're lonely. Because of this, and in order to maximize sales, merchants are to highlight the personal (cue the homey sofas and friendly baristas at Starbucks) and downplay the real goal, which is the sale of goods for cash. With the market having delved into the more private reaches of our personal lives, we're left with a situation in which our ties might *look* the same as they did fifty years ago, but *feel* quite different. Connections might remain in place, but there might be less heart and content to them. The culture overall, stress academics such as Hochschild, might become "cooler," offering us more chances to buy things, but fewer chances to connect.

And it's important to note that the market, which is gradually closing in on what used to be considered "personal," is quite rapidly eating away at the natural world. Over the course of just the last thirty-five years, populations of marine and terrestrial species have declined by a rate of about 30 percent. A conservative estimate of the extinction rate pegs it at about 800 species a day, or 27,000 species a year, with many estimates suggesting that *half* of the plants and animals in the world will be gone by the year 2100.

It may seem odd to drop an endangered pine marten into a discussion of loneliness, and this is because we usually conceptualize the state as a gap or shortcoming in interpersonal relations—we see it as a state of lacking intimacy with the people around us. While this definition is no doubt accurate, it can't be said to be exhaustive. When I was intensely lonely, I sometimes used to borrow my sister's bike and head down to a big, almost entirely unfrequented park that jutted out into Lake Ontario. The "spit," as it was known, was home to a few truly hardened homeless people, but also to red foxes, cormorants, Canada geese, and rabbits. I could bike for an hour or so, and stop to stare at spiderwebs, foraging ducklings, and the thousands of gulls that rested on a long strip of land near the water. I found that whenever I did this—when I stopped to really look at the world around me—my loneliness would abate. This wasn't just because I was managing to distract myself from my problems and pump myself up with exercise. It was because the natural world was providing me with a sense of connection.

There's an idea within environmentalism known as "biophilia," and it means that we're innately and emotionally linked to other living creatures. And this sense of connection—which has developed over millions of years of interacting with other species—means that, as the world around us begins to thin out and suffer, we're going to begin to feel the gaps in our own lives.

Biophilia is essentially the emotional counterpart to biological arguments about a healthy environment being necessary for us to breathe properly, and to drink what we need, and to grow the crops we rely on. Without species diversity, environmental psychologists warn, we'll necessarily feel more alone. It's for this reason that E. O. Wilson, a Harvard professor who is one of the world's leading conservationists, has described ours as the "Age of Loneliness." He's not speaking metaphorically. He means that, as we continue to let species perish, we're inevitably going to feel more isolated and bereft in the world they've left behind. With loneliness conceptualized in this reasonable way—as a state that reflects, at least in part, our ties to the world around us—it's impossible to think that the extinction rate can climb upward while the loneliness rate remains unchanged. Environmental losses will translate into personally felt absences. What's different about environmental loss is its quiet nature. There's no one storming out, no one slamming a door or leaving a hastily written note. Rather, extinction is a gradual, perpetual, and silent good-bye—a disappearance we might not even notice until we start to feel empty, and then notice that the world we're living in has become quieter, less vivid, and a lot more lonely.

Species are perhaps the most obvious indicator of loss. It's relatively easy to estimate species diversity over time and then calculate what's gone missing. It's slightly harder to do this with personal relationships, but the same overall pattern of a slow vanishing appears if you compare sociability levels from the 1970s to those of today. Compared to thirty or forty years ago, we're spending more time alone, seeing less of our friends and family, spending more time at work, losing confidants at a greater rate, glorifying aloneness, and allowing the commercial to slowly undermine the personal.

What's important to note about many of these changes is that they're invisible—while the rise in single-person households might be evident, the slow climb in time spent alone generally isn't. And the invisibility of much isolation means that the highly sociable world the media presents us with can start to seem true. Because, everywhere one looks today, one finds representations of a close and easily achieved togetherness. The whole time that I was lonely, I was routinely presented with images of sociability, with Brad and Angelina leading their big brood of children through a playground, or Tom Cruise and Katie Holmes holding up little Suri for the cameras. These images of togetherness had a pronounced effect on me. Namely, they made me feel as though my isolation was strange and exceptional.

"I try to avoid it," says Rachel, the homemaker from Florida, referring to pop culture. "But I can't. I watch TV, I look at magazines, I read the paper. And you'll always hear about some supermom who has a huge network of friends, and she's running in the breast cancer marathon with about twenty friends, and it's sort of like . . ." Rachel stops, sighs heavily, and pauses before starting again. "I'll rationalize it. When I think of it with an intelligent mind, I'll ask, 'Does it even matter if I have friends or not?' But at an emotional level, I'll think, 'What's *wrong* with me?' "

"It doesn't fit," agrees Sonia, the copywriter, describing her experience of isolation. "It doesn't fit with society, it doesn't fit with how we're supposed to be." My own aloneness had precisely this effect on me: it made me feel like some sort of emotional throwback. Even though I was in many ways the archetypal twenty-first-century citizen—litigious, vegetarian, worried about trees—my loneliness made me feel like a nineteenth-century shepherd or eighteenth-century lighthouse keeper. My state didn't seem to fit within a world that prided itself on twenty-four-hour communication, instant messaging, and speed dates. I grew lonelier and lonelier in a culture that suggested connection had never before been so easy to come by.

It took me some time to realize that the displays of togetherness I was being subjected to were more smoke screen than fact. It was the late, great Susan Sontag who noted that images of something will proliferate just as the real object begins to disappear. An image, Sontag stressed, can "exorcise some of the anxiety and remorse" we feel about an object's disappearance; it can keep something alive as an idea even as it begins to disappear in reality.

If you want to test the truth of Sontag's remark, consider the number of polar bears that have sprouted up recently—sliding down snowbanks in Coke ads, or posing as stuffed toys, or playing leading roles in films such as *Arctic Tale*. Just as the number of real bears collapses—there are now fewer than 15,000 bears in the Canadian Arctic, and numbers are expected to drop by 75 percent in the next fifty years—images of them have multiplied, making it seem as though populations are more vibrant and healthier than they really are.

A similar reversal effect is currently at work with images of connection and sociability. Just as confidant networks have shrunk, we've been exposed to images of rich social ties. As households have become increasingly inhabited by just one person, we've been presented—via everything from commercials to cooking shows—with images of big, intergenerational families. What's important to recognize is that isolation is one of the factors driving these representations. As we start to feel more alone, we're being comforted with images of what we've lost. But these representations of togetherness—while in some ways alluring—can be confusing. They can leave the lonely person convinced that loneliness is not a pervasive problem, and that it's their own emotional excesses that are to blame for the state. I was struck, in my talks with lonely people, at how many of them pointed to something being wrong with their *needs*. "I think my level of connection might be too much for others," says Adam, the illustrator, referring to what he sees as an "inappropriate" need for others, one so pronounced it's somehow unsuitable. "I think I have stronger needs than I'd ever admit," agrees Rachel, adding that she doesn't want the depth of her needs to become known for fear of looking "weak."

When the culture we're living in succeeds in portraying itself as socially abundant—there are, after all, all those Internet dates you can go on, and the high school friends you can look up on Facebook, and the people you can contact through Meetup.com—then the problem of loneliness emerges as an individual failing. The difficulty becomes not the fact that our needs aren't being met, but rather the nature of those needs in the first place. Within this context, the lonely person emerges as the one who needs "too much," who can never be satisfied, and who can't seem to get by on the minimum others seem to accept. While Cacioppo has noted that the lonely person might actually need a lot of contact, he hasn't remotely suggested that there's anything wrong with this need. On the contrary, Cacioppo—and most other social psychologists—stress that our need for others is basic, something as fundamental, unexceptional, and unquestionable as our need to sleep or eat.

What our culture has done is make lonely people see their own needs as problematic, when the real problem lies in our culture's diminishing ability to meet those needs. We're currently being asked to make do with less and less. There's the solitary households we're supposed to adapt to, and the shifting workplaces we're being asked to accept. There's the growing number of hours alone and the gradual disappearance of both confidants and species. And just as these absences in our lives become insurmountable—as we become lonely—we're encouraged to internalize those feelings of absence through blaming the self.

"I often wonder if my loneliness is the result of something that's wrong with me," says Ray, the fundraiser, rather hesitantly, as he casts around for a way to explain the state. "I'll wonder whether the problem is me, and as a result, I'll just think, 'Maybe no one wants to spend time with me.' "

Loneliness and isolation are not nearly as exceptional as the media would have us believe. Whichever rate you go with— the U.S. rate of 25 percent, the British rate of 29 percent, or the Australian rate of 33 percent—you're left with the fact that about a quarter to a third of the population struggles with loneliness on either a long- or short-term basis. And the data showing growing rates of loneliness among today's elderly suggests that the problem is getting not better but worse.

As I noted in chapter 6, it might be argued that our culture isn't getting *lonelier*, it's just connecting in a different way. Gone, this argument goes, are the time-consuming lunch dates and family birthday parties. In their place are neat, highly personalized, and convenient updates on Facebook. Even if we're seeing less of people, some suggest, we've never been so endlessly available: never before has a child alone in hospital been able to connect with a whole host of similarly ill children in similar hospitals all around the world, just by hitting the on switch of her computer.

Findings on loneliness and technology are inconsistent. Some individuals say that adding people as "friends" on social net-working sites leaves them feeling more connected. Others, like many of the lonely people I spoke to, say it leaves them feeling worse, or at best makes no difference. Digital technology and Internet connections likely ally themselves with the way a mind is already tilted. To the victor, in a sense, will go the spoils, with the nonlonely reaping more benefits from such sites than the lonely. "It just feels like an individual thing, where you're by yourself, in a big pool," says Milton, a lonely engineering drafter from Ontario, describing his time on Facebook in the same terms that he uses to describe his off-line relationships.

The best description of Internet "relationships" I've ever seen is that offered by the psychologist Kenneth Gergen, who describes them as "absent presences." Someone might say that they're a part of your life if they e-mail you, or if you can read about them on MySpace, but this is a long way from having someone literally on hand. To state the obvious: you can't cry on a digital shoulder, you can't hold a digital hand, you can't take comfort in a presence that isn't actually there. As humans, we're hardwired to seek out a sense of togetherness and com-munity, and it's unlikely that Internet communications can satisfy this need. If you're staring down a lion, what you need are other people on hand with tranquilizer guns. The fact that someone might be sending encouragements on their Black-Berry doesn't really cut it.

Many commentators, such as the sociologist Zygmunt Bauman, have noted that we're in the midst of an uncontrolled experiment on the effects of new technology, and that some as-pects of this technology will likely undermine our intimate ties. It's not possible, says Bauman, to enjoy the ease, brevity, rela-tive anonymity, and selectivity that technology offers, and not come to value these same principles off-line as well. Someone who loves the simplicity of disconnecting a "friend" on Facebook might come to resent the complexity of real friendship. Someone who loves the short, stripped, and slightly impersonal nature of communication on social networking sites might start to find real communication—with its pain, depth, and complexities—an unnecessary drag.

Sociologists such as Miller McPherson and Lynn Smith-Lovin, who analyzed the 2004 U.S. General Social Survey data on our declining social ties, point specifically to the Internet as a possible reason for the drop. The Internet, they say, allows us to create networks that aren't tied to place, but it reduces the likelihood of (and need for) face-to-face visits with family and friends. One thing that is clear is that the Internet—with its endlessly trumpeted ability to transcend geographical space and link us in previously impossible ways—hasn't reduced loneliness rates. Although the studies in question are admittedly difficult to compare, the loneliness rate has likely risen from the mid-1960s to the present day, and this is the case despite the fact that we've been able to avail ourselves of the Internet. Some researchers would say that it's risen in part *because* of the Internet. Others would simply say that the Internet has, despite the claims being made for it, done little to increase our sense of social cohesion.

I don't know if our era is the loneliest ever, and such sweeping historical comparisons—even if they could be constructed—are probably not very meaningful. What matters about loneliness today is that it's hard to pin down. I'm feeling very, very cautious about what I'm about to say, but when someone like Tolkien writes, "By 1918, all but one of my close friends were dead," he's pointing not just to the experience of isolation but to the reason for it. Previous generations were certainly lonely, but they were also able to externalize the state. There were the huge migrations to point to, the dust-bowl relocations, the terrible wars. Loneliness in previous eras didn't present the problem of dissonance—it didn't seem like a state that didn't make sense.

It's our own era that's made loneliness seem out of place and exceptional, like an emotion that doesn't add up. The period we're living in is interesting in that it's the first that's been able, through the media, to obscure the real extent of isolation and loneliness. It might be argued that the media has always been obsessed with images of sociability, but those images are working differently today. For at least the last four decades, togetherness has been portrayed against a backdrop of growing isolation: after all, what I did when I was alone as a child was try to take comfort from the togetherness presented on *Gilligan's Island*. We're growing more alone, and lonelier, in the face of representations—on television, in the movies, and in magazines—concerned with close and convenient togetherness, and in the face of assertions—usually from Yahoo and MSN Messenger—that it's never before been so easy to get and remain in touch.

And those images and messages are confusing. They inevitably make us wonder what it is about our own lives that's leaving us so exceptionally lonely. We're left clouded and unclear. Even if we tell ourselves—as I actively did—that the ties on *The L Word* are as fictional as those in *The Hobbit*, it's hard to shake the sensation that we ourselves are somehow uniquely out of step.

It's time we expanded the lens on loneliness and began recognizing the ways in which our culture is vastly more lonely than it tends to admit. A person who feels lonely today may very well have a genetic tendency toward the state, but he's also living in an environment that's more likely to trigger the tendency in question. At a time when we're being told that our needs are being met and that sociability is easy to achieve, we need to recognize a more complex truth. This truth involves us being alone more, confiding less, and getting caught up in the wheel of active socializing. Loneliness today is being egged on and aggravated by culture. It's probably time we saw this, and stopped portraying the state as something that's somehow the lonely person's fault.

Chapter Eight

TABOO

---

*Loneliness as the state you're
not supposed to name*

In the spring of 2006, as I was sketching the first outlines of what would become this book, I was walking from the library to a nearby subway stop. Tucked against my chest schoolgirl style were a number of books on loneliness, including some of my early favorites: *Loneliness and Love, Conquering Loneliness, Loneliness and Spiritual Growth.* Up ahead I saw Colin, an athletically built and slightly giddy prof who'd taught me tax law in school. I'd always liked Colin, and he'd always liked me. I admired him for his open enthusiasm about teaching, and he'd warmed to me for something of the reverse: I never had a clue what was going on in tax law, and my obvious hopelessness must have been endearing; he was always very nice to me.

So it was pleasant to see him there on the path. We stopped to talk, and when I told him I'd started writing a book, he voiced a reasonable question that I was to hear countless times in the coming years.

"So," he asked, as we stood beside a chestnut tree, "what are you writing about?"

I've since gotten used to the question—I've come to predict it—but I think that moment on the path was the first time anyone had asked it of me. I'm a terrible liar, and have never been quick on my feet, and these shortcomings meant that, when I was confronted with Colin's question, I blushed a sharp red and began to stammer.

"Oh, nothing," I said, somewhat illogically.

"No, really," he continued, not seeming to notice how flustered I'd become. "What's it about?"

"I can't tell you," I replied, cringing at a response that sounded so openly childish.

He laughed, and reached for one of the books I was holding. I had a vision of Colin glancing from a title—*Loneliness*—to me, and back again. Not being able to stand the thought of Colin gaining insight into what I was still thinking of as "my problem," I pulled back, and we fell into a short, ungainly struggle. From a distance, I probably looked like I was being mugged. Realizing how absurd the situation had become, we both stepped back, flushed and embarrassed.

"I'll send you a copy when it's done," I said, trying to sound, despite our recent scuffle, queerly carefree and professional.

"Sure," he said, backing away uncomfortably. "Just let me know."

As I continued down the path, panting slightly, I told myself, actually shaking my head back and forth, *That can't happen again.* By the time I reached the subway, I realized I needed a strategy. The quickest solution—tell people the truth—seemed obvious, but I couldn't bring myself to do this. Admitting to the subject of my book meant admitting to loneliness, and outside of Genevieve's consulting room, admitting to loneliness still seemed to mean opening up my personality to wide-ranging scrutiny and dismissal. It didn't seem as though I could admit to loneliness and remain myself. Naming long-term loneliness as a problem seemed poised to turn me, in the eyes of others, into someone dowdier, dour, more dull-witted. It was as though I couldn't admit to loneliness and remain the high-achieving, more or less acceptable, and reasonably cute person people generally perceived me to be.

Part of the problem confronting me might have been that, as a friend of mine once commented, I suffered from a slight case of golden girl complex. Since life had been so kind to me, I felt the need to return its generosity by being mildly perfect, and guilt overwhelmed me the moment I had to confront shortcomings other people saw as mundane. The "golden girl" hypothesis that had been spelled out to me in the law school cafeteria was in many ways an attractive theory, since it meant that all of the problems attaching to the word *loneliness*—the way it made me feel stressed and embarrassed and slightly out of control—were entirely my fault, and flowed from some misguided sense of myself as flawless.

The difficulty with seeing my silence in this light was that I readily admitted to other things. I'd been admitting to depression for years, and—while I tended not to bring the subject up—the topic didn't make me stammer or blush. I could rhyme off the mood's symptoms, list the various antidepressants I'd swallowed, and provide the name and address of the psychiatrist I'd seen. Even more significantly, I'd told people I was *gay*. If there's anything that's famously hard to admit to, it's homosexuality. But after I came out at thirty-five—using fictional characters such as those in *Oranges Are Not the Only Fruit* and *Dykes to Watch Out For* as substitutes for the social circle I would have otherwise defined myself against—I found

I didn't really have many problems spitting the words out. "No, I don't date men," I'd say, matter-of-factly. "I'm 'that way.'" Now, being gay is something that some people will judge you for. It's still, in some circles, seen as proof of moral corrosion, something guaranteed to earn you a place in some grade-school vision of hell. And the odd thing was that none of this—not the hysterical campaigns against gay marriage or the subtle linkage of homosexuality with infection—bothered me in the least. My usual response, when I saw another piece against civil unions, was to flip the page and stare out the window, my attention already on something else.

So, while I'll admit to some degree of golden girl complex, it's not monolithic. There are other states—depression, anxiety, homosexuality—that I'll freely admit to. I don't simply bow down before negative evaluations. On the contrary, I'm usually able to put a healthy degree of distance between myself and whatever generally held belief or misconception I'm being exposed to.

The problem with loneliness is that it seemed, and continues to seem, somewhat different from the things I'm able to discuss. There's a concept in law called "sui generis," and it means that an idea has to be treated separately, even if it seems quite similar to other ideas. (It's in this way that the Native American interest in land is sui generis—something that differs from the non-Native interest, even if we're talking about a single piece of land.) It seems to me that loneliness has emerged as a sui generis emotion. Even though it bears a similarity to depression and a resemblance to grief, it has to be hidden more, suppressed more aggressively, and discussed less often. I'm willing to accept that I might have had some unique problems in admitting to loneliness, but I've talked to too many lonely people with similar worries to see my concerns as mine alone. For the vast majority of people I spoke to, the mere possibility of their loneliness becoming known made them anxious. Although I knew the real identities of the people I was talking to, my promise to camouflage these identities was critical. With one or two exceptions (in both cases, where someone had overcome their loneliness), no one would have spoken to me if their real name were to be disclosed.

I've come to think that concerns about being known to be lonely are as central to the experience of loneliness as is the feeling of disconnection. That is, people struggling with a sense of isolation feel pressured to keep the fact of that isolation to themselves. In some senses, it's easy for lonely people to do this. We've worked so hard to eliminate the stigmas attaching to depression, social anxiety, and even bipolar disorder that we don't notice we've left loneliness behind. So much ink has been spilled about the need to not *judge* the depressed or socially anxious person, and to not see emotional problems as indexes of flawed characters, that many people don't notice that these misconceptions—mood as character flaw, the sufferer as somehow *off*—are still alive and well when it comes to loneliness. Loneliness is still judged harshly in our society, and it's the trick of balancing this judgment against their own experience that lonely people have to confront at every turn. The lonely, in other words, have to do battle not just with their state, but with the very loud and widely communicated sense that there's something wrong with them for feeling it in the first place.

One of the more fixed ideas about loneliness is that it's something glaring and obvious about a person, something as easy to detect as weight or hair color. The general notion is that we can tell if someone's lonely just by looking at him, or—if the situation really can't be avoided—by spending time with him. "The lonely tend to project a demeanor and aura that repels people," says one online therapist. "After all, who wants to hang out with a lonely person?" Presumably no one, because, in addition to being repellent, the lonely are, in the words of one scholar, writing in *Canadian Counsellor*, "more impatient with others' mistakes, more self-seeking and sarcastic, more often unfriendly, and more frequently outspoken and angry."

Loneliness, in other words, is something that we can supposedly spot about someone—all we have to do is look for the negative aura, or the anger, or the unfriendliness. These traits have a strange stickiness to them. They can attach to a lonely person overtly, and emerge as a defining aspect of her character, as in (as one self-help book puts it), "The personality she presented was that of a whining, self-centred, lonely person." Alternatively, they can have nothing to do with how the lonely person is actually behaving, but persist regardless. When I told an acquaintance that I was interviewing lonely people, he replied that the calls must be complete downers.

"No," I said, quite honestly. I'd grown so used to enjoying my talks with lonely people that I'd briefly forgotten about stereotypes. "Everyone's pretty cheerful."

"Of *course* they're cheerful," he replied, laughing at the witticism I belatedly saw coming. "They've finally got someone to talk to!"

The lame joke was one I couldn't quite dismiss. Although I didn't say so, I was struck by the way my acquaintance's comment aligned with research that was coming out of Keele University in England. Ken Rotenberg has shown that if someone is told that their conversational partner is lonely, they'll behave in more remote and antisocial ways, regardless of how sociable the "lonely" person is actually being. That is, the stereotype of loneliness is more powerful than overt behavior, since the behavior in question—cheerfulness, curiosity, charm—can simply be fed back into the stereotype. *Of course they're positive, they're desperately trying to make friends.* Or, *Of course they're trying to sound interesting, they want to draw your attention to them.*

The fact that the stereotype about lonely people can override overt behavior means that ideas about lonely people can become, in their own way, detached from reality. They can start to refer not to the characteristics lonely people actually exhibit, but rather to the characteristics others *think* they should exhibit. In experiments, for instance, subjects have been provided with the following description of a lonely person:

> *Michelle is a freshman in college. She chose an out-of-state college because it offered the major she wanted. She was assigned to live in a large dorm in which she knew no one. Michelle envies and admires others in her dorm who seem to have no difficulty finding friends. She feels isolated with no one to talk to or share her ups and downs with. She watches TV, goes to classes, and attends a movie occasionally, but she pretty much keeps to herself.*

When people at Purdue University and Lakehead University were asked to describe the person in question, the terms that emerged were: *unintelligent, unsuccessful, passive, unattractive, uncoordinated, insincere.* These traits seem to flow naturally from the portrait of isolation, but the description hasn't actually commented on any of them. We don't know what Michelle looks like, or how smart she is, or how well she can throw a ball. But as soon as an observer is provided with information about her loneliness, they *think* they know all these things.

And this means that loneliness possesses the classic properties of a stigma: knowledge of one aspect of a person's life—in this case, a sense of isolation—tips over like a pot of coffee and stains everything else, such as looks, personality, and charm. There's a blotting-out function that attaches to stigmas: a trait goes from being an aspect of personality to something that engulfs the personality as a whole.

Stigmas are problematic because they feed into stereotype. That is, we go from *feeling* a certain way about someone to *thinking* a certain way about them. And loneliness is interesting and possibly unique in that it gives rise to two distinct and contradictory stereotypes, depending on the gender of the lonely person. Lonely men tend to attract a particularly brutal response, and that's because they're associated with a particularly disturbing set of ideas.

"How does the gunman get described by the family next door?" asks Adam, the illustrator from Rhode Island, sounding frustrated at the ideas stacked up against him. "A loner. *Inevitably*, he's a loner." I've looked at what are probably hundreds of loneliness papers, and I haven't seen anything linking loneliness to violence. In fact, John Cacioppo, in an offhand comment, notes that it's probably people who *don't* feel lonely who are likely to become sociopaths, largely because they don't have any need for others. It's people who never struggle with loneliness, he says, who are "kind of scary." The fact that no research or coherent theory supports the lonely-men-as-crazy hypothesis, however, doesn't stop those unfamiliar with the field from casting loneliness as something wildly threatening. In the *International Journal of Offender Therapy*, for example, two academics don't hesitate before attributing the surreal violence of Jeffrey Dahmer—who killed and dismembered his victims—to his supposed loneliness. "Dahmer's feelings of loneliness were so strong," the authors note, citing little in the way of evidence, "that his destructive fantasies . . . became reality." Similarly, in a notorious Ontario case involving the murder of a nine-year-old girl, the accused was wrongfully convicted in part because his neighbors felt he spent too much time alone—a sure sign, the court accepted, of risk and evil lurking within him.

The corrosiveness of the stereotype about lonely men— Watch out! They're like Jeffrey Dahmer!—probably accounts for the difference in disclosure that exists between men and women. When men are given the UCLA Loneliness Scale, which doesn't actually contain the word "loneliness," they test as slightly lonelier than women. When men are given direct measures of loneliness, however, such as, "To what extent is loneliness a problem in your life?" they test as less lonely. In other words, when it's a matter of naming loneliness as a problem, men are more likely to pretend that the state doesn't affect them, even if they're slightly more likely (on the basis of the UCLA Loneliness Scale) to suffer from it.

Women have a slightly easier time of it when it comes to loneliness, in that they aren't portrayed as ax-wielding maniacs. But the stereotype of the lonely woman is perhaps a little too tame and peaceful. If lonely men are presented as *too much*, lonely women are presented as the opposite. "It's someone sitting in her house with twenty-five cats and a rocking chair," says Anne, the social worker from Illinois. As she sketches out the stereotype of the lonely woman, she comes up with the exact image—an old lady alone with too many cats—that many other lonely people instantly hit on as well. I'm not sure about the cat angle (I know many cat lovers who are highly sociable people), but all of the really classic images of lonely women involve those who are dusty and old. There's Miss

Havisham in her wedding dress, Emily Dickinson in her later years, the famous Miss Eleanor Rigby (buried along with her name), and—in a lively enactment of the stereotype—Judi Dench in the hit movie *Notes on a Scandal*, in which she portrays someone aged and frozen with loneliness, who spends her time plotting the downfall of a younger, more sexually active and socially embedded friend.

A key point about stereotype and stigma—one that stereotype researchers like to stress—is that lonely people know the content of the stereotype. Just as Adam could instantly reach for the image of the gunman next door, lonely people *know* that others see the state in ways that are off-putting. "People have this image of lonely people," notes Rachel, the homemaker from Florida. "And it's that you want to stay away from them, because they're going to start becoming needy, and sort of cloying to you, and you're going to be expected to take over their social life. And that's not *true*," she emphasizes.

"I worried I'd seem needy and just unpleasant to be around," adds Frances, the physiotherapist from Missouri, explaining why she couldn't tell others about her loneliness. It was as though, in admitting to the state, she'd turn into a downer, into a problem others had to deal with. "It was that I'd just be a drain on their happiness, or their satisfaction, or whatever."

It's because lonely people know that they're going to be met with stereotypes—lonely person as needy, lonely person as cloying—that they keep the fact of their loneliness to themselves. "Even one-on-one with friends," stresses James, the Quebec engineer, who hasn't told anyone about a loneliness that has lasted for over a decade, "it's not something I'd discuss or even think of discussing. It's very much a pride thing.

It's kind of like, don't tell the neighbors we're having trouble. Don't show weakness."

"There's a stigma," agrees Claire, the financial services employee from Saskatchewan. "I'd be a bit embarrassed. I would feel a bit self-conscious, and sort of pitied. I wouldn't want others to have the knowledge that I'm suffering from chronic, long-term loneliness."

It's because lonely people don't want to be pitied or maligned that they actively deny that the state is a problem for them. Claire notes that she "absolutely" makes efforts to hide loneliness. "I'll sort of embellish. If I weren't out on a Saturday night, I'd say, 'Oh, I had too much work to do,' or I'd kind of make up some activity to make it sound like I was busy. Or if I went and talked to someone on the phone, I'd kind of embellish that a bit, and make it sound like I had more interaction than I actually did."

"Most people who know me wouldn't associate me with loneliness," stresses Trevor, the businessman from Minnesota, referring to the state that's been a problem since childhood. "They think I'm relaxed and easygoing. And when I'm with them, I am. But it's not the whole truth. I just know how to hide my loneliness really, really well."

In my case, even when the subject of loneliness was raised, I refused to name the state as a personal problem.

"We get really fucking lonely sometimes," said my friend Simon, one summer evening when I was over for a barbecue. His wife, Monique, was in the doorway, heading in to check on one of the kids, and she paused to nod in agreement. For a moment, I was surprised and confused. From the perspective of my single state, it didn't occur to me that happily married couples could *get* lonely. I quickly saw that the loneliness Simon was referring to was situational. He was talking about the loneliness of having his social circle submerged into that of his kids, of having other parents forced upon him, and of not having time for the people he used to socialize with. Simon had been a friend of mine since 1989—we met in front of a pop machine at our university—and the fact that he struggled with difficult moods and hard-to-realize ambitions made him empathic and easy to talk to. He wasn't one to pass judgment. But my loneliness seemed to differ from his—his was explicable, mine was not—and this made me hesitant to admit to it.

"Gotta get out more, my friend," I said casually, and Monique called from the doorway to say that if anyone needed more time out of the house, it was *her*. A swift little argument ensued about who spent more time caring for the kids, and I was relieved to be able to duck down into my seat, loneliness having dropped from its brief and sudden spot on the conversational radar.

Now, theoretically, lonely people—including myself—shouldn't be able to hide their state. If there were any truth to the stereotypes, the lonely should be caught out immediately—they'd be the aggressive ones, the frigid ones, the ones with the ax. But researchers who work with lonely people stress that the state is much easier to hide than we generally think. "Loneliness is an internal thing in a lot of ways," notes the University of North Carolina's Daniel Perlman, "so it might be hard for others to spot."

Many lonely people have had the experience of being met with surprise after finally outing themselves and admitting to loneliness. Several people who were planning on speaking to me used the fact of our impending conversation as a jumping-off point in telling others about the state. The response they tended to receive was one of flat-out disbelief.

"I had dinner with this friend last night," says Adam. "I was telling him about you, and the Craigslist ad, and I told him about being lonely, and he *laughed*. He said, '*You??*' And I said, 'Yes.' And I was trying to be very matter of fact about it, and he was still incredulous, like, 'Are you *serious?*' "

Rachel, who's been married for over a decade, decided—on the day before she spoke to me—to tell her husband about the loneliness that's been with her since childhood. "I disclosed it to him when I told him I was participating in this interview. And he was shocked. He was like, 'Huh? Really?' He didn't see it coming."

Even lonely people, who might be considered experts in identifying the state, can have trouble spotting it in others. "I had a friend come visit," says Rachel, "and she's younger than me, but she's never been married, and she has no children, and I was telling her about being lonely, and she said, 'Oh, I'm terribly lonely.' And I said, '*You?*' I mean, she has enough friends to fill a cruise ship. And I'm thinking, 'You're just agreeing with me.' But she said, 'No, I feel terribly alone, and terribly lonely, and I feel dread and panic when I think of it.' And I'm looking at her and thinking, *Really?*"

The reason loneliness is hard to spot is that it doesn't actually manifest itself in the ways we normally think of. If one were to take a cursory run through the Internet or self-help aisle, for instance, it wouldn't take long to construct the idea that the lonely are: sartorially challenged ("many lonely people dress in a drab, unexciting way"); horrible to be around ("demanding, critical, needy, ungrateful, boastful, nosey, stingy, and selfish"); fundamentally lacking drive ("lonely people are frequently lazy people"); and egocentric ("loneliness is, in large measure, related to an excessive concern with oneself").

Notions such as these are almost irresistible to researchers, because, if they were true, they'd make the entire phenomenon of loneliness easy to understand. If the lonely really could be shown to behave egregiously, their sense of emotional isolation would make sense. Simply put, no one would want to be around them. It's for this reason that many of the stereotypical notions about loneliness have been tested, invariably with counterintuitive results.

One way to assess the notion of the lonely as cold or critical, for instance, is to measure popularity. *Popularity* is a bubble-gum word, a high school measure of how acceptable someone is, but it's an interesting standard in loneliness research, largely because the stereotype of the lonely is that they're socially unacceptable. Lonely people themselves insist that popularity's not a problem. "My loneliness hasn't been because I don't have friends or social skills or anything like that," notes Frank, the freelance journalist. "I've always had a lot of close friends." Researchers in Finland have born Frank's assertion out. When psychologists at the University of Helsinki had participants in a co-op program list their friends, and then ranked each student in terms of how often the others had named him or her, they found the lonely students emerging pretty firmly in the middle of the pack. They weren't the most popular, but they were hardly at the bottom of the list. The lonely students might have felt isolated, but "unpopularity" wasn't their problem.

Another idea about the lonely is that they're somehow less attractive than the nonlonely. None of the people I spoke to mentioned their looks, because it's a slightly absurd thing to talk about, but—for people who wrote in—their appearance was often the first thing they mentioned. "I'm not lonely because I'm unattractive," one person stressed. Or, "I'm usually described as really good looking." These statements are more than likely true. In an experiment from the early 1980s that probably wouldn't be allowed today (because of its preoccupation with hotness), researchers in Tulsa stationed observers outside the door of a room where a loneliness experiment was being conducted. The observers—who didn't know which of the participants were lonely—were asked to rate each person on the basis of looks as they emerged from the room. When the ratings for the lonely and nonlonely were compared, it was found that the lonely were ranked as just as good looking, or as slightly *better* looking, than the nonlonely participants.

Finally, there's the persistent notion that the lonely are somehow unpleasant, that they're not as friendly, smart, or agreeable as the nonlonely. However, in an experiment at Texas A&M University, in which lonely and nonlonely participants were asked to do group work and then rate their colleagues on a variety of traits such as friendliness and intelligence, the lonely were rated as just as smart and generally *more* friendly than their nonlonely counterparts.

"I couldn't tell one person from another," says Niels Christensen, the psychologist who conducted the experiment at Texas A&M. What someone might pick up on, Christensen notes, are what he calls "micro-level" behaviors, such as how much someone might be frowning, or speaking less, or how defensive their posture might be. "And in those situations, yes," says Christensen, "you can probably identify the sociable people and the nonsociable people, and loneliness might be correlated with that. I think that's absolutely possible. It can be done. But in everyday life, we're not walking around saying, 'Which one's the lonely person here?' I mean, we usually have a million different things going through our head when we're having a social interaction. Other people are not really paying attention to information in that way. So can people do it? Absolutely. Do people in fact make those distinctions? I'd say probably not."

The fact that loneliness doesn't align with stereotype, and that there's nothing obvious about the state, is, in a sense, good news for lonely people, because it means they can avoid stigma by simply not telling others about their loneliness. In stigma terms, this is known as "passing," and there are a couple of ways to achieve it. One way is to simply pretend there's no problem at all. "I don't let it show," says James, referring to the management technique he's devised. "I stick on a smile and take a deep breath and try to be part of the group." A second route is to pretend that the loneliness is actually depression, which can be openly discussed. "Sometimes I let them call it depression," says Anne, referring to her friends' diagnoses of her. "It's just easier than trying to explain."

Hiding loneliness, or passing it off as something else, might seem like a workable strategy, but the problem is that passing can make loneliness even more difficult to contain. Laura Smart Richman, a psychologist at Duke University who studies stigma, notes that keeping a stigmatized trait hidden can make it seem more pressing than it actually is. "When people try to keep something hidden," she says, as she explains her research to me, "they end up thinking about it more. So they can become kind of obsessed with what they're keeping hidden." Not talking about loneliness, in other words, can make the state loom up even more largely in your life. The more you try to pretend it's not a problem, the more central and significant it might begin to seem.

It's also the case that, unless someone is willing to name loneliness as a concern, they're not going to be in a position to seek or receive treatment for it. "People don't want to tell you that they're lonely," says Keele University's Ken Rotenberg.

"And that's the problem of even getting people into therapy if they require it. Because loneliness becomes very, very hidden and embedded, and not disclosed." Many of the lonely people I spoke to mentioned that they wouldn't be opposed to receiving counseling for loneliness, but the subject had never come up. Either they had never mentioned it, or their counselor, out of a misguided sense of tact or politeness, hadn't asked. While talking about loneliness can be difficult, it's not the case that the lonely don't want it named. "I think it would have been kind of cathartic for someone to have asked about loneliness and just recognized that it was an issue," says Claire. "I don't think it would have made me feel bad. I think it would have helped."

Hiding loneliness at the individual level can also make it seem, of course, as though most people aren't really lonely, or that the state is an entirely personal problem, one that others don't struggle with. The response I received from many people who read my blog was simple relief, as in, "I read some of the posts on your blog, and, honestly, felt a great sense of relief that it wasn't just me." It shouldn't take a slightly anonymous blog to provide people with this sense of comfort and belonging. I enjoyed my talks with lonely people, but there was a strange, one-by-one aspect to them. I felt as though we were each giving the other the chance to talk about the state, but that no larger discussion was taking place. Given the time zones involved—from eastern Canada to Oregon, and to New Zealand—it often felt as though the conversations were happening in a sort of no-man's-land, unconnected to reality. It's shouldn't be the case that lonely people are on the phone, sometimes late at night, with a stranger who's giving them permission to discuss their loneliness, and then—when they hang up the phone and return to their real lives—the state is once again off limits.

In fall of 2006, after I'd sold an outline of this book to a publisher, I realized I'd have to come up with a new strategy for discussing my research. Notices about the book were beginning to appear on publishing Web sites, and my blog would soon be up and running. A state I'd worked very hard to hide was on its way to becoming public knowledge, and I knew I'd have to start admitting to loneliness—if not as a profound, personal, long-term problem, then at least as the subject of my book. I wasn't sure *how* to mention my loneliness, however, so I had a prep talk with Laura, my friend from law school, who had some advice.

"It's all about tone," she said soothingly. "If you present it as something you're comfortable with, people will respond by being comfortable themselves. If you're a wreck, they're not going to know how to respond."

I wasn't sure that the part about comfort was entirely true, but I knew Laura was right about anxiety. If I betrayed my discomfort, I'd inevitably unsettle the people I was speaking to.

And so I began practicing my tone. I mean, I practiced *out loud*. "I'm writing about *loneliness*," I said, sounding upbeat and cheerful, as though my subject were puppies, or baby seals. Too cute. "About *loneliness*," I said, my voice becoming deeper and more academic, as though I were delivering a paper on the Hapsburg empire. Too dull. "*Loneliness*," I said, looking at myself in a mirror, and I knew I had it just right. My topic could have been my interest in publicly funded spay-and-neuter programs, or the time I took the ferry to Alaska, or the dream I'd had the previous night—something personally compelling but opaque to the people around me. I liked the way I managed to sound as though I were revealing something about myself while at the same time remaining matter-of-fact. This balance is harder to achieve than it might seem. *Think cookbooks*, I told myself, aiming for neutrality. *Think embroidery*.

With my tone hammered out, I had to focus on content, on message. There were a couple of key features that I needed to control. The first was duration. My loneliness had been life-long, but I knew from talking to Ken Rotenberg that people who present as having short-term loneliness attract much less censure. With this in mind, I shelved my present and went with my past, settling on an alternative version of my life in which I'd been lonely at some distant time, but wasn't currently having trouble with the state. I also knew that I had to shift the focus of my loneliness away from *trait* and toward *situation*. I needed to present the state as arising from circumstance, not from my genes. My psychiatrist had once told me that lawyers were the least happy of any occupational group he saw, so I decided to peg the state to my work.

"I got really lonely practicing law," I finally heard myself saying, not to myself, but actually to another person. This was at a craft fair, where I was selling literary magazines at a card table covered with a shiny red scarf. There were hand-carved caribou statues to one side of me, furry, scratchy-looking children's sweaters to the other. I was talking to an acquaintance from the writing world, a young woman I hoped to turn into a friend. The time had come for the talk all writers have. It was my tax prof's question all over again, only this time I was prepared. Helen was writing a romance novel set, for reasons I was too nervous to fully register, in the mid-1980s. I heard myself deliver my well-practiced line before launching into a hurried discussion of all the loneliness research being carried out. Even with my message hammered out beforehand, I could feel my face flush and my heart rate quicken. *Sound neutral,* I told myself. *Embroidery, cookbooks.*

I want to say that nothing changed, that Helen hugged me and shouted, "That's terrific!" Everything, I'd like to say, remained A-OK. But there were some slight changes, some distinct shifts in what Christensen has called micro-level behaviors. Helen's curiosity perked up. As I listened to myself talk—"Some really amazing research going on at the University of Chicago"—I realized that the heart of the story had gone missing. She was looking at me as though I were lying, as though there had to be something I wasn't telling her. And then, either because of my falsehood or because of my loneliness, her attitude toward me began to tilt. There seemed to be a quiet reclaiming of ground. She began to seem slightly distant, as though she needed to create a bit of space between the two of us.

"Loneliness," Helen said, looking around. "How, um, interesting." She seemed in desperate need of a new topic. I think she would have been pleased if one of the wooden caribou beside us had stood up and started to walk.

"It was just something that caught my attention," I said, hastily. "You know, something I decided to explore." I sounded as though I were asking for forgiveness, as though I weren't *really* interested in what I'd just said I was interested in. That is, I managed to make myself look not just lonely but unfocused, as though I were the sort of person who started writing books about random subjects they came across in passing. My next book, it seemed, might be about tea leaves, or public transit, or anything my scattered mind might hit on.

Helen's husband appeared, and the conversation ended. I took my leave, feeling torn. I'd admitted my subject, but the reaction had been precisely the one I'd been worried about:

an almost imperceptible but undeniable removal, an eyebrow raised. The suggestion—not named between us—that maybe there was something just a little bit off about me, a little bit suspect. There are many possible explanations I could fasten on, but I have to note that she never became my friend.

One of the main reasons it's hard to talk about loneliness is that the state is relational. It's a private feeling that inevitably refers outward to our relationships with others. "People get hurt by the word *lonely*," notes Rachel astutely. "They think, 'Oh great, thanks a lot.' " Rachel has told me about an episode where, as a child, she told her mother that she felt lonely, only to have her mother take offense. "And that always comes back to me, that feeling of 'Thanks a lot,' or 'What am I? I don't help?' And you think, But that's not what I said." It was precisely because I couldn't untangle blame from loneliness that it was hard for me to tell my family about either the state or the book. This didn't mean they didn't know. While the online notices about the book might not have been accessible to my mother and stepmother, who didn't spend time trawling the Internet, they were certainly available to my sisters, who were fully computer-savvy.

"One and only *LONELY* heart's club band," my nine-year-old niece sang, rushing past my sister and me one afternoon as we were coming home from brunch. *They know*, I realized instantly, as Theresa quickly told my niece to be quiet.

It was interesting for me to note that, even with an opening provided to us, both Theresa and I hurried to talk about other things. I couldn't take advantage of this very obvious entry point—one that came complete with a sunny sidewalk, a sated autumn afternoon, and the peace and space of outdoors—

because I was anxious about sounding as though I were some-how pointing a finger.

"It's as though it's a way of saying I don't like their friend-ship, or don't appreciate them," says Adam, who's faced the dilemma I did. "It's a way of saying I feel disconnected from them, when they might not have that feeling at all."

The asymmetry of the state was one of the problems I faced with Theresa. As though to debunk the idea of loneliness being handed down in a uniform manner, my sister was a poster child for extroversion. In high school, she could organize a party in the late afternoon, and by nine in the evening, there'd be people spilling off the lawn and into the street. The differences in our temperaments were so marked that I found she was a great one to turn to when the problem was depression. I knew her innate optimism would balance my pessimism, and that her bright objectivity could clear up my dark thoughts and distor-tions. The difficulty with loneliness was that she *didn't* feel a sense of disconnection, and so any allusions on my part to a feeling of isolation would start to seem like finger-pointing, as though I were accusing her of having failed me in some mys-terious way. It was precisely because she'd been, for years, so kind and generous toward me that I couldn't imagine uttering the word *lonely*.

It was also the case that I couldn't tell her how to fix it. "If I asked him to do something," says Rachel, referring to her hus-band, "he'd do it. Like, if I said to him, 'OK, this is what you need to do to make me feel less lonely,' he'd do it. But I don't know what the answer is."

It's partly because lonely people can't provide solutions to solving the problem that it can start to seem easier to duck the issue. It's also the fact that, when lonely people do force them-selves over their apprehension and name the state, they tend to get the wrong advice. "They just say, 'Try to go out and meet new people,'" notes Ray, the fundraiser from Philadelphia, who's told a few family members about his loneliness. "And I've never really understood how that's exactly done, I guess," he adds with a quiet laugh. "It's almost like saying, 'Well, if you feel like playing baseball, why don't you go and join the major leagues?' It just seems like such a huge thing to do."

"It doesn't really get to the heart of the problem of being lonely," agrees Frances, the physiotherapist from Missouri, who told her mother about being lonely. "Her reaction was 'Well, if you just go out and meet some people, you'll be fine.' But it's not that you don't know people, it's that you don't feel connected to them."

One reason people are able to talk about depression is that we know how to discuss it. Years of research, hundreds of hours of talk-show discussions, and written materials ranging from memoirs to public information posters have given us a way of framing the conversation. People related to or living with a depressed person know that they shouldn't see the mood as a comment on the nature or health of their relationship, they know not to offer pat solutions, and they know they should offer support. We're all, when we talk about depression, actually taking part in a much larger discussion, one in which many key facts have already been filled in for both parties.

The problem with loneliness is that, with no larger cultural discussion in play, people have to do, in a sense, too much talking. The lonely person has to resolve every issue that arises. She has to deal with the problem of blame, and somehow reassure whoever she's talking to that it's not a case of relationship failure. She has to know how to respond to unsolicited advice, and handle the inevitable question, What next? And the fact that these conversations are happening on a strictly one-to-one basis makes the matters that arise even more difficult to deal with. It's hard, for instance, for someone who has no real knowledge of loneliness to hear that his wife is lonely and not think, Is it me?

Talks about loneliness could be more effective and economical if there were a larger discussion in place. It would have been helpful, as my sister and I walked down her street, for me to simply step into a larger dialogue, and have some key facts already known and on the table—about how the state doesn't necessarily correspond to problems in a relationship, about how it can be chronic, and about how it is in fact widely felt. With no broader discussion taking place, however, all of these issues fell to me, and—that afternoon on the sidewalk—it all simply seemed too much. And this meant my sister and I let my niece run on ahead of us, both of us pretending not to have heard the word *lonely*.

Decades ago, the late Canadian sociologist Erving Goffman asked himself what purpose concealable stigmas were serving. Why, in other words, would people who carry a stigmatized trait go to such efforts to hide it? The response might seem self-evident—to avoid censure, of course—but that answer begged the question of what purpose the censure was serving. It wasn't possible, Goffman argued, for there to be broad-scale disapproval attaching to a specific trait or experience and not have that disapproval *mean* something.

Loneliness researchers themselves point out that there's something odd about our general tendency to criticize the state. "Loneliness," notes Ken Rotenberg, "is a subjective state, rather than an objective one. And that's where the strangeness for stigmatizing someone for loneliness comes in. You're stigmatizing them for how they *feel* about their relationships, for their perception of not being able to connect with others."

There's nothing, in other words, overtly *wrong* with loneliness. We rationalize the stigma by telling ourselves there's something flawed about lonely people—that they don't dress properly, or socialize properly, or that they're too hostile or self-involved. If these attributes were true, the stigma against loneliness might make some sense. In effect, we'd be criticizing not the state but the behaviors associated with it. If there aren't any observable differenc_s between the lonely and the nonlonely in terms of looks, intelligence, friendliness, or popularity, however, then the stigma has to be doing something much subtler.

One thing that becomes apparent, if a person—say, me—has spent years reading loneliness materials, is that the tone of the discussion surrounding the state has changed. Loneliness literature can be said to have been born in the old, acidified pages of journals such as *Psychiatry* and *Psychoanalysis*—periodicals from the 1950s devoted to detailing the neuroses of midcentury America. Some of these papers read quite strangely today. One writer, for instance, liked to link loneliness to premature weaning (the idea being that the experience of being pulled away from the breast gave rise to permanent feelings of being emotionally cut off). Despite the oddities that sometimes arise, though, the writings from the 1940s to 1960s are marked, overall, by a tone of inclusion and care. They aren't alarmist. Harry Stack Sullivan, for instance, one of the leading psychiatrists of the twentieth century, described loneliness as a state of simply not having one's emotional needs met, of being caught in a situation characterized by the "inadequate discharge of the need for human intimacy." Karl Menninger, founder of the Menninger Clinic and author of *The Human Mind*, described loneliness partly as the by-product of just being kept apart—of growing up poor, or different, or far away.

Around 1950, however, discussions of loneliness began to change. This was a shift that clear-sighted observers spotted right away. David Riesman, in his blockbuster *The Lonely Crowd*, stressed that only in the postwar era had loneliness become "a problem." People in previous generations, Riesman noted, hadn't tied themselves up into knots if they thought their children were lonely. It was only in the modern era that people were beginning to see the state as something in need of eradication.

Stigma researchers stress that the tone around a trait can change while the trait itself remains the same. An obvious example of this is disability, which has gone from something capable of blocking out an entire personality—rendering the person in the wheelchair supposedly humorless and passive— to something more active and nuanced. It's hard, for instance, to see the sprinter Oscar Pistorius racing on his carbon-fiber blades and not realize that his physical difference might not be a burden at all.

What changes in stigma terms isn't the trait itself, but rather our attitude toward it. A general rule of thumb is that stigma will increase as anxiety rises, with the traits that we're most anxious about giving rise to the harshest stigmas. It's helpful to keep this little axiom in mind when considering more recent statements about loneliness. Because if you shift from the 1940s and '50s to the present, what emerges is a distinct change of tone—a demonizing and marginalizing of the state. While loneliness according to Sullivan and Menninger was something that anyone might feel (since any of us might find ourselves cut off, and since we all possess a need for intimacy), loneliness in the modern age is presented in rather extreme terms.

For the psychologist James Lynch, writing in 2000, loneliness has graduated from being a feeling to being a "lethal poison," a state extreme and risky enough for someone in the text to refer to it, without irony, as "the new Black Death." David Burns, the pop psych sensation behind the *Feeling Good* books, carries on with the disease theme in describing the lonely as "grim and down on themselves, and about as marketable as lepers." Laura Papanno, a Boston journalist who wants to tell Americans why they feel so alone, seems so intimidated by the state that she actually redefines it. The lonely person *she's* talking about, she stresses, isn't "the Eleanor Rigby type, the lonely one missing out on the party of life, famished for human contact with too much time to wonder what's gone wrong." Instead, the lonely person she's addressing is a member of "the new lonely," someone "overstimulated, hyperkinetic, overcommitted, plugged in." I don't know whether I'm the old lonely or the new lonely, but I do know—from my talks with lonely people—that overcommitment and overstimulation generally aren't problems associated with loneliness. Papanno seems to be trying to distance herself from the very subject of loneliness, and the reason she needs to do this is that loneliness—the plain, stripped, "old" kind—is too difficult to talk about, too unhip, too embarrassing to even name.

It's interesting to note that the emergence of loneliness as a disease state—or as a state so taboo it can't be addressed without being redefined—has occurred just as isolation has become more prevalent. Or, to put the matter more precisely, the conceptualization of loneliness as something extreme and different has emerged *because* isolation has become more prevalent. Previous eras, which enjoyed less time alone, less objective isolation, and larger confidant networks, didn't have to demonize loneliness—they could treat the state for what it was, something that might be painful and difficult but not beyond the pale. It's our own era that's had to throw a wall up against the state. As we've become more alone, and as our vulnerability to loneliness has increased, we've put more effort into trying to push loneliness away, and turn it into something marginal, worrisome, and rare.

When we demonize loneliness on a broad enough scale—when most people feel it's something they can't talk about or admit to—then we've made social embeddedness seem much more common than it actually is. And it's this distortion function that Goffman decided was the real purpose of concealable stigmas: in hiding something, we make its opposite seem more prevalent and widely realized than it actually is. In this way, the stigma against loneliness dovetails with representations of sociability to make it seem as though embeddedness—at the turn of the somewhat fractured twenty-first century—is common, ordinary, and easy to achieve.

The stigma against loneliness is pushing loneliness off the cultural radar just as it's becoming a broader cultural problem. There's a rich discussion we could be having about loneliness—about prevalence, about responses, about cognition—but so long as loneliness remains unmentionable, this wider discussion can't ever occur. Depressed people might feel as though they can't mention their symptoms, as though there might be something failed or embarrassing about their condition. In one sense, however, individual depressed people don't *have* to talk about their condition—a much wider cultural discussion about remedies, characterization, and self-blame is already under way. Lonely people find themselves doubly silenced. Not only can they not talk about the state, no one *else* is talking about it either. Silence at the individual level is matched by silence at the societal level, creating the wildly mistaken notion that loneliness is not a problem, that it's not a state or condition requiring much in the way of thought or response.

And what's most distressing about this situation—aside from the fact that it's seeing loneliness getting pushed aside—is that lonely people *want* to talk about what's happening to them. It was very unnerving for me, over the course of the interviews that I conducted, to hear that I was the only person the interviewee had ever told about the state. Some of the people I spoke to had confided, with a greater or lesser degree of detail, to partners or parents. But for many, the opportunity to talk about loneliness had literally never arisen. "I would love to participate in your study," more than one person wrote, "just to have the chance to talk about this." Many people liked the anonymity of the phone calls, the judgment-free opportunity to talk about a problem that mattered. "I feel free to tell you things that my *mom* doesn't know about," said Katherine, the policy analyst from Nova Scotia, describing the interview as "safe."

There's an idea in circulation that loneliness is so shameful and embarrassing that lonely people will keep the state to themselves regardless of the situation—in other words, loneliness is something that people simply won't admit to in any circumstance. But I, with remarkably little effort, got people talking about the state. Lonely people *told* me they wanted to talk about it. "I appreciate just having the chance to talk about this," added Katherine. "Just having the chance to put words to it—for me, it gets easier to think about, the more I can express it and not keep it inside. So this has been tremendously helpful to me."

"Being able to talk about it lets me reflect in a way I just can't do on my own, or with a journal," agrees Sonia, the West Coast copywriter. "So it's interesting for me just to talk about this, and the questions you're asking are things I've never thought about. So I think it could be useful to have someone to talk to about loneliness, and for someone to understand, and to have the right questions to ask."

The argument that the lonely are so inveterately silent that they just won't talk about the state doesn't hold water. What many lonely people seemed to want—what I wanted—was the ability to talk about loneliness and have someone listen in an entirely judgment-free way. For Anne, the Illinois social worker, a friend had started the conversation about loneliness by gently suggesting that she thought it might be a problem in Anne's life. "And that kind of opened up the conversation," says Anne. "She's now someone I can be very open with about it. I can call her up and just say, 'OK, Sarah, this is one of those times when I feel alone in the universe,' and that gives me the sense of connection I'm missing."

The sense of connection that can come with having your loneliness recognized can be profound. Only once in my life, in the years before I started seeing Genevieve, had someone commented on my loneliness. In 2001, my father and I were having coffee at an outdoor café. It was a beautiful day in early spring. The sun was bright, the wind was light, and the air smelled of coffee, fresh soil, and melted snow. I must have said something about my sisters being so much older than me. My father didn't respond right away. He was stirring sugar into his coffee, and he seemed to be thinking about my comment. I hadn't meant it as anything significant or accusatory. I was, after all, just stating a fact. But he turned to me and said, "Your sisters always had each other when they were younger. At least they had that sisterly bond. But you were alone, and lonely."

It was a surprise to hear him say the word. There must have

been something about me that afternoon that troubled my father. Maybe he was worried about me, about my career path, about the dissatisfaction he said I'd feel as a lawyer. And it was just eight months before he died. He might have had a sense of being about to leave me, of needing to warn me about a problem he wouldn't be able to help me through.

I put my cup down and looked around. I wasn't prepared for the way in which the recognition of my loneliness would make me feel. If someone had told me that my father was going to comment on the state, I'd have felt anxious and worried. I wouldn't have wanted it to be seen. So it was a surprise to feel myself relax. I felt fleshed out, more fully there.

"Yes," I said, admitting to the loneliness. "I was."

That was the last spring of my father's life. We never returned to the subject of my loneliness, and he never knew I was going to write this book. But his acknowledgment has stayed with me. In some ways, his recognition is part of what's made it possible for me to take up and finish this project. Because his tone when he talked about my loneliness was one of acceptance and regret. He *saw* the state, and in so doing, he helped me shift my perspective on it. I'm not saying I didn't freeze or stumble later on, when I had to out myself to others as lonely—obviously, I did. But I think my father's recognition went some way toward offsetting the otherwise strong cultural condemnation of the state. In making loneliness seem *all right*, my father gave me something I could rely on in the face of a huge and engulfing stigma. It took me a long, long time to name loneliness as a personal problem—I think naming it is something I'll continue to struggle with throughout my life—but that initial recognition was part of what led me to eventually find my voice.

The stigma against loneliness does many things—it portrays individual lonely people as flawed and unattractive; it obscures the real extent of loneliness in society; and it chokes off discussion of a state that's becoming more of a problem. But what it does most of all is deprive lonely people of the chance to talk about what's important to them. No one should feel as though they can't air crucial aspects of their lives, but that is what's happened with loneliness. In casting the state as a shortcoming, as a *problem*, we've turned loneliness into something people can't admit to, and in doing this, we've silenced the discussion that could otherwise be taking place.

I know that lonely people have things to say about their loneliness—about how it makes them feel, and behave, and think; about how they feel walking into a room or bar; about how strange it is to unplug the phone after a weekend of loneliness. So long as we stigmatize loneliness, however, we're not going to hear about any of this. So long as the state remains taboo, there's a big wide stretch of human feeling and experience we're simply going to miss.

Part IV

RESOLUTION

Chapter Nine

PROMISES, PROMISES

Public and private ideas about
responding to loneliness

With the stigma against loneliness making the state hard to talk about, many lonely people are forced to rely on themselves in an attempt to overcome the affliction. It's worth noting that depressed people face a rather different scenario when it comes to seeking help. Someone struggling with depression might choose to rely on do-it-yourself manuals, such as *Mind Over Mood*, but they can also access doctors, therapists, public information brochures, and clinically tested medications.

The lonely person is confronted with a radically different situation. A lot of lonely people seeking resources online ended up contacting *me*, even though I'd made it clear in my blog that I was a lawyer, not a psychologist. At first, I couldn't understand why people would reach out to an unqualified stranger, but this was before I started looking for help myself. "At least you're not crazy," one person wrote, and as soon as I went online, I began to see what he meant. Missing, I discovered, were the symptom lists, the meds, the educational campaigns, and the support groups that depressed people can access. In their place was something almost medieval. The lonely person seeking a response to their state was presented with "cures," "secret elixirs," loneliness potions, self-hypnosis downloads, and "Magick Spells" promising to provide the precise incantation needed to break the state (just $40!).

To describe the market for loneliness cures as carnivalesque and unregulated understates the problem: it's a free-for-all. And the array of untested loneliness-ending potions and downloads is distressing not just because it speaks to an enormous need but because it underlines the lack of a coherent response. A flip through the Internet or a stroll through the self-help section of the bookstore is enough to demonstrate that loneliness is not a problem most governments or public health agencies feel particularly compelled to address. A sort of laissez-faire attitude permeates the entire field of loneliness reduction, with few public and authoritative voices emerging as sources of reliable information and help.

This silence persists despite the fact that many social service agencies are arguing that governments need to get involved. Lobbying groups such as the United Kingdom's Demos and Help the Aged have issued statements stressing that loneliness has to be seen as a public policy issue—that is, as something governments should focus on and address.

"We're now beginning to recognize just how common the phenomenon of loneliness really is," says William Lauder, a nursing professor at the University of Stirling in Scotland who's addressed the need to incorporate loneliness into public health plans. "And we're beginning to understand how it can directly or indirectly lead to a whole range of very common morbidities." Although Lauder notes that loneliness reduction is a "soft" goal—one that's somewhat difficult to implement and tricky to measure—he stresses that improved embeddedness and decreased loneliness are still goals worth pursuing. "When we look at social connections, they're associated with improvements over a whole spectrum, and that could include coronary heart disease, and reductions in stress-related illnesses. So I think a joint target of loneliness reduction and a broader sense of social connection has a potential benefit over a wide range of areas."

The Dutch sociologist Roelof Hortulanus, who recently completed a study showing that at least 30 percent of the Dutch population suffers from loneliness, has noted that loneliness tends to be seen as an issue too private for governments to interfere with. "We see social isolation as a personal matter," he writes, "as a phenomenon that is part of life." But Hortulanus notes that other phenomena—such as poverty and unemployment—are equally a part of life, yet governments have been turning their attention to them for some time.

The argument that loneliness differs from other issues because it imposes no public costs can't be right. The state, by virtue of its impact on blood pressure and the immune system, leads to increased health-care costs; distress translates into increased demands for social services; and the very nature of social isolation means that many members of society are not participating as fully as they could. Furthermore, failing to address loneliness directly means that the costs and problems associated with it can begin to spiral upward, when in fact the lonely could be positioned as part of the solution. In a pilot project in England, for instance, lonely individuals are being cast as supports to other isolated members of the community, meaning the local council is creating a low-cost buffer against social isolation and likely lowering health-care costs in the process.

The notion of loneliness as a public issue—as something that matters collectively, rather than just within individual lives—is slowly starting to register. In 2002, the World Health Organization recognized decreased loneliness and increased embeddedness as critical to a healthy older age, and loneliness reduction has been included as a goal in proposed or adopted public health plans issued by the governments of New Zealand, Canada, and Sweden.

One reason that governments are slowly turning their attention to loneliness is that they're beginning to understand the physiological impact it can have on a life. But another reason is that researchers working within the field have shown that there are effective ways of responding to the state.

"I think that, at all levels, something can be done about it," says Sean Seepersad, a psychologist at California State Fresno who's developed a loneliness-reduction program. "Even the more chronic types of loneliness—they might require a different type of intervention, perhaps therapy—but I don't think the chronically lonely person is necessarily stuck."

The idea of loneliness being responsive to treatment is what's fueled the work of the Dutch psychologist Nan Stevens, who's developed a loneliness-reduction program shown to cut loneliness rates in half. Stevens's program takes the form of weekly group lessons offered over the course of three months. Under the guidance of a social worker or peer leader, participants are encouraged to do straightforward things such as assessing their need for and expectations of friendships and mapping out relationships that already exist, in order to spot dormant potential friendships. Participants are supported as they devise ways of improving existing relationships, and they're encouraged—

throughout the program—to exchange stories about which techniques did or did not work, and to talk about successes and setbacks. The program essentially operates as a brake on the withdrawal loneliness tends to cue. With the group leader and other participants encouraging them to be more proactive, lonely people are given the support they need to overcome their feelings of threat and anxiety. It's also the case that simply being in a group allows lonely people to recognize they're not in any way unusual. "I think that being involved with a group of people working on loneliness provides learning and social comparison opportunities," says Stevens, "and it makes the participant realize she's not the only one without an ideal social life."

The difficulty with Stevens's program is that it's not widely enough available. "Articles about it will appear in the newspapers or in magazines," she tells me, "and then I get a lot of calls from those who would like to follow the program. But I often have to disappoint them when it's not offered in their town or city." Stevens's program is being implemented by social service agencies across Holland, kits have been sent to the United States, Canada, and the United Kingdom, and interest in the program has been expressed from as far away as Portugal and Australia, but most lonely people are still going to find themselves outside the catchment areas where the program is being offered.

Psychologists working in the field insist that a program of some sort—one that brings the lonely person into contact with other lonely people, and provides them with instruction and guidance—is key to successfully overcoming the state. "I think if people could fix loneliness on their own," says Sean Seepersad, referring to self-help strategies, "they probably would. But they need something else. They need a group process—say the sort that happens with the intervention program I do—so that they're able to connect."

The effectiveness of group intervention programs has been demonstrated. Certain programs, such as Stevens's, reliably drop rates, while other initiatives have been shown to offset the physiological changes caused by loneliness. When the Swedish psychologist Lars Andersson organized discussion groups for lonely widows and encouraged them—over a period of several weeks—to talk and open up lines of communication, he found that the widows involved in the groups displayed a 10 mm drop in blood pressure. The lonely widows who'd been left in an isolated state displayed no similar reduction.

The notion of loneliness as something the lonely need help overcoming is becoming increasingly accepted within the field. In England, for instance, the think tank Participle is looking at ways of bringing lonely individuals together. The old way of doing things was to create "social recreation groups" for seniors, and let people fend for themselves within an unstructured social zone. What Participle is trying to do, explains Chris Vanstone, a lead designer with the program, is arrange introductions on the basis of an individual's interests, background, and personality. That is, instead of letting the lonely person essentially scramble to overcome the state alone, Participle is stepping in to try to maximize the chances of a positive outcome. "The ideal," says Vanstone, "is that we connect people to form mutual friendships that provide mutual support—whether that's emotional support, or practical support, or both."

The idea that effective loneliness reduction requires *external* help and assistance is one that psychologists are increasingly stressing. They note that a lonely person needs some sort of structure and context. "I think with loneliness you have to be in a group, and you have to do it," says Seepersad, referring to some of the exercises covered in his seven-week loneliness-reduction program. "You need other people's support to help to you do it, and you need a safe environment to do it in, where people understand how you feel."

Leaving the lonely to simply fend for themselves tends to result in little in the way of change. "I was just seeing a huge amount of very socially isolated and lonely people," says Caroline Starkey, a former social worker in northern England. Frustrated that lonely people were being allowed to fall through the cracks, Starkey created what is probably the West's first isolation and loneliness resource kit—a thirty-five-page guide setting out all the ways in which caregivers, social workers, and health-care professionals can find social programs and help for the lonely. In an innovative twist, Starkey is even planning on holding training sessions for mail carriers, meter readers, and fuel deliverymen—the people most likely to encounter the socially isolated in their homes. The solution, Starkey emphasizes, is not to walk away, but to take active measures to try to help the lonely person. "It's a human right," says Starkey, passionately, referring to a sense of belonging. "And I think it should be a full society issue. This is an issue for everyone."

I'd done a lot of reading in self-help before I spoke to people such as Stevens, Seepersad, and Starkey. What I was struck by, in speaking with them, was the difference in what might be called emphasis. Within self-help, loneliness emerges as a state that must be responded to solo: the lonely person is supposed to call upon reserves of ingenuity and self-nurturance and somehow solve the problem of loneliness by herself. Every professional I spoke to, however, stressed the need for assistance and guidance. Experts such as Starkey positioned themselves firmly against the notion that the lonely should or could be left alone. The intellectual basis for Starkey's stance is easy to identify: if loneliness is a problem marked by feelings of isolation, then the best way to respond to that problem is through the guidance and assistance offered by another person. It doesn't make sense to try to remedy aloneness by asking the lonely person to draw even more deeply on the self.

But it's a sense of aloneness that much self-help advises the lonely person to embrace. I'd gone through a period, in 2007, of letting my hair down and scrolling through the loneliness collections of online bookstores. After plowing my way through countless articles on genetics, physiology, and behavior, it was time to have some fun. It was with a sense of glee that I clicked on books with titles such as *Positive Solitude: A Practical Program for Mastering Loneliness* and *Intimate Connections: The New and Clinically Tested Program for Overcoming Loneliness*. These books featured pink and purple covers, and were decorated with crayonlike heart outlines and pictures of flowers. Once they arrived, I curled up on the sofa with a mug of tea, ready to absorb whatever pop culture had to tell me about ending loneliness.

I quickly realized that the picture of the lonely person that emerged in the books was a rather contradictory one. The lonely person was, on one hand, someone badly in need of instruction, and on the other, a sort of superhero. The books seemed to suggest that the lonely person, like a child, didn't know what he needed to know, but that—once he learned the right lessons—he'd be invincible, and able to overcome loneliness on his own. And the way he was to subdue the state was through a process of meeting his needs *himself*.

"Put the word 'Self' rather than 'Alone' next to activities that you do by yourself," suggests David Burns in *Intimate*

Connections. "This will remind you that you're never really alone." The circular notion that the lonely person is the only person the lonely person needs is one that surfaces, in various forms, throughout much self-help literature. The lonely person can comfort herself by creating an Inner Adult to minister to an Inner Child—an approach advocated by the authors of *Healing Your Aloneness*—or she can treat herself as the friend she needs. "Start by going to the store and picking out your favorite foods," advises Burns in an address to the person who's eating all her meals alone. "Set a nice table for yourself, and put on some nice music, just as if you were having company."

Go sculling, adds Dr. Rae André in *Positive Solitude.* Sip a glass of champagne. Do some carving. And in the midst of these fascinating activities, if you still feel as though you need someone, remind yourself that this impulse is an instance of what André calls an "intrusive thought."

"Yes, it might be nice if someone were with you," she admits. "Yet, you are alone, with your own feelings and sensuality, and that is terrific, too."

Lonely people stress that they don't need instruction in being alone. Not only do they usually have solitude down to an art, it's not the case that they get bored and cranky the minute they're left to themselves. "I'm someone who's never really had trouble being by myself," notes Frank, the freelance journalist from Seattle. The problem he identifies isn't solitude, which comes quite naturally, but rather loneliness, which he can't escape. "I don't like the idea," he notes, rather mildly, "of finding myself in a situation where there's nothing."

But a denuded social world is what much self-help advises lonely people to accept. In 2007, I was making gentle fun of the books, grinning every time I read a passage such as "loneliness does not really exist," and "Ron is talking himself into his loneliness." In cheerfully mocking the texts, however, I was ignoring the fact that I had, during the worst period of my loneliness, actually embarked on a strategy very close to the one being advocated. In the late fall of 2005, after my subjective and objective isolation had lasted for more than three years, I'd started doing something I called "focusing in." The idea—which I had to struggle to articulate, since it didn't really make sense—was that I was supposed to ignore the social world, and concentrate solely on my own thoughts and feelings. On long evening walks, I'd ignore the sight of people indoors, cuddling on sofas, and tell myself that I was my own companion. Playing fast and loose with concepts from mindfulness meditation, I'd feel anxiety present itself after too much time alone and think, *That's good. You're communicating with yourself.* Trying to somehow multiply myself into a number greater than one, I'd tell myself, when writing in my diary, that there were actually three people involved: there was my present self, who was writing; a future self, who would read; and a past self, who appeared in older journals.

I told Genevieve about this parceling of myself into past and present, and she was clearly troubled by a scenario that seemed to come from *The Three Faces of Eve*. "The idea that we can meet all our own needs is just *wrong*," she said, rather quietly. Genevieve and her partner had three cats, and she nodded her head toward the door as though to indicate one of them. "Daisy is diabetic," she continued. "She needs insulin. We have to *give* this to her." Genevieve started making small up and down motions with her hands, as though outlining two silos. "She'd like to make the insulin herself," she said, pointing to one silo, "but it has to come from *outside*." Here she waved to the second silo. Then she looked at me and brought her hands together. "Some of the things we need most we can't manufacture ourselves. We need *other people* to give them to us."

I saw the point Genevieve was trying to make, but at the time I wasn't able to fully accept the notion that I needed someone else on hand. This was because, if I did away with the idea of myself as a support, I wasn't sure what I'd be left with. I knew, both emotionally and intellectually, that I needed the comfort and companionship of others, but with others not readily presenting themselves, I wasn't sure where to turn. In late 2005, I was stuck in the trap that so many lonely people find themselves in. I was deeply lonely, but the "cues" about my state, as the psychologist Daniel Perlman has referred to them, weren't obvious. Many of the people in my life weren't aware of what I was going through. This meant I had the choice of telling people about my loneliness, and asking for help, or simply continuing to rely upon myself, hoping that I'd somehow be able to summon up the resources necessary to make it through on my own.

One of the things I wanted to do in writing this book was to test some of the self-help remedies that were popularly available. I'll state at the outset that by the spring of 2007, when I was testing the remedies, my problems with loneliness were not as intense and debilitating as they had been. I was still lonely, but my loneliness had more to do with social than with emotional isolation—someone had come into my life, and the state was no longer as intense and all-encompassing as it had been. It was only because I was no longer feeling totally alone that I was willing to subject myself to various "cures." I would have felt too vulnerable to have tried these supposed remedies during my worst stretches of loneliness, and I'm glad now that I didn't try them. Because, even in 2007, with my loneliness having changed, the promise of a cure seemed immensely powerful. I couldn't fully divorce myself from the notion that, if I just tried the right thing, or swallowed the right drink, I'd eliminate the state for good. From 2002 to 2006, when my loneliness was at its worst, I might have believed in the idea of a cure even more strongly, and wound up feeling not just lonely but taken in and cheated.

It was with a sense of wanting to see what other lonely people might stumble upon that I donned my investigative journalism hat and set out in search of "loneliness cures." The first cures I explored were anti-loneliness potions. I'd heard about such potions from a friend who dabbled in homeopathy, and who liked to insist—probably rightly—that herbal remedies were at the forefront of pop culture. If you want to know what the drug companies will be pushing in five years, she'd say, look at what your homeopath is prescribing today. To this end, I went into my local holistic dispensary—a bright, airy place with the requisite big ferns and exposed ductwork—and asked for cures for loneliness.

"Loneliness," the skinny and extremely calm herbalist repeated flatly, as though he were asked about it ten times a day. Without further ado, he reached for a big volume, which I later learned was the *Flower Essence Repertory*. He cracked it open like a phonebook and pushed it across the counter. "Which one do you need?" he asked.

I was surprised to hear that there was more than one cure, but I quickly realized, in scanning the page, that loneliness was a more multidimensional state than I had appreciated. There were cures for excessive detachment, for feeling shy, for feeling paranoid, and for fearing rejection. I had to think quickly. With the herbalist looking on, I decided that my main "soul issues" were "feeling cut off from community and family ties," confronting "social barriers," and feeling "emotionally distanced." The herbalist pulled three cute stoppered bottles off the shelf— evening primrose, mallow, and sweet pea—and $40 later I was back on the street, clutching a bag of home remedies that I was jonesing to get to.

At home, I thought about blitzing myself with the stuff and mixing up a primrose-mallow-sweet-pea blast, but decided that I'd be cautious and address feelings of being cut off from community first. The drink, when I prepared it, tasted like the most watered-down cocktail I'd ever been handed—it was about four drops of brandy in a glass of water—but I stood at the counter feeling receptive. Even though I suspected that the whole process was nonsense, I was shocked at the powerful urge I had for the remedy to *work*. I was amazed by how much I was willing to believe, and how my innate cynicism seemed to collapse as I soon as I started drinking something that could only be described as faintly revolting.

I noticed nothing at first, but I continued with my new regime. Four times a day, and every day for a week, I mixed up the little concoction that promised to restore my "soul feeling for home." The online materials said that it was possible to notice changes within a month, but I didn't have to wait that long. By day five, I was becoming more relaxed. I'd sit on my bed and gaze out the window, admiring rooftops and the pattern of branches against the sky. I began to spend long moments staring at my feet, feeling mildly contented. One evening, with my journal on my lap, I wrote, "Rain." Then, about half an hour later, I wrote, "Pretty rain." Then I passed out.

For a while, it was a good place to be. I haven't done drugs— at least nonpharmaceuticals—since I was twenty-two, and it was enjoyable to feel myself drifting and spacing out again. The herbal remedy had a different effect than the clonazepam I'd been prescribed (and which I was still taking). I began to feel floaty; my limbs began to feel heavy; breaking with a lifetime of practice, I forgot to put milk in my tea and then couldn't figure out why it tasted so tart. But then bags began to appear under my eyes. Nausea struck. My friend Laura suggested that, as someone with a history of mood disorders, I might not want to fiddle with psychotropics. But I thought that maybe the soul feeling for home really *was* presenting itself, and that if I just kept taking the sweet pea—and added mallow and evening primrose to the mix—I'd have my loneliness completely conquered.

I wanted to continue in the name of research. I was like a twelve-year-old determined to get results from her first science fair project. I was, however, just too high to carry on. It was impossible for me to swallow the mixture and get any work done. I'd also gotten the point where the mere smell of brandy in water was making me want to heave. So I had to bid an ambivalent adieu to the world of herbal remedies, without having come to any firm conclusions. In part, since I was taking the remedy with other drugs, my results were dirty. It was hard to know whether the sweet pea was affecting me, or whether it was just wildly accelerating the effects of the clonazepam. What I can say is that herbal remedies are not, despite the cute little bottles, something you want to mess around with off-label. I packed the bottles away feeling a bit unsteady—it's hard to feel high without feeling low—convinced that, if the government wants to start regulating mind-altering substances, it might want to send representatives to the local health food store.

Having failed at adjusting my resonance, I decided to turn to an American psychologist who offered telephone counseling in ending loneliness. The online promise was that the state would simply disappear within two to four sessions, and all that was involved was learning to change my thought processes.

"Think of how you'd feel if someone hit you from behind," the therapist said, on the phone from her car. "You'd be angry, right, and possibly scared?"

I wasn't sure that I'd feel alarmed if someone hit me from behind—this happened as a matter of course on the subway—but I agreed that I would likely feel angry and scared.

"And now think about how you'd feel if you turned around and saw that someone was having an epileptic seizure, and that they'd hit you as they fell. How would you feel? Maybe compassionate? Sympathetic?"

For a moment I paused to consider the fact that I didn't know anyone who was epileptic, and that this was unusual. It made me wonder whether I really did know epileptics who were keeping their condition hidden. And this made me question if there was something about me that was prompting the secrecy—did I seem like someone who would react negatively?—but before I reached the end of this thought, the therapist was talking about my changed feelings.

"See how easy that was? All you had to do was change your perspective, and the negative feelings went away."

My overwhelming urge, once my perspective was brought into play, was to end the conversation. It seemed as though my loneliness was being blamed on me, on my thoughts and interpretive tendencies, and the assignment of blame made it hard to not to start feeling self-conscious and awkward. The therapist's goal had been to give me a sense of control (since perspective, according to pop culture, is something you can alter), but focusing in on it made my loneliness seem that much more uncontrollable. With the external factors of my life stripped away, the state began to seem ghostly, as though I'd made it up. Since I didn't need my loneliness topped with a garnish of unreality, it was a relief to have the therapist name her rate—$300 an hour—and be able to make murmuring sounds about having to "consider" continuing with treatment.

A much cheaper option was to go with self-directed hypnotherapy. I'd discovered hypnotherapy by doing what any normal lonely person might do: I Googled "loneliness" and "cures." The promise that I might "overcome" my loneliness through hypnosis was one of the first approaches that popped up, and—since the MP3 was priced at just $20—I decided this was an approach I could afford. With the MP3 playing on my laptop, I lay down beside my desk and let the message to "relax, relax, relax" wash over me. Generally, I'm the sort of person who tenses up when told to calm down, and the instruction to let go of stress was beginning to get on my nerves. The tape seemed harmless enough, however, sort of like a yoga session with a slowed-down Duran Duran sound track, and I reasoned that if the MP3 encouraged lonely people to take a break and focus on their breathing for twenty minutes, it could hardly be said to be a bad thing.

That was before the subconscious suggestions started. In a way that I couldn't immediately pinpoint, they seemed oddly familiar. The hypnotist was telling me to picture myself being "open and friendly," and to think about people responding positively to me. "They want to be with you," his soothing voice said. "They want to be near you. They want to spend time with you." As I pictured myself meeting people with a warm, friendly smile, and having them respond in a warm, friendly manner, I realized where the familiarity was coming from. I was, in a sense, just reliving the fantasies I used to engage in on my own, only this time I had prompts and structure to guide me along. The idea behind the suggestions was that the more I visualized myself being social, the more likely I was to actually become social. But in my experience, daydreams of sociability interfered with real sociability, because the ease of the former made the latter seem doubly complicated.

As I lay on my office floor in the spring of 2007, I was reminded of lying in the same spot in the late fall of 2005. I could remember the day quite clearly, because I'd recorded it in my diary in an anatomical way. The entry, from November of 2005, said that I'd woken alone, eaten breakfast alone, commuted to the college where I taught alone, returned home alone, went swimming alone, listened to a CD alone, cooked dinner alone, washed dishes alone, and paid some bills alone. I then, on my own, began to engage in one of the exercises Genevieve was always encouraging me toward. I tried to *visualize* what I was feeling. In my diary, I noted that the image that came to mind was of a cold, empty, gravel-floored space—a sort of variation on the crawl space I used to play in with my best friend Stacey as a child. There was an echoing quality to this space, as though an empty pop can were dropping and hitting the hard floor with a tinny, halfhearted sound.

I reflected in my diary about what this all meant—the emptiness, the coolness, the musty, unused atmosphere of what I was picturing. And I realized, with some surprise, that I was seeing the inside of my heart. In a cool, analytical way, I'd finished up my journal entry by saying, "That an empty cave is what my life has become."

Two years later, after the hypnotic suggestions had come to an end, I tried to imagine how I would have felt if I'd listened to the MP3 at the close of the day I'd written about. In November of 2005, I was no longer crying about my loneliness: since I was the only one around to pick up the pieces, I'd given up on falling apart. But I think the MP3—which someone in England was making money on—might have succeeded in pushing me right over the edge. After I had spent the day entirely alone, the suggestion that I simply picture my life as being full of people would have struck me as ghastly and mean. It would have left me alone on the floor, my heart feeling like an empty cave, struggling with talk of togetherness—all the while knowing that real togetherness was nowhere in sight.

A main idea running through self-help is that we choose and direct our own outcomes. This is the motivating principle behind books such as *The Secret* and *The Law of Attraction*, which stress that our thoughts inform events, and that we manufacture our own reality through a sort of psychic magnetism, in which we most attract what we most consider. The idea of creating your own reality nullifies the significance of material circumstances. If you find yourself facing a negative situation, it's because you've somehow willed it; if you didn't accomplish something, it's because your own negative thought patterns and negative "frequency" stood in your way. Rather cruelly, the facts of a difficult life—poverty, poor housing, a truncated education—can emerge as choices, as events entirely divorced from larger political currents and public-sector decisions.

Many people who write about loneliness fall into line with this way of thinking. They pretend that the material facts of our lives don't matter. "Blaming poverty, lack of education, age, illness, and other whims of fate for one's loneliness is a false charge," insists Chuck Gallozi, on the "Cure for Loneliness" page at personal-development.com. "Regardless of one's disadvantages and handicaps, there are always others that are worse off, yet successful. So it is not our circumstances but our attitude that decides our fate."

In fact, loneliness researchers have spent the past three decades arguing that circumstances—above and beyond attitude—play a major role in determining whether or not we're going to become lonely. One of the biggest determinants is a factor that doesn't even exist within the airbrushed world of self-help, and that's socioeconomic status. At the most general level, it's fair to say that, as income declines, self-reported rates of loneliness rise. In a recent study of over 1,000 individuals in Australia, for instance, researchers found that people earning less than $24,000 a year were twice as likely to be lonely than those earning over $50,000, with loneliness rates falling as income rose. We have a tendency to say that it's "lonely at the top," but researchers at the University of California who decided to test the maxim found that the opposite was the case: people with higher incomes and more prestigious jobs reported less loneliness. And contrary to the nonstop social activity presented on shows such as *Cheers*, research has shown that people in blue-collar or semi-skilled jobs are more likely to be confronted with longer periods of objective aloneness in the course of a day, and that people with less education are more likely to lack confidants than those with graduate degrees. In one study, for instance, one in three individuals with a high school degree were struggling with emotional isolation, compared to just one in ten with a master's degree or higher.

Reed Larson, the sociologist who conducted the original time-budget research in Chicago, noticed the link between income and loneliness right away, and stressed that companionship was at risk of becoming "a luxury more accessible to those with money and higher social status." As rates of objective isolation increase, it's those with disposable income and higher education who are going to be able to obtain contact in the form of classes, massage sessions, personal coaching, therapy, and e-mails. As some academics have noted, work itself, at least in the prerecession era, had turned into something of a social club, with the most advantaged employees being offered not just money but perks that take the form of structured togetherness—group vacations, wine tastings, in-house movie nights, sports outings, and fitness classes.

People who are unemployed, underemployed, or working in the home are cut off from this private form of sociability. For at least the past ten years, policy makers have been arguing that a new form of inequality is presenting itself. As the gap between high and low earners increases, so does the gap between those who are "network rich" and those who are "network poor," with the network poor finding themselves without the social contacts they need to ward off health risks and participate in the culture around them. To say that someone has equality rights in the classic sense of freedom from discrimination on the basis of race or gender is, legally speaking, not particularly meaningful if—like the 48 percent of older people in one British study—they're forced to rely on television as their main form of companionship. True equality, theorists argue, would require that everyone have at least a basic level of social connection, with the government creating and enforcing a floor of social support below which the most vulnerable individuals would not be allowed to fall.

Creating a minimum standard of interaction might sound like an abstract goal, but there are concrete ways in which it can be achieved: through increased funding to public transit (which is crucial in enabling people to get around); through a rethinking of welfare so that it's able to support a certain base level of socializing, such as meeting a friend at a diner once or twice a month; through government-funded respite programs for caregivers; through increased funding for community groups that lead home visits and personal assistance schemes; through government-led matching programs that pair widows with widows, and veterans with veterans; and through the insistence that budgeting become "loneliness-sensitive"—alert to the impact that cuts and reductions might have on a person's ability to sustain a network.

It's only possible to advocate for measures such as these, however, if you see loneliness and isolation as socially patterned—as states that correspond to certain circumstances in a life. And this is a point that self-help writers refuse to concede. For the majority of authors writing self-help today, loneliness is personal, not political. This means that fixing loneliness means turning to the self, through ingesting potions, or trying to hypnotize yourself out of the state, or trying to adjust your "attitude." Within this context, loneliness becomes a choice, something you've decided to feel or unconsciously produced through your own thought processes. And the corollary of this line of thought is that *ending* loneliness must be a choice as well, something you bring about by changing your perspective, or your frequency, or your relationship with yourself.

The question of how much the lonely person is "choosing" their loneliness is a tricky one. Self-help manuals, and the entire doctrine of personal "frequencies," suggest that loneliness is a state that the lonely person is somehow causing (through a poor wardrobe, negative thoughts, poor social skills), and that if the lonely person just decided to *change* these things, the loneliness would fade. Social network theorists, on the other hand, stress that a lot of external factors are at play when it comes to loneliness. Income partly decides who'll become lonely, as does your social status, your level of education, your job, and your age. These factors, especially factors we tend to inherit, such as social status, fall far outside the purview of what a person can readily or easily change about the self. Explicit in the self-help materials is the idea that loneliness—if it lasts—is something the lonely person has chosen to embrace; implicit in the social network studies is the idea that loneliness is something that might be entirely outside the realm of what we can control.

Choice is a dicey word within the language of loneliness. No one wants to think that they're bringing the state upon themselves. And I don't think it's accurate to suggest that anyone, to any extent, goes out and claims a state of painful isolation as their own. But I do think that, once loneliness has settled, the prospect of getting rid of it might indeed prove more difficult and counterintuitive than is generally recognized. Self-help writers encourage the lonely to simply *choose a life of connection*, but this is something that the lonely might not be able to easily do.

There's an old joke in the loneliness literature about something called the "anti-loneliness pill." The idea is that, if such a thing were invented, the lonely person could simply swallow a dose and watch their loneliness disappear. While there has been some slight movement toward the creation of such a tablet—researchers at the University of Illinois have identified a hormone associated with feelings of isolation—the prospect of medication (aside from the help offered by existing anti-anxiety drugs) still belongs to a far-off future.

But the idea of an anti-loneliness pill is a handy one when it comes to asking lonely people about ending their state. I closed each conversation with the same question: If an anti-loneliness pill were invented, would you take it? I was expecting people to say something along the lines of "I'd swallow the bottle," so it was a surprise to be met with indecision, hesitation, and wholesale rejection.

"Right now," says Anne, who's told me about feelings of loneliness that have lasted for most of her life, "I would have to say that, while I would think about it, and I'd probably think about it quite seriously, I doubt that I would take it."

"There might be some days," agrees Katherine, "when, if you offered me the antidote, I'd take it right away. But overall, I don't think I'd take it, if I knew I'd never feel lonely again."

Lonely people differed in their reasons for not wanting to take the remedy. For some lonely people, loneliness had lasted for so long, and had come to inform so many aspects of their lives, that the prospect of saying good-bye to it came to feel like a sort of betrayal of the self.

"I think of the kid I was," says Katherine, referring to a long stretch of loneliness that afflicted her in her early teens. "I was this girl who was always in by herself on Friday nights, plotting to go to university. And I think that girl would be, like, 'This is who we *are.*'"

If loneliness has informed a past, then facing a future without it can seem unnerving. Our past is one of the main sources of information we have to rely upon when it comes to making decisions about our future, and if loneliness is what the self has always known, then getting rid of the state can feel like shipping yourself out to sea without compass or anchor.

"It's always there," says Claire. "It's like a familiar thing, like a baseline. It's kind of like my mode of being, and I couldn't know what it's like *not* to feel it. It's always in the background, in every circumstance." If loneliness is ingrained right into a life, then getting rid of the state means changing that life, and changing a life is not an easy thing to do. Thinking about a life without loneliness can be both pleasurable and disconcerting: pleasurable because the sense of disconnection would be gone; disconcerting because a lonely person might lack the experience necessary to respond to life without it.

Like depression, loneliness presents problems of self-definition. How much is you, and how much is the state? And how much about yourself would have to change if you *didn't* feel lonely? Would giving up loneliness mean surrendering not just negative experiences—isolation, a persistent sense of marginality—but positive ones as well?

"It's part of who I am," explains Anne, stressing why she'd choose to remain lonely. "It's part of where my sensitivity to other people's emotions and relationships comes out of."

With research showing that loneliness really does focus one's attention more closely on the social world, and on social relationships, is that increased clarity something the lonely person is prepared to surrender? And what about the fact that, for many people, loneliness is tied to creativity?

"About three years ago, when I really started feeling this loneliness again," says Frank, "I suddenly started writing songs again. And I've done that constantly now for the past three years." Although not a single one of the lonely people that I spoke to characterized themselves as "artsy," I was amazed at the extent of the creative undertakings they were involved in. I very much doubt that in a random sampling of nonlonely people, I would have hit upon such a high degree of painting, writing, piano-playing, and diarizing. But the lonely people I was speaking to—almost without exception—were engaged in some form of artistic endeavor.

"I think loneliness probably feeds my creativity," says Katherine. "Some of the stuff I've been most proud of has come from times when I've felt really lonely. And that means ending the loneliness doesn't feel like an altogether completely pleasant prospect."

Talking to lonely people, it becomes clear that there might be legitimate reasons for them to "choose" to remain lonely: the state provides them with a muse, it gives them a degree of sensitivity and insight, and it's the basis of the self that they're used to. But it's worth noting that the question I was asking was an entirely artificial one. I didn't ask whether they'd trade their loneliness for a feeling of strong intimacy and embeddedness; I'd asked if they'd simply get rid of it. It was an erasure of loneliness that people were saying no to, and I think I know why.

At the beginning of 2006, as my loneliness was edging toward its fourth year, and as I was beginning to wonder how much more of it I could emotionally and psychologically endure, I began to refer to the affliction not as loneliness but as "emotional anorexia." I don't know where the phrase came from. It wasn't one I'd heard before. I do know that I'd been trying to come up with a way of conveying to myself how scrawny my life had become. The idea of someone slowly starving herself seemed to make metaphoric sense. Just as an anorexic turns down food, I was turning down social interactions; at the same time, I was beginning to obsess and dream and fantasize about those very interactions. My relationship with sociability was becoming as clouded and symbolic as an anorexic's relationship with meals.

There are many ways of talking about anorexia, and about why the state afflicts certain men and women but misses others. But one thing that many researchers agree upon is that anorexia is a form of communication. The anorexic is someone using her body as a way of getting a message across, both to herself and to others. And I think that loneliness, in a way, operates in a similar fashion. Loneliness *says* something. In fact, it announces what the lonely person herself might not be able to say. I'm quite certain that Cacioppo is right when he states that loneliness cues cognitive shifts that make togetherness seem threatening. It was partly for this reason that I found myself becoming so withdrawn. But to a certain extent, withdrawal was something I was quietly courting. Just as an anorexic winnows her body down to nothing, I think I subconsciously *wanted* my social life to become stripped and bare, and I wanted this to happen so that others would see what I was missing. As I let my social circle shrink more and more, and as I let in less and less emotional nourishment, I was hoping that others would notice something going awry. I needed my loneliness as a signal— as a way of communicating to myself, and to others, that my needs were not being met.

Laypeople often link loneliness to a sort of anger. The notion of anger gives rise to some nasty stereotypes, such as the lonely person furiously lashing out at others, or being horribly and meanly jealous of the love others seem to find. I don't think there's any truth to the stereotype of the lonely person as a sort of raging killjoy, but I do think that the notion of anger is intuitively right—just in a different and more subtle sense. Anorexia is, above all, a form of protest, a way of saying, "Look how far I'll go to show you that my needs have not been met." I think this same note of protest can come to underline a loneliness that lasts. The state, and the changes it cues, can become a silent way for the lonely person to express the fact that he's being forced to do without the social connections he needs and expects.

I think this is why lonely people, if you ask them, won't say yes to the possibility of simply giving up their loneliness. The state is doing something for them, it's communicating something. I'm not saying that lonely people choose loneliness. No one does. But loneliness, once it's in place, works as a signal, both to the self and to others. The lonely person might in fact let this signal gets worse and worse, just as a way of more loudly communicating what it is they're lacking. Loneliness, like the body, can become a sort of message board, holding and announcing all the things we're not supposed to say.

What I wanted when lonely was for someone to notice how little I had. My loneliness was a way of voicing—both to myself and to those around me—how badly I needed intimacy and companionship. The more pronounced these needs became, the more I might have cultivated absence, and this was to draw the needs into sharper relief, and turn the volume up on the signal. My loneliness was *articulating* something, and so long as my needs remained unmet, I wasn't prepared to give it up. If that decision can be shoved into the pop culture pigeonhole of "choice," then so be it. I didn't and don't see my loneliness in this light. I see the state as one that was trying to communicate something, and its message wasn't one I was prepared to surrender until others understood what I was trying to say. I didn't want self-help in ending my loneliness. What I wanted was for the state to be recognized, and for someone to extend the intimacy and connection my loneliness was shouting out for.

Chapter Ten

THE GOOD-BYE LOOK

Listing, luck, and a difficult change

Many lonely people stress that they want help and assistance from those around them—either in the form of recognition or in the more concrete form of a loneliness-reduction program. "Any government can go and do a survey," says Maggie, the New Zealander, "and say that 30 percent of people are lonely. But there's no point in spending all the money on the research if you're not going to then do something to try to *fix* the problem, to try and do something to make sure it doesn't get worse, or to put something in place that can try to help the people who are feeling like that. You can do all the surveys in the world, but unless there's some way that lonely people can get help, then you've gotten nowhere."

With lonely people saying they'd like to see more interventions, and with some successful blueprints for intervention available, one might think that there would be more interest and activity in developing additional intervention programs. One problem that everyone working in the field runs into, however, is money. "I think there's a real difference between recognition and action," says Caroline Starkey, referring to loneliness's new and enhanced place in the policy world. "Recognition is really critical, because that's never been in place previously. But I don't think there's any way you can have innovative and exciting projects when you haven't got the funding to do them." Starkey notes that other government priorities—such as military and "stimulus" spending—have squeezed the dollars available to the charitable sector, and that even if the dollars were available, it's not certain that they'd be devoted to loneliness reduction.

"It's amazing how many *billions* of dollars are spent figuring out how to treat depression," notes the University of Arizona's Chris Segrin. "And you can compare that to how many dollars are spent figuring out how to treat loneliness." He pauses for a moment to do the calculation. "I don't know if *any* dollars are spent," he concludes with a laugh.

One of the reasons there's not more money directed toward loneliness and its reduction is that funding is largely determined by government agencies, and the agencies want research to be "translational"—that is, they want to spend dollars on research that contributes to improving recognized clinical problems. "Any time you get funding," explains Radford University's Niels Christensen, "there has to be a clinical disorder, and you have to be working toward reducing that disorder." If a state, such as loneliness, isn't recognized as a serious clinical problem, it's hard to free up the money necessary to work on it, and this creates a classic chicken-and-egg dilemma: without the money, it's hard to prove how significant loneliness really is; without a demonstration of significance, it's hard to get the money. While funds have been awarded for specific loneliness projects, such as Andrew Steptoe's work on loneliness and physiological responses, the deep pockets that magically open for studies on depression close when the subject is loneliness. This means that loneliness researchers are often forced to spend time chasing down dollars to look at approaches and responses to a condition the government isn't sure is "problematic."

One possible, though surely controversial, response to this impasse would be to list chronic loneliness in the next version of the *Diagnostic and Statistical Manual of Mental Disorders*, which is due out in 2012. Since 1952, the DSM has been revised four times, with each change seeing the creation of new disorders, such as "nicotine dependence," "female sexual arousal disorder," and "caffeine-induced anxiety disorder." That is, if you think the manual limits itself to big-ticket items such as schizophrenia and psychosis, you're a bit old-fashioned in your thinking. In the past thirty years, the text has branched out into areas—such as occupational problems, voyeurism, and insomnia—that we don't typically associate with traditional concepts of mental illness.

The increasingly sprawling nature of the DSM has been roundly criticized by mental health critics such as Herb Kutchins and Stuart Kirk, who describe the DSM's tendency to absorb ordinary traits and occurrences as "the pathologizing of everyday behavior." According to Kutchins and Kirk, ordinary tendencies and moods are labeled as clinically deviant partly as a way of clearing a path for lucrative pharmacological interventions, and sometimes for political ends as well (in 1987, for example, it was suggested that there be an entry for "masochistic personality disorder," which, if created, would have cast the problem of spousal abuse as one in which the woman was staying with her partner for the sake of the masochistic enjoyment she received from being hurt).

There are definitely those within the loneliness research community who are uncertain about the notion of adding

loneliness to the list of disorders included in the DSM. "I hate
the medicalizing of the difficulties of life," says Robert Weiss
gently, after pausing to give the question of the DSM some
thought. "I've gotten involved with something like this with
severe grief—should persistent grief be in the next version of
the DSM? And I think it will be, but my feeling was ambivalence on the side of resisting it. And my reason for that is, even
though not everyone experiences persisting and intense grief
when someone close to them dies, nevertheless persisting and
intense grief seems to me well within the normal range of experience." A similar argument, Weiss suggests, could be made
in relation to loneliness. The fact that long-term, intense loneliness isn't a state everyone struggles with doesn't mean there's
something unusual or "disordered" about it; it can still be seen
an aspect of everyday life. "I'm just not comfortable," Weiss
concludes, "with the idea that you pick up the DSM and it's got
every trouble that could occur to anybody."

There are others, however, who see the very inclusivity of
the DSM as a good reason for loneliness to be added. "Through
all these revisions to the DSM," says Chris Segrin, "no one has
added loneliness. The DSM has things like caffeine addiction in
it. Why isn't *loneliness* in there? There's almost been something
of a bias against it. I think loneliness should be considered a
primary psychological problem that has its own set of theories,
causes, treatments, and so forth."

"With people who have been lonely for years and years,
you have to ask if there's underlying depression, or underlying social anxiety," agrees Niels Christensen. "And if there's
not, then there's something different there that's problematic."
Chronic loneliness, Christensen suggests, could be seen as
something that differs from other people's experiences, that in-
terferes with functioning, and that causes subjective distress. If

you take the DSM's own definition of mental disorder, which says that there should be "a clinically significant behavioral or psychological syndrome . . . that is associated with present distress or disability or with a significantly increased risk of suffering death, pain, or disability," then chronic loneliness meets the definition.

The notion of medicalizing loneliness becomes slightly more persuasive when one steps back and looks at the consequences of not doing so. "I would never do it, because it would crush my mom and dad," says Graham, a midforties information technology professional from New York who describes himself as "really, really lonely." "But I feel suicidal. If my mom and dad weren't in the picture, I don't know what I'd do."

Suicidal thinking occupies such an extreme position on the emotional spectrum that it's easy to view comments such as Graham's as uniquely distressing. But in toying with the notion of self-destruction, Graham might be uncommonly honest, but he's not unusual. In a study of 20,000 Quebec residents, researchers at the University of Montreal found that 21 percent of individuals who identified themselves as "feeling lonely very often" had thought of suicide, while 8 percent of the lonely had engaged in parasuicidal behavior such as cutting or swallowing sublethal doses of pills. While the relationship between loneliness, depression, and suicide is complex—in the Quebec study, feeling both lonely and depressed carried the highest suicide risk—the significance of loneliness and isolation as risk factors for suicide have long been recognized by mental health professionals. In 2007, the Samaritans—a leading twenty-four-hour suicide prevention and support hotline operating in the United Kingdom and Ireland—surveyed 500 individuals and asked them about the reason for their call. More than half of the callers identified loneliness as a problem, meaning that loneliness was the second reason (just behind depression) leading people to reach out for anonymous support and intervention.

It's also the case that loneliness is slowly *being* pathologized. Although there's no entry for "loneliness" in the DSM, the word comes up a lot when the diagnosis is "avoidant personality disorder." The disorder is a new one. It was created in 1980, just as objective isolation was beginning to increase and visits with friends and family were beginning to drop. According to the DSM, avoidant personality disorder is characterized by showing restraint in intimate relationships, viewing the self as socially inept, being preoccupied with the possibility of rejection in social situations, and being hesitant about getting too involved with others unless there's a certainty of reciprocity. The DSM refers to "avoidants" as "lonely" and "isolated," while Martin Kantor's *Distancing*—a text devoted entirely to avoidant personality disorder—describes avoidants this way: they live by themselves or with their family, they don't socialize very often or socialize only "within limits," they keep old friends but have difficulty meeting new people, they display a degree of "relationship anxiety," they dream about abandonment, and they possess remarkably good insight.

When I was reading *Distancing* at the med school library, I began to feel a slightly sick sensation, as though I were in a car that had hit a sudden dip in the road. Is there really something wrong with me? I thought, feeling immensely self-conscious. Is my problem really a personality disorder? Personality disorders refer to something inherently wrong with the self. Unlike depression or anxiety (which are seen as changeable states), personality disorders are viewed as ingrained, maladaptive aspects of identity that have lasted a lifetime, and which result in profound impairment in occupational functioning or interpersonal relationships. My loneliness has been lifelong, I thought, scanning the pages of *The Textbook of Personality Disorders*; it's impaired my interpersonal relationships.

As my queasiness intensified, I began to rifle through some of the personality assessment schedules a psychiatrist might use in making a diagnosis of disordered personality. Was I sensitive to setbacks in life? (This question struck me as odd: Was it possible for something to be a setback without arousing sensitivity? In any event, I wasn't particularly sensitive.) Was I an introvert? (Yes.) Did I spend a lot of time thinking? (Yes.) And then there were the million-dollar questions about sociability: Did I have many close relationships? Did it trouble me that I didn't have more? I was in the process of counting up my close relationships when I read the subscript: "If subject has few close relationships but definitely desires more, this item should not be scored." In other words, if one is distressed about the lack of close ties, then the absence of such ties shouldn't be seen as indicative of a disorder. And what was loneliness but distress about the lack of close ties?

I sat back, a bit relieved and confused. *Distancing* was telling me that loneliness could be indicative of a disordered personality, but the personality assessment schedule was telling me that loneliness was actually a sign of normality. I think this confusion about the role of loneliness runs right through the avoidant personality disorder diagnosis. It casts the "avoidant" person as pathological, but it doesn't ask what's cuing the avoidance. It might be loneliness that, in its paradoxical way, is triggering withdrawal, sensitivity to criticism, and unease around others. And if it's loneliness that's the heart of the problem, then the personality in question can't and shouldn't be seen as disordered, since loneliness is an innate, protective, and profoundly human emotion.

There's probably no easy answer to the question of whether or not to "medicalize" loneliness. On one hand, the state is so humane, so central to who we are as individuals, that it's hard to see it as something that requires inclusion in a guide to mental disorders. On the other hand, the impact loneliness has on a life is so profound that it seems as though *not* including it constitutes something of an oversight. If drinking too much coffee is in the guidebook, then a state that alters sleep patterns, disrupts the immune system, and triggers shifts in cognition should probably be there too.

"I think the psychological toll of loneliness is every bit as powerful as depression, or social anxiety, or alcoholism," emphasizes Chris Segrin. "But our society just doesn't recognize it as such." Including loneliness in the next version of the DSM would help us to recognize the impact loneliness can have on a life, and would reassure lonely people that they're struggling with an affliction others recognize as real. If one adds the possibility of increased funding to the list of advantages, as well as the subduing of avoidant personality disorder, then the argument for inclusion becomes even stronger.

I think that listing loneliness (or "chronic loneliness") within the DSM would be an important first step in seeing the state as a legitimate, recognizable affliction. This recognition would go some ways toward encouraging lonely people to self-identify with the problem, and would help them understand that they're dealing with something real. It's also the case that talking about a state in one sphere—say, a psychiatric manual—can open the door to talking about it in other spheres. Including loneliness in the DSM would open up discussion about loneliness in scientific and psychological circles, and this discussion—as it was picked up by newspapers and magazines—would probably spill over into a wider public discussion, one that might leave lonely people feeling more comfortable about admitting to the state. Including loneliness in the DSM would also encourage general practitioners to ask about it (in the way that they now routinely screen for signs of depression), and it might lead to an expanded emphasis on treatment options.

Ultimately, listing loneliness within the DSM might create a situation in which the state is taken seriously. Just forty years ago, people were writing about loneliness as a "blessing," as a sort of cognitive gift that allowed us to realize how alone we actually were. Loneliness, many authors insisted, was "transcendent," "exquisite," and "precious." Until recently, it wasn't unusual to see the state being characterized as "a point of intense and timeless awareness of the Self," as an affliction that possessed something of a cachet. "Loneliness is not a distinction given to all," wrote one commentator in 1961, making loneliness seem like musical skill or a knack for baking—something one is lucky to have.

We need to recognize that there's a cultural history attached to loneliness that doesn't attach to depression. While depression has been (and to a certain extent continues to be) glamorized as a source of depth, it hasn't been celebrated as a blessing, as something that makes us *better* than we would otherwise be. And this is the intellectual tradition that loneliness comes out of. So many people, for so long, have written about loneliness as a *good* thing, as a trait that feeds artistry, or connects us to our essential selves, or gives us important hints about our place in the cosmic order. People are still, today, writing about our need to embrace loneliness, to see it as a special message from God, or as a precondition to making lasting art.

Loneliness isn't a badge of creative prestige. It's not something sent from the heavens. It doesn't bring richness and knowledge. It undermines the body. It leads to dementia. It sucker-punches the immune system, cues self-defeating behaviors, and can last for years. Listing the state in a book dedicated to *afflictions* would help to erase the nonsensical ideas that have grown up around it. We now have a different, more scientifically grounded understanding of what loneliness is and what it does. An entry in a well-respected medical tome might help hammer this message home.

The fact that loneliness isn't currently listed in the DSM means that there's not a lot of funding available for treatment programs, and the absence of treatment programs leaves lonely individuals relying on hit-and-miss strategies in their attempts to overcome the state. A lot of lonely people have tried volunteering—which, many stress, can leave them feeling doubly alone—and others have joined groups, such as writing or watercolor classes, which often have the same effect.

What many lonely people have been forced to rely on, with few guided strategies available, is luck. "I don't know that when I've had a lot more friends and felt less lonely, it was because of something I was doing," notes Frank. "I think it was more that I was who I was, and the situation was different." The extent to which we control the situations in our lives is a subject of some debate. The academics behind the Luck Project in England say that everything we call "luck" is actually the manifestation of some effort we've made, and that nothing, in short, happens at random. But some lonely people I've spoken with, such as Frances, say that it was entirely luck that ended their loneliness. In changing her job, she—in one fell swoop—met the man who became her husband and also found her way into a full social circle that met her emotional needs. The change is so dramatic, says Frances, "that I'll surprise myself by thinking, 'I'm not actually lonely any more, am I?' "

People who like to rationalize luck away would say that I created the end of the worst part of my loneliness. In some ways, I did do certain things. At the beginning of 2006, I decided I *had* to do something about my loneliness. I forced myself over my tendency toward withdrawal and—almost choking with anxiety—made myself sign up for an intramural basketball league. (For the record: the fact that I'd paid a nonrefundable $150 registration fee meant that I was able to offset my anxiety with my innate refusal to waste money.) The league was a lesbian one, and I expected it to be a casual, dressed-down affair. I showed up in torn turquoise sweatpants, a baggy T-shirt, and a pair of ancient running shoes. I was shocked and horrified to walk into the gym and see most women dressed like Kobe Bryant. There were a lot of silky, knee-length basketball shorts, and flashy jerseys, and bright white ankle-high shoes. I was handed an orange team T-shirt—one that made my skin look sickly—and with a sense of being massively unprepared I retreated to the changing room.

The problem with an all-women's league, of course, is that retreating to the changing room just means you run into more of the people you're trying to avoid. I went into the locker room, clutching my orange shirt, and saw another woman with a short, salt-and-pepper crew cut, tying up her shoes. She was wearing an orange shirt, like mine, so I assumed we must be teammates. The locker room was small—during the days, the recreation center catered to kids—and I didn't have much room to maneuver. I sat down on a bench across from the woman and, to my surprise, found myself spilling out all my worries.

"I don't know that I'll be able to do this," I said in a hurry.

"I've never played before. I'm not even *wearing* the right thing."

Danielle had a quiet, reassuring manner to her. "You'll be fine," she said, with a little smile that showed off her dimples.

I asked her if she knew how to play, and without a hint of vanity she said yes, she'd played in the past. I felt like hanging on to her, as though she could lead me into the gym and through the game. I had an overwhelming urge to reach out to her, as though I were a little kid grasping at her mother's skirt. But doing so would have been foolish. We were two grown women in a changing room, and I had to dress.

"See you out there," Danielle said as she left, and I collapsed into a little bundle of worries in her absence, certain that others were going to make fun of my pants.

When Danielle said that she'd played before, she hadn't been kidding. I'd later learn she'd been a varsity athlete, a provincial MVP, and coach to the province-wide basketball team. At the time, I was just struck by the ease and grace she brought to the simple act of movement. She seemed to know exactly where the ball was at all times, how to get to it, how to handle it, and how to pass it along to the next person in line. She didn't drop things, she didn't stumble. She could score a basket after little more than a glance at the net. She played fairly—she never hogged the ball, even though she was the best player on the team—and she was encouraging to others, shouting (as I would learn to do) "Good D!" whenever someone managed a strong defensive move.

A lot of things went through my mind during that first game. I tried to spend as much time on the bench as possible. The game was rushed, and everyone was new, so it was hard for the team leader to keep track of who'd played when. Every time I was asked if I'd just been out, I tried to look winded and said yes. Not only was I alarmed at the prospect of playing with women who were good at the game, I liked the way my perch gave me the chance to quietly look around. I was able to take note of how the others were dressed (I wanted to fit in next time), and watch others as they played. After my fit of nerves in the changing room, it was relaxing to see everyone else hurry around and race. I liked the fact that, unlike my ill-fated bike trip, there was no expectation of—in fact, no possibility of—long conversations or intimate disclosures. Everyone was simply running and bustling, and I was relieved that very little was expected of me socially. The sound of women's laughter calmed me, I liked the high-pitched squeal of the refs' whistles, and I liked the warm sense of companionship that came from squeezing in knee-to-knee with others on the bench.

But what I liked most of all was seeing my teammates handle the ball. I watched everyone: the lovely Irish woman who'd been told to take out her earrings; the muscular Australian who looked as though she was ready to run right through her opponents; the small, pretty, and surprisingly tough-talking woman who was so quick on her feet. But my attention kept returning, time and time again, to Danielle. A lot of thoughts and ideas went through my mind during that first game, but one of the main ones—one that I'd come to rely on in the months and years to come—was, Someone that coordinated won't break my heart.

When research on loneliness first began, there was an idea that the state possessed a sort of off switch, that once the right relationship presented itself, it would simply vanish, as though it had never been. This conceptualization of loneliness as a state that simply disappears from one day to the next is rather different from how we conceptualize depression. With depression, we're encouraged to think of recovery in terms of weeks or months, with depressed people being cautioned against making major decisions during the recovery period, since it's hard to know how operative the mood might still be in their lives. Recovery from depression is seen as a gradual process, one in which the depressed person must slowly find her way back to a more balanced perspective, while recovery from loneliness is seen as a sort of instantaneous event, one that sees the lonely person traveling an enormous emotional distance in a matter of hours or days.

There hasn't been a great deal of research on recovery from loneliness, and this is because the state is seen as something one simply overcomes. The treatment programs that have proven effective, however, are those that unfold over a period of weeks or months, and this suggests that transitioning away from the state is a more gradual process than we generally conceive it to be. Furthermore, if the complexity of loneliness is fully acknowledged—if we recognize that the state can distort perception, disrupt sleep, undermine the immune system, reduce fluent thought, and cue fantasy—it becomes less and less plausible to see it as something that simply ends the moment a relationship is in place.

"It's definitely not easy to move from a lonely place to being with someone all the time," says Frances. When she met the man who became her husband, the worst part of the state subsided for her, but the transition away from loneliness was more complex than simply giving someone a good-night kiss. "Over time, it gets more comfortable, but it's very strange to start sharing your personal space and having a very intimate relationship when you're used to being alone and withdrawn."

Some lonely people specifically use what I'd call a pacing approach to try to encourage themselves away from the state. That is, they allow for days in which to be alone and lonely, and balance that out with days that are more social and embedded. "A little bit at a time," says Sonia, who is trying to make the transition to a more socially active life, "I'll try to adjust my schedule, so that I'm around people a lot more. But I find I get tired of it. Every few days or so, I just want to be by myself. And so I'll do that—every few days I just don't want any contact with anyone. I'll just hole up."

Part of the reason a back-and-forth between sociability and solitude is necessary is that the lonely person trying to lead a more social life is, in some ways, transitioning from one version of the self to another. "There's a kind of integration of the self that's associated with being lonely," says Robert Weiss, "and that's different from the integration of the self that's associated with membership in a community, or with being part of a partnership. And you may say, 'One of those is the real me, I really feel myself this way.' But they're both the real you. Except when you're in one of them, you don't have much access to the other."

A more realistic way of looking at the end of loneliness—if such a thing really exists—is to see it as a gradual movement from a self characterized by isolation to a self characterized by embeddedness, and this is hardly a simple transition to make. As Weiss notes, the self that's identified with loneliness might start to feel like the *real* self; feelings of connection—rather than simply displacing loneliness—might start to feel phony, or exhausting, or so far removed from the familiar that they can emerge as worrisome rather than welcoming. Moving away from loneliness, in other words, can start to feel like a movement away from the self that you know, and the emotional distance in question can leave you feeling cut off from who you used to be.

I started seeing Danielle after a springtime basketball party held in a coffee shop in Toronto's gay village. I'd asked her out as our subways came roaring into the station—she was heading south, while I was heading north—and in a week we met for our first date. I remember seeing her on the sidewalk, waiting for me outside the café, the sunshine seeming to gravitate toward the spot where she was standing, and I felt filled not just with desire but with something like hope, as though something critical about me might be about to change. The first date led to a second, the second led to a weekend in my apartment, and that lost weekend led to a series of trips between my place downtown and her apartment farther out in the suburbs.

My first few weeks with Danielle were spectacular. I'd read about the notion of the lonely person simply leaving loneliness behind, and I thought—with a great deal of self-congratulation—I've done it. That's over. But the Technicolor intensity of the first month or so began to blur into something more uneven. I was enormously happy to be with Danielle, but I noticed that this happiness was beginning to be marked by shifts and changes.

Togetherness, after such a long time alone, led to dreams in which I was surrounded by crowds, or shouting at people to get away from me. My appetite collapsed—I went from eating constantly to not being able to eat at all. I started skipping lunch and even dinner in favor of crackers and yogurt that I forced myself to swallow at the counter. I began to become persistent about my privacy: when my neighbor's new puppy let out small yelps in the morning, I was enraged, as though someone had just come charging into my apartment; after several years of leaving my curtains open, I began to close them, so that my neighbors couldn't see into any of my rooms. Heat and noise began to undo me. It was a hot summer—one of the hottest on record—and I felt as though I were permanently overheated: I'd slip into the cool tub to try to drop my body temperature back to normal; the racket of other people's air conditioners seemed overly loud and constant; and if I opened the windows, I couldn't stop listening to the sound of traffic. When I went for walks in the evenings, I found it hard to take note of my surroundings. It was as though the world around me were melting, as though it were gradually becoming less real and concrete than it actually was.

Three months into dating Danielle, I was seriously strung out, and the reason I was falling apart was that I was worried about her leaving. As I sat on the lawn at the University of Toronto with Laura, feeding the edges of our sandwiches to the starlings, she asked if Danielle had given any sign of dissatisfaction, if she'd given any hints about intending to leave.

"No," I said, lying back on the cool grass. "She's great. She's nothing but encouraging."

"So why are you so convinced she's going somewhere?"

"I don't know. I just can't get around it."

I found it hard to think about Danielle staying in my life, because—in my experience—staying entailed an eventual departure. I couldn't seem to fix Danielle in my imagination in a permanent way. It was also undeniable and painful for me to realize that, when I thought about the possibility of her leaving, I felt something close to relief, as though the inevitable were finally about to unfold.

"You could be alone for years and years," Genevieve said, when I settled myself on her couch. One of her cats was a fat brown tabby named Gordon, and I patted him as Genevieve tried to outline the problem. She'd told me that she was happy that I'd found Danielle, and she was, in that silent, therapeutic way, clearly cheering the relationship on. But my reluctance to fully engage with and trust Danielle seemed to frustrate her. "If you were alone," she said, trying to subtly trace the ins and outs of my flawed thinking, "it would be very comfortable for you. You could maintain it your whole life. It would be easy for you."

The word *easy* seemed to reverberate within me. There was something simple and uncluttered about my aloneness; in comparison, the relationship with Danielle seemed messy and complex. In response to what felt like a major upheaval, I became obsessively neat in my apartment, trying to keep everything as orderly as possible, and I canceled on family brunches, because I felt too emotionally overloaded to deal with even cursory social demands. There was a version of myself that I was used to, and it seemed to be under siege. Like other lonely people, it was a version of myself that I linked to creativity, to calmness, to certainty. In a strange way, I began to feel almost nostalgic for my loneliness. I'd been hanging on to it as a means of signaling an emergency, but—now that the emergency was being responded to—I felt as though my emotional center were crashing down. I'd been lonely for almost four years. Without the state to serve as my mental and emotional foundation, I felt ready to crumble. Every day that Danielle and I spent together was a day that saw me moving further away from the person I used to be, and I wasn't comfortable with an experience that felt like the emotional equivalent of continental drift.

———

I'd told Danielle, on one of our first dates, that I was writing a book about ecopsychology. Ecopsychology looks at the inter-relationship between our minds and the natural world, and—while it's a fascinating subject—it clearly wasn't my real topic. I wasn't sure how to tell Danielle that I was working on a book about loneliness. I didn't know how she'd react to the news. I worried about a scenario in which I'd say the word *lonely* only to be met with discomfort or disbelief. I worried about some of the ideas I'd seen floating around online—such as the lonely being stingy, mean, or (in a strange conceptualization) elit-ist. Above all, I worried about seeming unattractive. It was as though the lack of intimacy I was writing about might seem like proof positive of the fact that I didn't *deserve* intimacy, that announcing my loneliness would alert Danielle to the fact that I was supposed to be left alone.

About two months after our first date, Danielle and I were back in the coffee shop that had hosted the basketball party. It was during the Gay Pride weekend in Toronto, on the day before the huge parade. The street outside was filled with gruff-looking men holding hands, and gaggles of women in tank tops, and rainbow-painted display booths. Danielle and I were on tall stools near the window, relaxing after a walk along the parade route. She asked about my work.

There was a backstage atmosphere to that afternoon, as though we were being let in on a secret that—with the streets closed off in preparation for the parade—the rest of the city wasn't being allowed to see. This secrecy was mixed with a de-licious sense of openness, of being able, on that street and on that weekend, to hold hands and touch your partner in a close, protective way. Notions of privacy—of being out or being in, of telling people about yourself or keeping everything hidden—seemed to be floating on the breeze. The idea of having to keep hiding something about myself began to seem untenable. It's part of who I am, I thought.

"My book," I said, looking straight into my glass. "It's not really about ecopsychology." I was about to falter and say, "I'm writing a novel," but I decided the truth had to come out. "It's about loneliness," I said finally. I was so nervous my hands started shaking. I could hear the silver ring I wore start to rattle against the glass I was holding.

This is it, I thought. This is where she walks out.

"Loneliness?" Danielle repeated, sounding curious. "Why did you get interested in that?"

"I got really lonely practicing law," I said. Instead of an excuse, the statement sounded true. Struck by the notion that I might just be able tell someone what had happened, I continued. "I was really lonely, so I started to read about it. Then the reading sort of grew into the idea of a memoir, and well . . . Now I'm writing about it all the time." Here I lost my nerve. I sounded apologetic. But Danielle didn't seem to notice my change in tone.

"So you're writing about your own loneliness?"

I nodded.

"Good for you," she said. She reached over and pried my fingers off the side of the glass. My palm was slippery with sweat and condensation, and she started running her fingertip along the edge of my life line. "I think that's courageous."

"Do you?" I asked. It sounded as though I needed approval, but I *did* need approval. I needed to be able to have my subject—my condition—and Danielle at the same time. In my experience, other people and discussions of loneliness didn't really go together. Many people in my life—from friends to professionals—hadn't seemed to want to ask me about it. It hadn't seemed like something they wanted me to name.

"I think it's great," she said, sounding completely truthful. "It's not something most people would do. It's sort of strange," she conceded, in an amused, surprised tone. "But it's interesting. Tell me more about it."

And so I started to talk.

One long weekend in late August, after Danielle and I had been together for four months, we borrowed a summer house on Lake Erie from one of Danielle's colleagues. We ate peaches and nectarines we'd bought from a fruit stall, and spent our days walking along Crystal Beach, where the shoreline was filled with young men throwing footballs, little kids putting on water wings, ice cream sellers, beach chairs, and coolers of beer. At night, we laid on our backs on the wooden deck, with Danielle lifting her hand up against the sky to try to trace the constellations. We woke late, sneezing with dust and mold allergies triggered by the old house, and drank strong coffee out of heavy mugs.

In the course of one of these lazy mornings, Danielle's cell phone rang. I heard a hurried voice on the other end, and Danielle went into the living room for better reception. I heard her saying, "That's right. Two years ago." It wasn't clear to me what it was she was talking about.

"That was MUN," she said, coming back into the kitchen and looking dazed. "That job I applied for two years ago? They just got funding for it. They want me to start in April."

Memorial University of Newfoundland is on the east coast. In fact, it's as far east as you can go in pursuit of higher education and still remain in North America. I'd never been to Newfoundland, and when I thought of the place, all I could do was conjure up stock images of whales, cliffs, and raging waves.

"Would you come with me?" Danielle asked, tilting her head toward mine so that our foreheads were touching.

"To Newfoundland?"

People often talk about being of two minds about something. When they say this, they're usually referring to religious education in schools, or donating money to Planned Parenthood. I meant it more literally. The prospect of a move to the east coast seemed to split my life in two. I drew up lists of pros and cons, and tried to picture myself standing on a rock, staring out at the waves and mist of the Atlantic, wearing (for some reason) a hood. But I could never come up with a list convincing enough, or a vision romantic enough, to overcome my uneasiness. I knew that if I went, it would be for cohabitation, a shared life, and love; it would be the end of the loneliness that I'd been trying to fight off for so long. If I stayed, it would be for the simplicity and familiarity of aloneness. On the facts, the choice seemed easy. I could almost, as I tried to puzzle it out, see it as a sort of blindingly obvious LSAT question: A lonely person is offered escape from her loneliness. She (a) moves to the east coast to be with the person who she loves and who makes her feel connected, or (b) remains in Toronto, where a lack of emotional connection is driving her loneliness toward the pathological.

From an analytical perspective, I could see the answer. Of course the lonely person should move to the coast, should dive right into that more connected life and leave loneliness behind. But—and this is what self-help books and urges to "just get over it" seem to miss completely—it's hard to do that when loneliness is what you're used to. If part of your self has been shaped by loneliness, it's hard to step away from the state and do something that you have, in a sense, little emotional training for. It's hard to turn into that other person, the nonlonely self, the one who feels connected.

One hot night in early September, more than four years after my loneliness had set in, I had a dream in which an older woman said, "You want your old life back, don't you?" The woman in the dream was blond, like me, and mildly attractive. I knew I was partly in love with her. We were in my bedroom, and she'd just climbed out of bed and was dressing to go back to her own house. Her tone, in the dream, was judgment-free. It was as though she was finally naming something that we'd both been aware of but were too cautious to mention.

"Yes," I said, with enormous relief, thinking I could just get back to things. And I felt—both within the dream and upon waking—as though solidity were being presented to me after weeks of half-measures and anxiety. I felt as though I could go back to being myself.

There were seven months between the time that Danielle got the call about the job and the time that she'd have to leave to drive to Newfoundland. We spent a lot of this time talking, debating, and weighing pros and cons. I think it was here that a lifetime's experience with sports came to Danielle's advantage. She didn't try to rush me; she picked up a conversation wherever I left it; she subtly followed me wherever my emotions led.

"I can't do it," I said one night in February, a month before her departure. I was lying on my back on the bed, sobbing. I was trying to picture myself leaving everything that was familiar— family, friends, city—and embarking on a life of uncertainty.

"Shhh," Danielle whispered. She was lying beside me, gently stroking my hair.

"I can't. I'm sorry, but I can't."

"You'll know what you need to do," she said.

Danielle was still playing basketball in the women's league every Saturday night. I'd quit playing—to be honest, I was hopeless—but I accompanied her to all of the games. The basketball court had an observation deck attached, but the deck was behind glass, and you had to reach it by leaving the gym and heading up a flight of stairs. At the top of the staircase was a big, empty area that felt like a waiting room, with old chairs and couches scattered randomly around.

On the night that I'd told Danielle I couldn't go, I went up to the lounge area. The glass muted the sound of the game on the court below, and the whole area was dimly lit; since I was the only person upstairs, I didn't bother searching for the light switch. I began pacing from one end of the observation area to the other, each time turning to look at Danielle on the court as I passed the glass. Exhausted by my own emotional calculations, by my sadness, and by my inability to commit to a different sort of life, I threw myself into one of the dusty, battered armchairs and let my head fall against the headrest.

This is what you'll have when she leaves, I thought, looking around at the shadowy light, the ugly furniture, the emptiness. There were two security guards downstairs, but their conversation barely reached me. Between their muffled talk and the blotted-out sounds of the game, I felt as though I were cut off from communication itself, as though I might never talk to anyone again. A searing sense of aloneness came rushing back to me, a feeling that had started to ease in my time with Danielle.

And in that moment—alone in that strange, ugly, unlit place—something gave way. Some fear or reluctance, some childhood failure to attach, some sense of dread about being with someone—it gave way to a greater fear, which was that of continuing to be on my own. The paradox of my own loneliness finally, as I sat in the dismal lounge, collapsed. Disconnection began to seem more threatening than connection, aloneness more frightening than a life with someone else. I began to see that my loneliness, while it felt comforting and familiar, was actually killing me, and that I'd have to challenge it to overcome the pain I was in. I knew that facing the unknown would be hard, making emotional changes would be hard, and leaving would be hard, but nothing would be harder than continuing to live a life with loneliness, a life without Danielle. Feeling as though I had to step away from myself in order to save myself, I came to my decision.

"I'm going with you," I said, when we were back in the safety of the car.

Danielle stopped at a light and turned to look at me. "I knew you would," she said, softly.

I think that we need to start seeing the end of loneliness as a process, not a step, and as a process that the lonely person might not successfully emerge from. In my experience, the immediate feelings associated with loneliness—the persistent sense of being alone—those feelings can ebb and abate quite quickly. But in their place can come anxiety, uncertainty, indecision. These were the emotions that could have engulfed me; they could have left me locked in a lonely life. It was by no means guaranteed that I was going to go to Newfoundland. The indecision I faced was real, and the decision was ultimately made by a sort of desperation, by a quick flashing reminder of what my life had been like. If this hadn't happened, if I hadn't been able to recognize the lure of my loneliness and remember my loneliest self, I might have remained in Toronto, safe with but troubled by my state.

We need to recognize that loneliness, if it's lasted for a long time, can leave a person with behaviors and beliefs that can become deeply rooted. The fact that Danielle left me feeling less alone, for instance, didn't change the fact that I was used to thinking of myself as solitary. Her presence didn't touch on what had become an ingrained tendency to keep my feelings and convictions to myself, and to see myself as my sole source of support in times of strain. If there's a self that's associated with loneliness, and a self that's associated with sociability, then it takes time to make the transition from one to the other, just as it takes time to journey from a nondepressed perspective to a more hopeful and uplifted one. I'm not suggesting that the transition can't be made, or that every journey will be as hard as the one I experienced. But I am saying that we need to see the movement away from loneliness as much more complex than is generally thought, and we need to give lonely people help in making the transition. We have to start seeing loneliness as a state that might dig itself in with claws. When I made the decision to leave Toronto, I felt as though I were ripping something away from me, as though, if I were to look down right now, I'd see the scars and scrapes where it had tried its best to dig itself in.

I arrived in Newfoundland in early June, shocked to find it still cold. Danielle had rented a house that sat on the edge of a park. It was a sunny day, I was jet-lagged, and I felt as though I were surrounded by too much light. Mumbling something about the need to retreat, I wound my way to an upstairs bedroom and curled up not on the bed but on the dusty, carpeted floor.

I could hear kids playing in the park outside and could smell the salty sweetness of the air. I told Danielle that I thought I was in shock, and asked if she could make me some sugary tea. From my spot on the floor, tucked up in a fetal position, I could hear her running water and stirring a spoon against a cup in the kitchen downstairs. Then I heard her mount the steps and return to the room where I was resting.

"Drink," she said. "Sit up and sip." The tea was hot and strong; it seemed to focus my attention. Sitting up, I drank my tea and nibbled at the blueberry muffin Danielle had bought me. We sat like that for a while, silently. I was more than a thousand miles from home, in a city I'd never seen before, in a house owned by someone else, with most of my possessions packed into duffel bags. I was propped on one elbow, not yet entirely upright, and I kept dropping my head to the carpet between sips and bites. Gradually, I relaxed enough to stretch out, and I turned over on my back.

The house was over a hundred years old. The ceilings were high, and the whole place smelled fresh and yet somehow lived in, as though I were surrounded by the presence of all the people who'd been in that room before me.

Danielle lay down beside me, and we listened to the children shouting outdoors. I was wearing clothes that were a bit too light—it had been much warmer in Toronto when I'd left—and I felt as though I'd fallen into a different dimension, as though I'd left one medium, like air, and had landed in an entirely different one, like water.

"You made it," Danielle said. "You're finally here."

I opened my eyes to get a better sense of my surroundings. The floor felt solid; the light seemed to have settled down and was bright and clear. I felt suspended between one world and another; not yet departed, not yet fully arrived. But I knew I'd made a transition, one more difficult than packing my bags and boarding a plane seemed to suggest. I knew I'd started on the journey from one self to another, from a lonely life to a life marked by more of a sense of connection. I wasn't sure what the future would hold in terms of loneliness, but I knew I'd slayed one dragon. The worst part of my loneliness had receded, and I'd survived.

"Yes," I said, feeling suddenly grounded. "I made it."

Epilogue

LONELY

Clinicians who work with the depressed often warn that depression serves a kindling function, with each depression making it easier for future depressions to present themselves. I wonder—though there's no research on the subject—whether loneliness works in the same way. I wonder whether, in becoming and staying lonely for so long in my early to midthirties, I essentially tilled the ground, and created a situation in which loneliness now has an easier time asserting itself in my life.

Because my loneliness, even though I'm now in a partnership, isn't gone. It's just different. In this sense, the handles I taught myself at the University of Toronto library have proven useful. I know that I've gone from a situation in which I lack a close emotional connection to one where I lack a strong sense of community and collegiality. To put the matter more concretely, I've found it somewhat difficult to make friends on this remote, rocky island. And that's not because I lack the social skills, or because opportunities haven't presented themselves. It's because certain behaviors that developed during my years of loneliness continue to be rooted within me. I'm shyer than I

was before chronic loneliness hit; I'm more hesitant in engag-
ing with others. I'm more reluctant—even in situations where
I have to interact with people—to force myself to connect; I'm
less showy. Some of these changes are no doubt due to maturity,
to turning into someone who feels less of a need to be glossy
and pert. But I have to wonder whether long-term loneliness
hasn't changed me, and turned me into someone I didn't used to
be—into someone who is, in fact, an easier target for the state,
someone who has fewer defenses to rally against it.

In some ways, I've gone back to being the person I was in
my late teens and early twenties, not in terms of sociability but
in terms of my outlook toward loneliness. Twenty years ago, I
saw loneliness as something I was destined for. Now that a terrible interval of loneliness has ended, it's left me with the same
sense of expectation and vulnerability, as though it might be
waiting to settle again.

And what strikes me as peculiar about this situation is that,
even though I know that the state is out there, even though
I understand that it's written into my DNA, and that its lifetime will necessarily correspond with my own, I can't bring
myself to take many of the steps that might keep the state at
bay for good. For reasons that are partly related to loneliness,
I've made the decision not to have children. I've left family and
friends for a province two time zones away. I've chosen work
that's entirely solitary, work that sees me spending day after
day on my own. I live in one of the most remote and inacces-
sible parts of North America, an island that can only be reached
through expensive flights or long, choppy ferry rides.

What's curious about this situation, and what sets it apart
from the feeling of foreboding that found me in my teens and
twenties, is that I'm now supremely educated on the subject of
loneliness. If there were an honor roll created for the field of

loneliness research, I'd be on it. I've spent years reading and writing about the state; I've interviewed experts about it; I've spent hours on the phone talking to other lonely people. The last several years of my life have been organized around what struck me as an urgent principle: I needed to find out everything I could about my loneliness.

Looking back, I think I did this work with the vague and never fully articulated notion that if I could just learn enough about the state, I'd never fall victim to it again. I had the idea that if I could just see my loneliness clearly enough and understand it fully enough, I'd be able to outsmart it, or at least lower my risk of encountering it. In the tug-of-war against loneliness that I'd been waging my whole life, education was going to be my strongman, my defense, my final rally. It was going to keep loneliness at bay.

So what mystifies me about my situation now is the fact that, knowing what I do about loneliness—how it can lead to early death, and dementia, and illness, and cognitive changes, and headaches, and stress, and threat—I haven't tried to organize my life in a way that might keep it away. I should be out there in a gregarious job; I should be on the phone long distance every week; I should be mingling, and going to parties, and socializing at the lesbian dances that sometimes spring up in this small town. Instead, I embrace solitude, take walks by myself, and tell myself I have Danielle—recognizing that, if Danielle were to leave, I'd be utterly and unmanageably alone.

What I'm doing now is playing a sort of Russian roulette with loneliness, telling myself it won't find me, and that it won't settle again, all the while knowing that it probably *will* find me, and *will* settle again. A pop psychologist would say that, deep down, I *want* to be lonely, that the state is so familiar to me that I can't really conceptualize my life without it. But I *don't* want to be lonely. The loneliness that found me in my thirties was so harrowing and horrid I never want to go back to it again.

So why do I leave myself so open to the state? Why don't I go out and foster children, or adopt, or devote at least one day a week to the difficult work of making friends and connections? Why don't I start attending church and begin going to religious seminars and after-mass socials? The list of possibilities is endless: I could join a rowing team, or a running group, or a belly-dancing class. I could do anything that might, in time, help create the sort of social circle I need to keep loneliness from settling again.

And I might do these things. I keep telling myself that next month, or the month after that, I'll be more purposeful, I'll put more safeguards in place. But whether I eventually do these things is an open question. It's quite possible that my state of relative aloneness will simply persist, with nothing acting as a buffer between me and long-term loneliness but my own crossed fingers, a blind hope in continued luck, and a bit of a prayer.

There's more than a hint of fate to my relationship with loneliness today. Even after years of researching the state, I still see it as something that will take me if it wishes. And the problem with seeing something as fated, of course, is that measures against it start to seem futile; once you're convinced of the futility of a response, you almost guarantee the advent of what you're worried about. This is the trap I've found myself in with loneliness. The less convinced I am that I can do anything about the state, the more likely it is to become a reality.

Almost three years ago, when I first started this project, my agent and I were tossing around possible titles. She suggested

An Unhaunted Place. The phrase was from a John Donne poem, and she thought it did a good job of communicating the sense of no one being present. But the title struck me as immediately and intuitively wrong. I was sitting in my kitchen, thinking about the word *unhaunted*, and found myself saying, "No. It's not unhaunted at all. It's as though I *am* haunted."

My agent didn't struggle with loneliness, and she fell silent as she tried to understand what I'd just said. I couldn't properly explain it to her. I wasn't sure how to say that loneliness felt like a ghost in my life, that I wasn't sure I'd ever move entirely away from it, and that I wasn't certain of what steps to take to fully end it. It was as though, with all my education, I'd failed to learn some trick, as though some crucial piece of information had not been passed down to me. I didn't know *what* to rely on in keeping loneliness at bay; I wasn't sure I possessed the emotional resources necessary to fight it off. And the effect of all this not knowing was to feel exposed, to feel as though the state, even when it wasn't presenting itself, was something I could see out of the corner of my eye, just on the edge of my existence.

"It's more like *is* with me," I said. "It's not like being without."

We settled on *Lonely*—the word certainly got its point across—but I'm not sure I want it to be the word that defines my life. I really do want a future in which loneliness is not a problem, one in which *lonely* doesn't continue to appear near the top of a list of my attributes. The word seems like a taunt, an incantation, a phrase that somehow contains and creates my future. And I want my future to proceed down a different path. In a way, I'm not asking for much. I remember Martin, the boyfriend I dated so long ago, effortlessly belting out the song "Unlonely," and I know I'll never turn into someone like that, someone so endlessly and easily embedded. I'll never be able to say the word *lonely* as if it's a curiosity or trifle. But what might be possible—what I modestly hope for—is a sort of truce. Loneliness and I have been antagonists for so long now. The state has hovered about my life for decades, either attacking directly or lurking off to the sides. And what I want is a laying down of arms. My fortieth birthday is approaching, and I'm trying to see the milestone as hopeful, symbolic. Having spent so long struggling with loneliness, I feel as though, by age forty, I might be considered to have paid my debt to the state, that whatever emotional sentence I was handed at birth might be regarded as served.

From where I sit, I can hear Danielle typing in the next room, and I like to think that she's writing out a different sort of future for me, one my own writing hasn't quite led me to. And maybe this was where I went wrong. Perhaps all my studying and thinking and reasoning about loneliness was based on the wrong premise. I thought I could somehow subdue the state myself. But I couldn't. I can't. What I need is the comfort that can be provided by someone else. I'm not, despite adequate skill or powerful desire, able to write an end to my own loneliness story. This ending has to come from outside, from someone else, from someone who takes me by the hand and leads me away from the state, away from the word, away from the feeling that's been mine for so long.

ACKNOWLEDGMENTS

Many thanks to my agent, Suzanne Brandreth, and to the smart, capable women who guided this book to publication: Jennifer Lambert, Susan Renouf, Nancy Miller, and Jeanette Perez. To A.C. and J.B., for years of encouragement and support; to D.C.W., for her constant kindness; and to my mother, for typing at night, and for showing me how important writing could be.

SELECTED SOURCES AND
FURTHER READING

There is much fascinating reading that can be done on loneliness. Below, I list some of the sources that were key to my research, or which I simply enjoyed. For a full bibliography, please go to www.lonelythebook.com.

A book that I took an enormous amount of inspiration from was Robert Weiss's *Loneliness: The Experience of Emotional and Social Isolation* (Cambridge, Mass.: MIT Press, 1974). This book is often referred to as the bible of loneliness research, and it provides a wonderful introduction into ideas such as the evolutionary basis of loneliness, as well as loneliness and attachment.

Additional early works that contain a wealth of information are Letitia Peplau and Daniel Perlman's *Loneliness: A Sourcebook of Current Theory, Research, and Therapy* (New York: Wiley/Interscience, 1982) and Mohammadreza Hojat and Rick Crandall's *Loneliness: Theory, Research, and Applications* (Newbury Park, Calif.: Sage, 1989).

The scale that made loneliness research truly possible was Dan Russell's UCLA Loneliness Scale. I've presented a modified version of this scale at the beginning of this book. A full, twenty-item version of the scale can be found in "UCLA Loneliness Scale (Version 3)," *Journal of Personality Assessment* 66, no. 1 (1996): 20–40.

A thoroughly researched paper stressing the need to see loneliness as a psychological problem in its own right is Liesl M. Heinrich and Eleonora Gullone, "The Clinical Significance of Loneliness: A Literature Review," *Clinical Psychology Review* 26 (2006): 695–718.

There are numerous papers on loneliness and health. A few of the most essential are:

John T. Cacioppo, John M. Ernst, et al., "Lonely Traits and Concomitant Physiological Processes: The MacArthur Social Neuroscience Studies," *International Journal of Psychophysiology* 35 (2000): 143–54;

Louise C. Hawkley, Mary H. Burleson, Gary G. Bernston, and John T. Cacioppo, "Loneliness in Everyday Life: Cardiovascular Activity, Psychosocial Context, and Health Behaviors," *Journal of Personality and Social Psychology* 85, no. 1 (2003): 105–20;

Sarah D. Pressman, Sheldon Cohen, et al., "Loneliness, Social Network Size, and Immune Response to Influenza Vaccination in College Freshmen," *Health Psychology* 24, no. 3 (2005): 297–306;

Andrew Steptoe, Natalie Owen, Sabine R. Kunz-Ebrecht, and Lena Brydon, "Loneliness and Neuroendocrine, Cardiovascular, and Inflammatory Stress Responses in Middle-Aged Men and Women," *Psychoneuroendocrinology* 29 (2004): 593–611; and

Robert S. Wilson, Kristin R. Krueger, et al., "Loneliness and Risk of Alzheimer Disease," *Archives of General Psychiatry* 64, no. 2 (2007): 234–40.

A paper I quite like, since it shows I wasn't alone in losing control of my eating when lonely, is Ken Rotenberg and Darlene Flood, "Loneliness, Dysphoria, Dietary Restraint, and Eating Behavior," *International Journal of Eating Disorders* 25 (1999): 55–64.

The research linking loneliness to genetics can be found in Dorret I. Boomsma, Gonneke Willemsen, et al., "Genetic and Environmental Contributions to Loneliness in Adults: The Netherlands Twin Register Study," *Behavior Genetics* 35, no. 6 (2005): 745–52.

The idea of the lonely being highly attuned to the social world around them is presented by Wendi Gardner and Cynthia Pickett in "On the Outside Looking In: Loneliness and Social Monitoring," *Personality and Social Psychology Bulletin* 31, no. 11 (2005): 1549–60.

The really interesting study showing that lonely people actually possess good social skills is John Vitkus and Leonard M. Horowitz, "Poor Social Performance of Lonely People: Lacking a Skill or Adopting a Role?" *Journal of Personality and Social Psychology* 52, no. 6 (1987): 1266–73.

John Cacioppo's hypnosis experiments are described in "Loneliness within a Nomological Net: An Evolutionary Perspective," *Journal of Research in Personality* 40 (2006): 1054–85. Cacioppo and Hawkley's ideas about loneliness as an agent of change are also set out in "People Thinking about People: The Vicious Cycle of Being a Social Outcast in One's Own Mind," in *The Social Outcast: Ostracism, Exclusion, Rejection, and Bullying*, edited by Kipling Williams, Joseph Forgas, and William von Hippel (New York: Psychology Press, 2005).

The links between loneliness and instability in childhood are described in Carin Rubenstein and Phillip Shaver, "The Experience of Loneliness," in Peplau and Perlman, *Loneliness: A Sourcebook*, and in Diana T. Hecht and Steven K. Baum, "Loneliness and Attachment Patterns in Young Adults," *Journal of Clinical Psychology* 40, no. 1 (1984): 193–97.

For information about increasing depression rates, and the idea of a cohort effect, see Gerald L. Lerman and Myrna Weissman, "Increasing Rates of Depression," *Journal of the American Medical Association* 261, no. 15 (1989): 2229–35, and Cross-National Collaborative Group, "The Changing Rate of Major Depression," *Journal of the American Medical Association* 268, no. 21 (1992): 3098–3105.

Information on loneliness rates for various countries can be found in different sources. The U.S. rate of 25 percent is in Norman N. Bradburn, *The Structure of Psychological Well-Being* (Chicago: Aldine, 1969). The UK rate of 29 percent can be found online at www.mind.org.uk. The Australian rate of 33 percent is from William Lauder, Siobhan Sharkey, and Kerry Mummery, "A Community Survey of Loneliness," *Journal of Advanced Nursing* 46, no. 1 (2004): 88–94.

The data about elderly people being lonelier today is from Christina V. Victor, Sasha J. Scrambler, et al., "Has Loneliness amongst Older People Increased? An Investigation into Variations between Cohorts," *Ageing and Society* 22 (2002): 585–97.

The intriguing findings about shrinking confidant networks in the United States can be found in Miller McPherson, Lynn Smith-Lovin, and Matthew Brashears, "Social Isolation in America: Changes in Core Discussion Networks over Two Decades," *American Sociological Review* 71 (2006): 353–75, and also in Miller McPherson, Lynn Smith-Lovin, and Matthew Brashears, "The Ties That Bind Are Fraying," *Contexts* 7, no. 3 (2008): 32–36.

A great paper on our need to belong as basic and *not* something (as we're sometimes told) "inappropriate" is R. F. Baumeister and M. R. Leary, "The Need to Belong: Desire for Interpersonal Attachments as a Fundamental Human Motivation," *Psychological Bulletin* 117 (1995): 497–529.

The notion of someone behaving in a "cooler" manner when told that their conversational partner is lonely is from Ken J. Rotenberg, Jamie

Gruman, and Mellisa Ariganello, "Behavioral Confirmation of the Loneliness Stereotype," *Basic and Applied Social Psychology* 24, no. 2 (2002): 81–89.

For the idea that men are less likely to disclose loneliness, see Shelley Borys and Daniel Perlman, "Gender Differences and Loneliness," *Personality and Social Psychology Bulletin* 11, no. 1 (1985): 63–75.

The rather fun experiment in which observers were asked to rate lonely people on the basis of looks is at Warren H. Jones, J. E. Freemon, and Ruth Ann Goswick, "The Persistence of Loneliness: Self and Other Determinants," *Journal of Personality* 49, no. 1 (1981): 27–48.

For the need to treat loneliness as a public policy issue (rather than as a strictly personal problem), see the discussions in Helen McCarthy and Gillian Thomas, *Home Alone: Combating Isolation with Older Housebound People* (2004), www.demos.co.uk; and Help the Aged, "Isolation and Loneliness: Policy Statement 2007," policy.helptheaged.org.uk.

A description of Nan Stevens's very effective loneliness intervention program can be found in "Combatting Loneliness: A Friendship Enrichment Programme for Older Women," *Ageing and Society* 21 (2001): 183–202.

Caroline Starkey's social isolation and loneliness resource kit is at www.opforum.webeden.co.uk/#/socialisolation/4522666178.

The *Diagnostic and Statistical Manual of Mental Disorders* can be found at most major reference libraries. The personality assessment schedules I refer to are included in Peter Tyrer, *Personality Disorders: Diagnosis, Management, and Course* (Oxford, England: Butterworth-Heinemann, 2000).